REFORM IN
GREAT BRITAIN
AND GERMANY
1750–1850

PROCEEDINGS OF THE BRITISH ACADEMY · 100

REFORM IN GREAT BRITAIN AND GERMANY 1750–1850

Edited by
T. C. W. BLANNING & PETER WENDE

Published for THE BRITISH ACADEMY
by OXFORD UNIVERSITY PRESS

Oxford University Press, Great Clarendon Street, Oxford OX2 6DP

Oxford New York
Athens Auckland Bangkok Bogota Bombay
Buenos Aires Calcutta Cape Town Dar es Salaam
Delhi Florence Hong Kong Istanbul Karachi
Kuala Lumpur Madras Madrid Melbourne
Mexico City Nairobi Paris Singapore
Taipei Tokyo Toronto Warsaw

and associated companies in
Berlin Ibadan

Published in the United States by
Oxford University Press Inc., New York

British Library Cataloguing in Publication Data
Data available

ISBN 0–19–726201–5
ISSN 0068–1202

Typeset by Alden Bookset, Osney Mead, Oxford
Printed in Great Britain
on acid-free paper by
Creative Print and Design Wales
Ebbw Vale

Contents

Notes on Contributors   vii

Introduction   1
T. C. W. BLANNING & PETER WENDE

Why does Corruption Matter? Reforms and Reform Movements in
Britain and Germany in the Second Half of the Eighteenth Century   5
ECKHART HELLMUTH

The Whigs, the People, and Reform   25
L. G. MITCHELL

Legal Reforms: Changing the Law in Germany in the *Ancien Régime*
and in the *Vormärz*   43
DIETHELM KLIPPEL

The Prussian Reformers and their Impact on German History   61
HAGEN SCHULZE

Reform in Britain and Prussia, 1797–1815: (Confessional)
Fiscal-Military State and Military-Agrarian Complex   79
BRENDAN SIMMS

The English as Reformers: Foreign Visitors' Impressions, 1750–1850   101
PAUL LANGFORD

Riding a Tiger: Daniel O'Connell, Reform, and Popular Politics in
Ireland, 1800–1847   121
K. THEODORE HOPPEN

1848: Reform or Revolution in Germany and Great Britain   145
PETER WENDE

The Idea of Reform in British Politics, 1829–1850   159
DEREK BEALES

Index   175

Notes on Contributors

T. C. W. Blanning is Professor of Modern European History at the University of Cambridge and a Fellow of Sidney Sussex College. He is also a Fellow of the British Academy. His recent publications include *The French Revolutionary Wars* (1996); (ed.) *The rise and fall of the French Revolution* (1996); (ed.) *The Oxford illustrated history of modern Europe* (1996); *History and biography: essays in honour of Derek Beales* (edited with David Cannadine); and *The French Revolution: class war or culture clash?* (1998).

Peter Wende is Professor of Modern History at the Johannes Wolfgang Goethe-University, Frankfurt am Main, and since 1994 Director of the German Historical Institute, London. His recent publications include *Geschichte Englands* (2nd edition, 1995) and (ed.) *Englische Könige und Königinnen* (1998).

Eckhart Hellmuth is Professor of Modern History at the Ludwig-Maximilian-University at Munich. His main field of interest is eighteenth-century German and British history. His publications include *Naturrechtsphilosophie und bürokratischer Werthorizont. Studien zur preußischen Geistes- und Sozialgeschichte des 18. Jahrhunderts* (1985); *The transformation of political culture: England and Germany in the late eighteenth century* (1990); *Rethinking Leviathan: the eighteenth century state in Britain and Germany*, edited with John Brewer (1999); and *Nationalismus vor dem Nationalismus*, edited with Reinhard Stauber (1998).

L. G. Mitchell is Fellow and Praelector in Modern History at University College, Oxford. His most recent publications are biographies of Charles James Fox and Lord Melbourne.

Diethelm Klippel holds the chair of Civil Law and Legal History within the Legal and Economics Faculty at the University of Bayreuth. He has published on German civil law, legal history and eighteenth- and nineteenth-century political theory. His most recent publications are *Naturrecht — Spätaufklärung — Revolution*, edited with Otto Dann (1995); and (ed.) *Naturrecht im 19. Jahrhundert, Kontinuität — Inhalt — Funktion — Wirkung* (1997).

Hagen Schulze holds the Chair of Modern German and European History at the Friedrich Meinecke Institute, Free University of Berlin. Among his recent publications are *Staat und Nation in der europäischen Geschichte*, (3rd revised edition, 1998), translated as *State, nations and nationalism* (2nd edition, 1998); *Kleine deutsche Geschichte* (1996), translated as *Germany: a new history* (1998); and *Phoenix Europa. Die Moderne von 1740 bis heute* (1998).

K. T. Hoppen is Professor of History at the University of Hull. He has published extensively in modern British and Irish history and his books include *Elections, politics and society in Ireland, 1832–1885* (1984); *Ireland since 1800: conflict and conformity* (1989; 2nd edn, 1998), and a volume in the *New Oxford history of England*, entitled *The mid-Victorian generation, 1846–1886* (1998).

Brendan Simms is a Fellow of Peterhouse, Cambridge. His recent publications include *The impact of Napoleon: Prussian high politics, foreign policy and the crisis of the executive* (1997); *The struggle for mastery in Germany, 1780–1850* (1998) and numerous articles on Germany in the eighteenth and nineteenth centuries, British foreign policy, the Weimar Republic and the Third Reich.

Paul Langford is Professor of Modern History in the University of Oxford and a Fellow of Lincoln College. He is also a Fellow of the British Academy. He has published numerous works, including *A polite and commercial people: England, 1727–1783* in the *New Oxford history of England*, in 1989, and his Ford Lectures, *The public life of the propertied Englishman, 1689–1798*, in 1991. He is General Editor of *The writings and speeches of Edmund Burke* for Oxford University Press and is in the process of launching a new series aimed at the student and the general reader, 'The short Oxford history of the British Isles'.

Derek Beales has been a Fellow of Sidney Sussex College, Cambridge, since 1955 and was Professor of Modern History at Cambridge from 1980 until 1997. He is also a Fellow of the British Academy. He has written extensively on eighteenth- and nineteenth-century Europe, including Britain. His biggest enterprise has been a biography of Joseph II, of which the first volume appeared in 1987. He has published many articles on British politics before and after the first Reform Act, and a general survey *From Castlereagh to Gladstone, 1815–85* appeared in 1969. A *New dictionary of national biography* entry for Canning, and an essay on Gladstone and Garibaldi, are in the press.

Introduction

T. C. W. BLANNING & PETER WENDE

HELD AT CORNWALL TERRACE on 26 and 27 September 1997, the conference on 'Reform in Great Britain and Germany, 1750–1850' was a joint initiative on the part of the British Academy and the German Historical Institute. Its organizers were motivated by the belief that in the historiography of late eighteenth-century Europe the concept of 'reform', both in theory and in practice, had been neglected, especially when compared with the attention lavished on its more glamorous relation 'revolution' (the bicentenary of the fall of the Bastille engendered no fewer than 170 conferences across the world, the central event, organized at the Sorbonne in July 1989, alone producing nearly 300 papers). Yet it was reform not revolution which characterized the experience of both Great Britain and Germany during the late eighteenth and early nineteenth centuries. The British ship of state sailed untroubled through the turbulence created by the French Revolution without having to do much more than take in the occasional sail and flog the odd mutineer. Germany was certainly revolutionized after 1789, not least by the destruction of the Holy Roman Empire, but it was change imposed from outside, not generated from within by domestic subversion. Indeed, the various forms of exploitation suffered at the hands of the French revolutionaries and their heir, Napoleon, only served to strengthen a long-established German preference for gradual change through reform.

If violent and rapid change naturally appears more exciting than gradual adaptation, the papers delivered at the conference revealed that a study of the latter can stimulate just as much intellectual excitement. The ten papers were divided into three sessions. The first, chaired by T. C. W. Blanning (Sidney Sussex College, Cambridge), comprised Eckhart Hellmuth (Munich) on 'Reform movements in Great Britain and Germany in the later eighteenth century', Leslie Mitchell (University College, Oxford) on 'The whigs, the people, and reform' and Diethelm Klippel (Göttingen) on 'Legal reforms: changing the law in Germany during the *ancien régime* and the *Vormärz*'. All three revealed fundamental differences between the British and German political structures. If the popular notion of the former being characterized

Proceedings of the British Academy, **100**, 1–3. © The British Academy 1999.

by a weak state and the latter by omnicompetent bureaucracies has to be abandoned, the fact remains that in most German states it was the path of reform from above that was followed, while in Great Britain most reforming energy came from below and was directed against alleged abuses and corruption at the centre of government. Whig aristocrats were particularly anxious to seek legitimacy by associating their programme with the people.

In the second session, presided over by Rudolf Vierhaus (Göttingen), there were two comparative papers on Great Britain and Prussia — Hagen Schulze (Free University, Berlin) on 'Napoleon, the Prussian reformers and their impact on German history' and Brendan Simms (Peterhouse, Cambridge) on 'Facing Napoleonic France: reform in Britain and Prussia, 1797–1815' — and two neatly juxtaposed contributions on perceptions — Paul Langford (Lincoln College, Oxford) on 'The English as reformers: foreign perceptions, 1750–1850' and Rudolf Muhs (Royal Holloway and Bedford New College) on 'The Germans as reformers: British perceptions, 1750–1850.'* Some important similarities became apparent here, notably the importance of the 'primacy of foreign policy' in both initiating and shaping reform. In neither country, however, was the pressure exerted by the Revolutionary-Napoleonic wars sufficient to impose radical change in the distribution of power or to bring the two political cultures closer. Germans gradually ceased to see Great Britain as the exemplar of modernity, while the British continued to associate Germany with authoritarian politics.

It was the third component of the United Kingdom of Great Britain and Ireland which proved — and has continued to prove — most intractable in the face of metropolitan attempts at reform. However, in the third session, chaired by Roy Foster (Hertford College, Oxford), Theo Hoppen (Hull) showed how Daniel O'Connell was able to lead a movement of rural protest to become a highly effective reform movement. His marriage of Catholicism and liberalism achieved astonishing success in Ireland but could not be exported to the rest of Europe. In the final two papers — Peter Wende (German Historical Institute, London) on 'Chartism and German reformism in 1848 compared' and Derek Beales (Sidney Sussex College, Cambridge) on 'The idea of reform in British politics, 1829–1850' — attention was focused on the meaning attached by contemporaries to the word 'reform'. For German liberals it meant a non-violent revolution, to be secured by negotiation between government and opposition. It was a strategy which collapsed in 1848, frustrated by the intransigence of the *Vormärz* regimes. In Great Britain too, 'reform' had radical connotations, implying a degree of change which just stopped short of revolution. For that reason it was used

---

* We regret that a publishable version of Rudolf Muhs' paper was not available when we were finally obliged to go to press.

almost exclusively to denote parliamentary reform and more specifically the Great Reform Act of 1832. Conservative social reformers therefore chose a vocabulary with less disturbing associations.

That 'reform' has no reason to feel over-awed by 'revolution' in any conceptual battle was also shown by the lively discussions which followed each of these ten papers. Seventy-odd scholars filled the Cornwall Terrace lecture room on each of the two days and engaged in vigorous debate, both with the speakers and each other. The organizers take the opportunity to thank them for making the conference such a stimulating occasion. They also thank the British Academy and the German Historical Institute for their material and moral support.

Why does Corruption Matter?
Reforms and Reform Movements in
Britain and Germany in the Second Half
of the Eighteenth Century*

ECKHART HELLMUTH

I SHALL START BY MAKING A STATEMENT that could not be more banal: the
second half of the eighteenth century, in Britain and Germany alike, was a
time when things began to be in flux. Reform, improvement, transformation — these are the terms in which historians frequently try to capture the
spirit of the times. Of course, there is also another school of historiography,
the one which subsumes conditions of the later eighteenth century under the
category *ancien régime*. Since Jonathan Clark, this heuristic concept has even
been applied to conditions in Britain.[1] None the less, the fact remains that the
majority of historians see the period after the Seven Years War in particular
as a period of change. Yet when they describe this change in Germany and
Britain, they concentrate on very different things. Those who deal with
Germany look at, for example, Frederick the Great, Joseph II, and the
problem of enlightened absolutism. Those who deal with England write,
among other things, about John Wilkes, Major John Cartwright, Tom Paine,
and the movement for political and economical reform. We are obviously,
therefore, dealing with two quite different historical landscapes which,
moreover, do not lend themselves easily to comparative examination. Yet
it is not only the different realities of life that make a comparison difficult.

* In revising this paper for publication, I have preserved its original character as a lecture. As a
result, references have been kept to the necessary minimum. In the process of revision, I have
taken into account at least some of the contributions that were made in the discussion at the
conference. I was particularly grateful for the comments made by Joanna Innes, Professor Derek
Beales, and Professor Peter Dickson. The paper was translated by Dr Angela Davies, whom I
should like to thank here. Thanks are also due to Christoph Schroer for his help in procuring
literature, and for his critical reading of the present essay.
[1] J. C. D. Clark, *English society 1699–1832: ideology, social structure and political practice during
the ancien regime* (Cambridge, 1985).

Proceedings of the British Academy, **100**, 5–23. © The British Academy 1999.

Added to this is the fact that historians dealing with German and British conditions in the eighteenth century often operate within quite different heuristic horizons.[2]

Another problem also deserves mention. In order to understand the will for change in the late eighteenth century, and its objects and objectives, it would really be necessary to examine the discourse of this age with the greatest care. This would also mean looking at how language changed, and reconstructing the contemporary vocabulary of reform and its semantic content. At present, it is only possible to say that, at least in Germany, the concept of 'reform' entered the language of politics as a contrast to that of 'revolution'. *Begriffsgeschichte* (the history of concepts) as pioneered by Reinhard Koselleck teaches us that 'reform' signifies

> change in the framework of the existing system, improvement by the abolition of obsolete forms and ones that have been overtaken by contemporary conditions, adaptation to new conditions, constitutionality, lack of violence, necessary interventions undertaken carefully and with caution, implementation over a long period of time, initiatives by the legal constitutional organs, the need for the concept of reform to concur with the general conviction.[3]

While such attempted definitions are useful, they cannot disguise the fact that we know comparatively little about the vocabulary that the advocates (and opponents) of change in Germany and Britain used in their language games. Yet it was these language games that, at the end of the eighteenth century, often opened up or blocked possibilities for reform.[4]

Thus the difficulties confronting any comparison are enormous. I shall, nevertheless, attempt such a comparison, not least because historical sociologists have always regarded England and Germany as the two main alternatives on the path to modernity.[5] Before I embark on my analysis, however, I must make a few general provisos. First, I shall develop my argument in a schematic way, deliberately dispensing with nuances. Second, I shall have to refer to some things which are well known. Third, my remarks encompass actual reforms, failed reforms, and attempted reforms. Fourth, I understand

---

[2] Some comments on this can be found in E. Hellmuth, 'Towards a comparative study of political culture: the cases of late eighteenth-century England and Germany', in idem, ed., *The transformation of political culture: England and Germany in the late eighteenth century* (Oxford, 1990), pp. 1–36, esp. 10ff.

[3] Eike Wolgast, 'Reform, Reformation', in O. Brunner, W. Conze and R. Koselleck, eds, *Geschichtliche Grundbegriffe. Historisches Lexikon zur politisch-sozialen Sprache in Deutschland* (8 vols, Stuttgart, 1972–97), v, pp. 313–60, esp. 344.

[4] Some fundamental considerations on this can be found in W. Steinmetz, *Das Sagbare und das Machbare. Zum Wandel politischer Handlungsspielräume England 1780–1867* (Stuttgart, 1993).

[5] On this see T. Ertman, 'Explaining variation in early modern state structure: the cases of England and the German territorial states', in J. Brewer and E. Hellmuth, eds, *Rethinking Leviathan: the eighteenth-century state in Britain and Germany* (Oxford, forthcoming 1999), pp. 23–52, with references to further literature.

'reform' to mean what historical research has defined as reform, although I am aware that phenomena which historians analyse as 'reforms' would not necessarily have been subsumed under this category by eighteenth-century contemporaries.

In order to make clear what I am talking about in this paper, I should like to refer briefly to a present-day episode. If we look at the political debate that has been conducted in the media of the Federal Republic of Germany over recent years, we keep coming back to one catchphrase: 'Reformstau'. Those who use this word deplore the indeed hopeless situation of almost total paralysis in many areas of reform. Above all, people are chafing at the fact that it is at present impossible to bring down tax rates in the Federal Republic, to cut back bureaucratic regulations, and to put limits on the state in its role as the shaper of social and economic life. 'Reformstau' has become the battle cry of those who want to combat Leviathan. And many observers in the Federal Republic who are seeking alternatives look with envy at a Britain which was subjected to a radical cure by Margaret Thatcher. This is not without irony. At that time, the interventionist state in the Federal Republican mould was held up by many Britons as a model for orientation. I am referring to this episode not only to make clear that what has just been praised as a model of reform can quickly end up in the dustbin of history. Something else is more important. To think about reform is to think about the state. This is as true of the present day as of historical contemplation of the eighteenth century. It is tempting to bring the state into our consideration of reform not least because our image of Leviathan in the eighteenth century has changed considerably over the last decade. I shall therefore start by making a few brief remarks about recent research on the state in the eighteenth century (I). Thereafter I shall deal with reforms in eighteenth-century Germany (II), before turning to conditions in Britain (III). And I hope that in this last section the reason for calling this paper 'Why does corruption matter?' becomes clear.

I

Over recent years an astonishing phenomenon has been observable. Historians and historical sociologists have rediscovered the early modern state as an object of investigation.[6] Moreover, they are in the process of departing

---

[6] Among recently published works the following deserve special mention: T. Ertman, *Birth of the Leviathan: building states and regimes in medieval and early modern Europe* (Cambridge, Mass., 1997); M. Greengrass, ed., *Conquest and coalescence: the shaping of the state in early modern Europe* (London, 1991); B. Downing, 'Constitutionalism, warfare and political change in early modern Europe', *Theory and Society*, 17 (1988), pp. 7–56; idem, *The military revolution and political change: origins of democracy and autocracy in early modern Europe* (Princeton, 1992); Richard Bonney, ed., *Economic systems and state finance* (Oxford, 1995); W. Reinhard, ed., *Power elites and state building* (Oxford, 1996).

from the well-worn paths of analysis in two respects. First, they are attempting to free themselves from the interpretative patterns that are more or less associated with the name of Max Weber.[7] And secondly, they are generating empirical findings that are forcing us to dispense with familiar assumptions. This applies to British and German conditions.[8] Thus the assumption that in the eighteenth century the state apparatus was especially 'strong' in the German territories and Prussia while it was 'weak' in Britain has increasingly come under fire. We have been taking leave of these entrenched clichés for some time. John Brewer's book *The sinews of power*,[9] published almost ten years ago now, provided an important boost to this new way of thinking. Building on the earlier work of Daniel Baugh,[10] Gerald Aylmer,[11] and Patrick O'Brien,[12] Brewer presents the eighteenth-century English state as a powerful and efficient machine. By comparison with its contemporary European counterparts, argues Brewer, the English state was an extremely modern institution. The starting point for Brewer's ideas is the explanatory model which postulates a connection between war, finances, and bureaucracy. From Otto Hintze to Charles Tilly, this model was generally applied to continental states. One of Brewer's points is that the English state of the eighteenth century was able to siphon off large amounts of tax revenue which it needed to finance numerous wars and to maintain its formidable military apparatus. An efficient and highly professional fiscal system was required to collect these large amounts of tax. Thus we are confronted with the paradox that the presumably weak English state had at its disposal a fiscal administration unmatched anywhere in Europe.

This new view of the English state corresponds to an increasingly critical assessment of the German state of the eighteenth century. Scholars are distancing themselves from the image of a highly efficient absolutist state

---

[7] For this see, among others, J. Brewer and E. Hellmuth, 'Rethinking Leviathan' in Brewer and Hellmuth, eds, *Rethinking Leviathan,* pp. 1–21. On Weber's understanding of the state see Roland Axtmann, 'The formation of the modern state: a reconstruction of Max Weber's arguments', *History of Political Thought,* 11 (1990), pp. 295–311.

[8] For this see E. Hellmuth, 'Der Staat des 18. Jahrhunderts. England und Preußen im Vergleich', in Günter Birtsch, ed., *Reformabsolutismus im Vergleich = Aufklärung,* 9/1 (1996), pp. 5–24.

[9] J. Brewer, *The sinews of power* (London, 1989). Some of the implications of Brewer's book are discussed in L. Stone, ed., *An imperial state at war: Britain, 1689–1815* (London, 1994).

[10] D. Baugh, *British naval administration in the age of Walpole* (Princeton, 1965).

[11] G. Aylmer, *The king's servants: the civil service of Charles I, 1625–1642* (London, 1974); idem, *The state's servants: the civil service of the English republic, 1649–1660* (London, 1973); idem, 'From office-holding to civil service: the genesis of modern bureaucracy', *Transactions of the Royal Historical Society,* 5th ser., 30 (1980), pp. 91–108.

[12] P. O'Brien, 'The political economy of British taxation, 1660–1815', *Economic History Review,* 41 (1988), pp. 1–32. See also idem, P. Mathias, 'Taxation in England and France, 1715–1810: a comparison of the social and economic incidence of taxes collected for the central governments', *Journal of European Economic History,* 5 (1976), pp. 601–50.

pervading all areas of life, such as was found in the works of Gustav Schmoller, Otto Hintze, and Fritz Hartung. The insight that in the eighteenth century 'broad areas of social life were beyond the direct reach of the territorial ruler'[13] is at present accepted as a commonplace of history. The organs of the estates continued to have a large part in the administration of the territories. Thus almost thirty years ago Rudolf Vierhaus wrote: 'Nowhere was public life completely permeated by the political will of the ruler as, according to the theory of absolutism, it should have been. Nowhere were the old corporatist institutions completely abolished and replaced by territorial ones. Their co-existence was still . . . part of social reality.'[14]

But it was not only the continued existence of intermediary powers that contradicts the ideal-typical image of the absolutist state to be found in eighteenth-century Germany. The at least partial morbidity and inefficiency of the state apparatus of enlightened absolutism points in the same direction. Christof Dipper has recently drawn some highly sobering conclusions. 'By the eighteenth century', he argues,

> society had reached a degree of complexity which was beyond the capacity of autocratic rulers to deal with. Many, especially in larger territories, remained dilettantes, and their interventions often did more harm than good. Thus despite the numerous decrees which it produced, the eighteenth-century state apparatus was concerned mainly with itself, in both theoretical and practical terms . . . Thus it is hardly surprising that attempts at intervention had such meagre results. Only too often, multiple administrative restructuring ended up in total confusion . . . In practice, this meant that no distinction was drawn between important and unimportant matters. Anyone today leafing through the decrees issued by German territories is surprised by the huge range of subjects to which the administration addressed itself . . . From the sublime to the ridiculous, from university reform to dog-catching was only a small step.[15]

It is obvious that historians are increasingly coming to doubt the efficiency of the eighteenth-century German territorial state. This applies in particular to the states organized in a bureaucratic-absolutist way. It is generally assumed that their internal constitutions, 'rationalized' throughout, along with the taxation systems associated with this form of organization, placed them in a position to maintain a formidable military apparatus

---

[13] R. Vierhaus, 'Ständewesen und Staatsverwaltung in Deutschland im späteren 18. Jahrhundert' (1966), in idem, *Deutschland im 18. Jahrhundert. Politische Verfassung, soziales Gefüge, geistige Bewegungen. Ausgewählte Aufsätze* (Göttingen, 1987), pp. 33–49, esp. p. 40. W. Neugebauer, *Politischer Wandel im Osten. Ost- und Westpreußen von den alten Ständen zum Konstitutionalismus* (Stuttgart, 1992), pp. 1–27 provides an excellent overview of the present state of research on the estates.

[14] Ibid., p. 35.

[15] C. Dipper, 'Government and administration — everyday politics in the Holy Roman Empire', in Brewer and Hellmuth, eds., *Rethinking Leviathan*, pp. 204–23, esp. 207, 221, 215.

which, in turn, raised their status within the circle of European powers. Yet
was this particular variant of the eighteenth-century German territorial state
really suited to increasing political and military power? The answer most
recently provided by Thomas Ertman is deeply sceptical.[16] Using the
example of Prussia, Ertman demonstrates that specific structural deficits
meant that the states that were organized on a bureaucratic-absolutist basis
were capable of asserting themselves within the concert of the European
powers only within limits. The basic problem, he argues, was the inability of
the Prussian state to establish a stable taxation and credit system which
would have allowed it to survive longer-term conflicts. The reason Ertman
gives is as follows:

> None of the Prussian monarchs were [sic] willing to tolerate representative
> assemblies, even if only to provide independent loan guarantees to potential
> lenders, yet without such guarantees the creation of a public credit market, a
> *sine qua non* of military effectiveness over the long term, was beyond reach. The
> belief that this contradiction — which lay at the heart of all fully absolutist
> regimes — could be overcome by building up cash hoards or invading neigh-
> bouring territories proved to be an illusion.[17]

The difficulties which resulted from this structural deficit of the Prussian state
were enhanced by the fact that the antiquated economic system, which was in
thrall to a society of orders and the manorial system, lacked any of the
dynamism that a military great power needed. Thus the reason for the
collapse of the most powerful eighteenth-century German territorial state in
1806, a collapse that had already been prefigured in its conflict with the
French revolutionary troops a good decade earlier, was to be found, among
other things, in its bureaucratic-absolutist state structure. This collapse can
be regarded as symptomatic of the weakness of the German territorial state
of the eighteenth century.

II

The eighteenth-century German states, whose internal condition, it seems,
was rather different from what earlier scholars had assumed, made serious
efforts at reform during the second half of the eighteenth century.[18] This
applied to the large powers Austria and Prussia, as well as to the smaller

---

[16] On this see Ertman, *Birth of the Leviathan*, pp. 224ff.

[17] Ibid., p. 262. Ertman expresses this insight against the background of his analysis of the
British state (ibid., pp. 156ff.).

[18] As my concern here is with the reforms undertaken within the context of the German
territorial state in the eighteenth century, I do not take into account the efforts directed at a
reform of the empire. On this see, most recently, W. Burgdorf, *Reichskonstitution und Nation.
Verfassungsreformkonzeptionen für das Heilige Römische Reich Deutscher Nation im politischen
Schrifttum von 1648 bis 1806* (Mainz, 1998), esp. pp. 131ff.

German territories generally known as the 'third Germany'. The reform programmes of territorial rulers and their enlightened bureaucracies were inspired by extremely diverse intellectual traditions, including cameralism, natural law, physiocracy, pietism, enlightened Catholicism, and Christian patrimonialism. The spurt in reforming activity which many German states experienced during the second half of the eighteenth century was not least the result of rivalry between states.[19] Thus the reforming efforts of the Habsburg monarchy were essentially inspired by the fact that it had been beaten in the Silesian wars by Prussia, the parvenu among the European powers. And the course of the Seven Years War made it abundantly clear to Maria Theresa and her advisers that the Austrian state machine required a thorough overhaul. War, or the effort of dealing with its consequences, was undoubtedly one of the forces driving on the reform process in many German territories. The larger and middle-sized states within the Holy Roman Empire tried to prepare themselves for possible encounters with other states.[20] This meant, above all, raising the finance that was necessary for them to stay in the power game of the eighteenth-century states. Rivalry between states included the ability to learn from competitors. The classic example of this is the Habsburg monarchy's partial adoption of the Prussian military system.

The most ambitious reform programme was undoubtedly set in motion in the Habsburg monarchy.[21] I shall give a brief outline of this activity here in order to demonstrate the areas in which reforming absolutism was active.[22] The following comments are intended not as a subtle analysis of Habsburg reforming absolutism,[23] but as a reminder of the scope and character of the

[19] On the connection between domestic politics and power politics and foreign policy, see B. Simms's comments in *The impact of Napoleon: Prussian high politics, foreign policy, and the crisis of the executive, 1797–1806* (Cambridge, 1997), pp. 2ff. (with references to further literature).

[20] On the contemporary scenario for conflict, see, most recently, P. W. Schröder, *The transformation of European politics, 1763–1848* (Oxford, 1994), pp. 24ff.

[21] I refer to the model of reform in the Habsburg monarchy because reform was pursued there with particular dynamism and consistency, and because it was especially broadly based. I am aware, however, that the ethnic plurality of the Habsburg monarchy means this reform model can only to a limited extent be described as 'German'.

[22] The following, among others, provide good overviews of this reforming activity: H. M. Scott, ed., 'Reform in the Habsburg monarchy, 1740–90', in idem, ed., *Enlightened absolutism: reform and reformers in later eighteenth-century Europe* (London, 1990), pp. 145–87; W. Demel, *Vom aufgeklärten Reformstaat zum bürokratischen Staatsabsolutismus* (Munich, 1993), pp. 83ff., and C. Ingrao, *The Habsburg monarchy, 1618–1815* (Cambridge, 1994), pp. 150ff.

[23] On the issues that are being discussed in the research see e.g. Christine L. Mueller, 'Enlightened absolutism', *Austrian History Yearbook*, 25 (1994), pp. 159–83; D. Beales, 'Was Joseph II an enlightened despot?', in R. Robertson and E. Timms, eds, *The Austrian Enlightenment and its aftermath*, Austrian Studies 2 (Edinburgh, 1991), pp. 1–21; L. Bodie, 'The Austrian Enlightenment: an essay on publications, 1975–1990', ibid., pp. 171–87; G. Birtsch, 'Der Idealtyp des aufgeklärten Herrschers. Friedrich der Große, Karl Friedrich von Baden und Joseph II. im Vergleich', in G. Birtsch, ed., *Der Idealtyp des aufgeklärten Herrschers = Aufklärung*, 2/1 (1987), pp. 9–45.

reforming efforts that were usual on the continent. It is therefore not necessary to distinguish between the regime of Maria Theresa, who from 1766 shared responsibility for government with her successor, and the sole rule of Joseph II between 1780 and 1790.[24] Rather, we should assume that there was a continuum of reform stretching from Maria Theresa to Joseph II. The reform projects which Joseph II pushed forward with characteristic determination and dynamism during his period of sole rule were frequently prefigured in policy before 1780.

The main objective of all reform attempts was to confer a greater degree of coherence on the Habsburg monarchy which, as a result of the way in which it had grown, contained a large number of territories with diverse constitutions. This meant, among other things, placing limits on the power of the estates and the church, strengthening the role of central government, and imposing greater uniformity in administrative, military, legal, and financial matters.

Consequently, one of the main fields of activity was administrative reform. After the Silesian wars had clearly exposed the shortcomings of the political-administrative system which had been cultivated within the Habsburg monarchy, the first large administrative reforms were undertaken. In 1749 the *Directorium in Publicis et Cameralibus* was established, and at the same time, subordinate officials were reorganized into *Representationen* and *Cammern*. This new administrative structure, however, proved to be relatively short-lived. In response to the lessons of the Seven Years War, it was dismantled after a few years. The *Staatsrat* (council of state), which had been set up in 1761, now became the centre of political-administrative power. In 1763, finally, a new intermediate tier of officials was created in the form of *Gubernien*. Until the end of the Josephinian regime, these were to play a key role in the implementation of social, economic, educational, and agrarian reforms.

These administrative reforms were accompanied by legal reforms. From the late 1740s, there was an increasing awareness that the existing legal chaos needed to be unified; this applied to civil and criminal law alike. The *Codex Theresianus* of 1766 was the first attempt to create a modern system of civil law for the Habsburg monarchy. In 1769 a criminal code followed, known as the *Nemesis Theresiana*, which was criticized by contemporaries for its draconian punishments. Thus it was not surprising that Joseph II introduced a new penal code as early as 1787. The *Allgemeines Gesetzbuch* was much more humane than its predecessor. Among other things, it did away with archaic offences such as sorcery and witchcraft. Joseph II had abolished the

---

[24] The differences in the attitudes and policies of Maria Theresa and Joseph II are perceptively analysed by D. Beales in *Joseph II*, vol. I: *In the Shadow of Maria Theresa, 1741–1780* (Cambridge, 1987), pp. 439ff.

death sentence with the exception of martial law as early as 1781, and torture had already been abolished under Maria Theresa in 1776.

The reform of the church, starting from the premise of the supremacy of the state over the church, was a further focal point of Theresian-Josephinian reform policy. This policy comprised a wide spectrum of measures, from the dissolution of numerous monasteries to the struggle against traditional forms of piety and the establishment of a priesthood whose life centred on community and pastoral work. Closely associated with the reform of the church was educational reform, in two respects in particular. First, the reduction in the influence of the Jesuits made possible a reorientation of higher education, especially the universities and *Gymnasien* (grammar schools). Secondly, the money released by the abolition of monasteries allowed a network of primary schools to be established, and attending them was made compulsory.

In addition to administration, the law, the church, and education, a number of other areas were included in the Habsburg monarchy's reform programme. Joseph II's policy of toleration in particular should be mentioned here. It largely ended discrimination against Protestants and Greek Orthodox. The sensational patent of toleration of October 1781 not only permitted Lutherans, Calvinists, and followers of Greek Orthodoxy to practise their own forms of worship, but it also granted them civil freedoms which had previously been denied to them. These included *Bürgerrecht*, the right to become a master craftsman, the right to take academic degrees, and to become a civil servant. And against the sometimes determined opposition of the people, the first steps towards the emancipation of the Jews were taken from 1782/3. The worst forms of discrimination were abolished, and measures designed to promote the civil equality of the Jews were implemented.

Probably the most radical part of this ambitious reform programme was intervention in the traditional agrarian system. In the 1770s and 1780s Maria Theresa and Joseph II made serious attempts to reform this sector. Initially their efforts were directed at curbing the worst excesses of serfdom; later they worked towards its abolition in certain parts of the monarchy. Finally, brief reference should be made to five further fields in which the Habsburg monarchy initiated reforms.

(i)   From 1748 a number of military reforms clearly inspired by the Prussian example were put in motion. These included setting up a recruiting system in the hereditary lands in the early 1770s, which in many respects resembled the Prussian system of cantons.

(ii)   From 1781 censorship was clearly relaxed, if only temporarily.

(iii)   In parts of the country the Customs system was simplified in order to stimulate the economy.

(iv)   The infrastructure was developed.

(v)   And welfare reforms were made, such as the establishment of hospitals and asylums.

What this outline is intended to show is the simple fact that the Habsburg monarchy undertook a broad spectrum of reform measures. If these failed at the first attempt, it tried again. This situation can be regarded as typical because other German territories — not only Prussia, but also many of the smaller and middling territories — acted in a similar way during the second half of the eighteenth century. Thus there can be no doubt that the German territories undertook serious reform attempts during the second half of the eighteenth century. The question is, how successful were they? In looking for an answer, we are confronted with two different narratives. The first is a story of success; the other is a story of failure, chaos, and disaster. Although there is a degree of overlap in historiographical practice, I shall present them separately here for the sake of clarity.

To start with the success story: those historians who see the history of these reforms as a success point above all to the example of the smaller German territories. They start from the position that the structural conditions in the 'third Germany' were particularly suitable for the implementation of reforms. Several arguments are generally put forward to substantiate this thesis. The smaller territories, it is said, were able to concentrate on domestic policy because they were not involved in the great conflicts of the time; their state budgets were not strained by a bloated military apparatus; the small size of the bureaucracies simplified decision-making procedures; and finally, the smaller territories did not have the regional and thus constitutional diversity which complicated the policy of reform in larger territories such as Prussia and Austria. Charles Ingrao, for example, has drawn up a scenario of reforming success along these lines. 'In purely economic terms', he points out,

> they [the reforms] generally helped increase agricultural output, improve the availability and distribution of food, and laid a firmer basis for subsequent industrialisation. More rational and responsible fiscal policies enabled a great many states to restore their finances, thereby enabling them to fund more and better domestic services. By providing greater public assistance, better justice, religious toleration, and limited protection from manorial exploitation, these domestic reforms also alleviated much of the suffering of the common people. Moreover, by making education more widely available they provided the key to even more rapid progress in the following century.[25]

---

[25] C. Ingrao, 'The smaller German states', in Scott, *Enlightened absolutism*, pp. 221–43, esp. 242.

Incidentally, these are more or less the arguments that are also used by historians who assess reforms in the large territories positively.[26]

Next to such a positive view, it is easy to place an interpretation of reform policy in the German territories which emphasizes its limitations and the partially chaotic character of the reforms.[27] This is the other story which will be told here. Scholars have regularly pointed to the miserable failure of Joseph II's policy of radical reform. It is becoming increasingly clear that it was not only the opposition of the traditional powers and the complexity of the Josephinian reform programme that led to disaster, but that the excessive demands placed on the state apparatus also contributed crucially to the failure.[28] In any case, recent research has shown that the agencies working at local level, which were regularly inundated by streams of edicts, were only to a limited extent able to put the ruler's will into practice. It cannot be said that Josephinian reform policy was implemented in a directed and controlled fashion. This was not least related to the fact that the state apparatus was not properly balanced. Too many civil servants were occupied with the paper rituals of the Leviathan: too few worked on pushing ahead practical reform policy.[29] It is also interesting to note that Peter Dickson, in his masterly work, *Finance and government under Maria Theresia*, adopts a rather sceptical tone when it comes to weighing up success and failure. He writes, among other things:

> Again, while the power of the state undoubtedly increased during the period, there is much evidence that government showed a progressive tendency after 1763 to become bogged down in detail, to lose the power of decision, and to substitute argument for action. It also has to be recognized that the reforms of central authority 1747–9 and 1761–3, while impressive in scope, were to a large extent less the deliberate and far-sighted assertion of fundamental principles of government than desperate expedients provoked by the justified fear of total political collapse.[30]

---

[26] A nuanced balance, positive in this sense, is drawn by H. Möller, *Fürstenstaat oder Bürgernation. Deutschland, 1763–1815* (Berlin, 1989), esp. chs. 3 and 5. A positive assessment of Prussian conditions can be found in C. B. A. Behrens, *Society, government and the Enlightenment: the experiences of eighteenth-century France and Prussia* (London, 1985), and T. C. W. Blanning, 'Frederick the Great and enlightened absolutism', in Scott, *Enlightened absolutism*, pp. 265–88.

[27] J. J. Sheehan, *German history, 1770–1866* (Oxford, 1991), pp. 11–71, for example, tends towards this view.

[28] On this see R. Stauber, *Auf der Grenzscheide des Südens und des Nordens. Administrative Integration, Herrschaftswandel und kulturelle Grenzen im Südalpenraum 1750–1820*, Habilitationsschrift der Philosophischen Fakultät für Geschichts- und Kunstwissenschaften der Universität München, 1997, pp. 235ff.

[29] On this see P. G. M. Dickson, 'Monarchy and bureaucracy in late eighteenth-century Austria', *English Historical Review*, 110 (1995), pp. 322–67, where he makes some fundamental observations.

[30] P. G. M. Dickson, *Finance and government under Maria Theresia, 1740–1780*, vol. 1: *Society and government* (Oxford, 1987), p. 14.

Even the myth of Frederick the Great and his reforms is beginning to fade. Yet as long as twenty years ago Hubert C. Johnson pointed out that the constant reorganization of the Prussian bureaucracy during the eighteenth century can hardly be seen as an expression of planned reforms. Rather, he suggested, it revealed a certain lack of direction in Prussia's internal administration.[31] A number of projects which the monarch set in motion with the assistance of his administration were obviously non-starters.[32] The state seems to have achieved only limited control over fundamental problems such as taxes and duties. And it is becoming increasingly clear that sections of the urban and rural population were able to avoid intervention by the authorities. There was obviously a large gap between the claims of absolutist regimes and the situation on the ground in certain parts of society. Recently, historians have described this discrepancy even in policy for schools, an area which has generally been regarded as the classic example of the Prussian state's success in implementing a policy of modernization.[33]

In the smaller German territories, too, which so fascinated Charles Ingrao and others, reform attempts during the eighteenth century do not seem to have made as much progress as is occasionally assumed. Here, too, the reforming-regimenting will of the authorities frequently failed in the face of traditional ways of life.[34] This also applied to attempts to eliminate particular forms of popular piety.[35] Wherever the process of reform is examined more closely, shortcomings and frictions appear. This becomes clear, for example, in Mary Lindemann's fascinating work, published in 1997, *Health and healing in eighteenth-century Germany*,[36] which looks at health reforms in the duchy of Brunswick-Wolfenbüttel, among other things. The scenario that Lindemann draws up shows a ducal administration which was prevented by a lack of resources and inadequate information, among other things, from reforming medical practice. Moreover, the will of the authorities to implement change was often frustrated by local conventions. Under these circumstances, there could be no question of a consistently

---

[31] H. C. Johnson, *Frederick the Great and his officials* (New Haven, 1975).

[32] On the following, see Hellmuth, 'Der Staat des 18. Jahrhunderts', pp. 14ff., with references to further literature.

[33] On this see the seminal study by W. Neugebauer, *Absolutistischer Staat und Schulwirklichkeit in Brandenburg-Preussen* (Berlin, 1985); cf. also J. Van Horn Melton, *Absolutism and the eighteenth-century origins of compulsory schooling in Prussia and Austria* (Cambridge, 1988).

[34] For this see e.g. C. Zimmermann, 'Grenzen des Veränderbaren im Absolutismus. Staat und Dorfgemeinde in der Markgrafschaft Baden', in Birtsch, *Reformabsolutismus im Vergleich*, pp. 25–45, in which he makes a number of excellent general observations on the reforming practice of enlightened absolutism, taking the relevant literature into account.

[35] For this see C. Dipper, 'Volksreligiosität und Obrigkeit im 18. Jahrhundert', in W. Schieder, ed., *Volksreligiosität in der modernen Sozialgeschichte*, Geschichte und Gesellschaft, Sonderheft 11 (Göttingen, 1986), pp. 73–96.

[36] M. Lindemann, *Health and healing in eighteenth-century Germany* (Baltimore, 1997).

implemented, coherent policy of reform. What Lindemann shows goes beyond the bounds of her case study. Obviously, historians should not take the laws and ordinances which eighteenth-century authorities produced in such large numbers at face value. At most, they signalled what the state intended to do; they did not show what was actually achieved. Behind the numerous laws and ordinances lay concealed a reality which posed a real challenge to reform-orientated authorities.

Naturally, the question now is: which of the two readings of reform policy in the German territories which I have introduced here is the correct one? I do not wish to conceal that I am inclined to take a sceptical view of things. The assumption that the German rulers and their administrations were only to a limited extent capable of conceptualizing and implementing reforms would, to a certain degree, correspond to the idea of the weak German state which I have already referred to above. Ultimately, however, in my opinion this question is irrelevant. Something else is much more important. In the German territories, almost all reform projects — the successful and the less successful alike — were initiated by the state.[37] If projects failed, or did not have the intended effect, the ruler and his administration frequently started again. Myriads of officials or would-be officials thought and argued about what the world should be like. The simple fact that within the borders of the Holy Roman Empire hundreds of state apparatuses, some of them only partially developed, existed side by side, meant that German territory in the eighteenth century provided a unique experimental area for policies of state intervention.

This policy of reform was accompanied by an intense debate conducted by journalists about individual reforming measures. Anyone who leafs through the journal articles, the works produced by the academies, the tracts and treatises of the late eighteenth century, comes across a remarkable catalogue of proposals for improvements and concepts for reform.[38] Sensible proposals were often mixed up with the bizarre. The spectrum of subjects ranged from instructions for public entertainments to proposals for the laying-out of public parks and the topics which, in our eyes, are typical of the age: plans to reform the education system, proposals to make the criminal

---

[37] Naturally there were exceptions within the German context. For example, conditions in Hamburg were different. See F. Kopitzsch, *Grundzüge einer Sozialgeschichte der Aufklärung in Hamburg und Altona* (Hamburg, 1982).

[38] On the public debate in Germany during the second half of the eighteenth century, see e.g. H. E. Bödeker, 'Journals and public opinion: the politicization of the German Enlightenment in the second half of the eighteenth century', in Hellmuth, ed., *The transformation of political culture*, pp. 423–45 (with references to further literature), and E. Hellmuth and U. Herrmann, eds., *Aufklärung als Politisierung — Politisierung der Aufklärung* (Hamburg, 1987).

justice system more humane, suggestions for the improvement of industry and agriculture, public health measures and so on. In many cases, these proposals built upon ideas which had been developed during the first half of the century in the handbooks of *Polizeiwissenschaft* and *Kameralwissenschaft*, of politics and natural law.[39] Thus there was a continuous stream of literature in which the state was reminded of its reforming task, in which reform was thinkable only as state reform. This literature was often still under the influence of a practical philosophy of Wolffian provenance, which regarded the perfecting of people, society, and the economy as the responsibility of the state and the authorities.[40]

We can now, of course, ask why the theory and practice of reform in Germany during the second half of the eighteenth century were so much under the sway of the state. The simple answer that there was no alternative is correct, but in my opinion this is a bit too simple and does not go quite far enough. There was something more. In the German territories of the late eighteenth century, the anti-governmental public which plays such an important part in Habermas's concept of the 'structural transformation of the public sphere' was not a very strong force. In other words, the members of the reading societies, the patriotic and enlightened associations which, in Jürgen Habermas's concept,[41] represented a critical social catalyst which was not bound into the state, were exactly the same people who sat in the government offices of late eighteenth-century Germany. We are thus dealing with a closed circuit within which there was practically no space to look for non-state alternatives to reform. And under these conditions, the principle of a state policy of reform was accepted as a cultural commonplace and produced the ideologization of the idea of reform from above.[42]

---

[39] There is a voluminous literature on this topic. I shall mention just the following: H. Maier, *Die ältere deutsche Staats- und Verwaltungslehre* (Munich, 1980); J. Brückner, *Staatswissenschaften, Kameralismus und Naturrecht. Ein Beitrag zur Geschichte der politischen Wissenschaften im Deutschland des späten 17. und frühen 18. Jahrhunderts* (Munich, 1977); B. Stolberg-Rillinger, *Der Staat als Maschine. Zur politischen Metaphorik des absoluten Fürstenstaates* (Berlin, 1986); and D. Klippel, 'Reasonable aims of civil society: the state and the individual in eighteenth-century German political theory', in Brewer and Hellmuth, eds, *Rethinking Leviathan*.

[40] On this see E. Hellmuth, *Naturrechtsphilosophie und bürokratischer Werthorizont. Studien zur preußischen Geistes- und Sozialgeschichte des 18. Jahrhunderts* (Göttingen, 1985).

[41] J. Habermas, *Strukturwandel der Öffentlichkeit. Untersuchungen zu einer Kategorie der bürgerlichen Öffentlichkeit* (Neuwied/Berlin, 1962), pp. 87ff. On the debate about Habermas, and criticism of him, see, among others, Craig Calhoun, ed., *Habermas and the public sphere* (Cambridge, Mass., 1994) and Andreas Gestrich, *Absolutismus und Öffentlichkeit. Politische Kommunikation in Deutschland zu Beginn des 18. Jahrhunderts* (Göttingen, 1994).

[42] On this see, among others, R. Vierhaus, 'The revolutionizing of consciousness: a German utopia?', in Hellmuth, ed., *The transformation of political culture*, pp. 561–77.

III

I shall now turn to conditions in England. While England had no programme of reform as comprehensive as that pursued by the larger German states during the second half of the eighteenth century, it did experience individual reform measures, attempted reforms, and above all, calls for reform. The reform laws passed by Parliament included the Penitentiary Act of 1779, which provided the impetus for a modernization of the prison system, the Catholic Relief Acts of 1778 and 1791, the Friendly Societies Act of 1793, and the Dissenters Relief Act of 1779. In addition, there was a series of reform projects which were not passed by Parliament, for example, the repeal of the Test and Corporation Acts and parliamentary reform in the 1780s. Moreover, a number of extra-parliamentary organizations were set up with the aim of achieving specific changes in politics, society, and the law. Compared with the continent, British society had a remarkable capacity for self-organization,[43] and this allowed large numbers of such movements to emerge. We could name the Reform of Manners Movement, the Sunday School Movements, the campaign for the repeal of the Test and Corporation Acts, and the Society for Charitable Purposes. As a result, reform projects which were regarded as a state responsibility on the continent were undertaken by private initiatives in Britain. One example is voluntary hospitals.[44] In general, there seems to have been a greater number of reform initiatives at local level in Britain than in Germany.[45] Joanna Innes provides this telling description of the situation on the spot:

> Justices of the Peace tightened licensing laws, inaugurated anti-vagrancy campaigns, and commissioned the building of new prisons. Gentlemen, farmers, tradesmen, and industrial employers reorganized parish poor-relief administration, established new workhouses, served in volunteer forces to facilitate the policing of towns, set up societies for the prosecution of felons, and promoted the establishment of Sunday schools.[46]

Browsing through the eighteenth-century literature on reform, one gains the impression that, at least at national level, the most significant topic in the reform debate was political or parliamentary reform. Greater autonomy for

---

[43] On this see, most recently, P. Langford, *Public life and the propertied Englishman, 1689–1798* (Oxford, 1991), esp. ch. 8.

[44] On this see K. Wilson, 'Urban culture and political activism in Hanoverian England: the example of voluntary hospitals', in Hellmuth, ed., *Transformation of political culture*, pp. 165–84.

[45] This was, it seems, connected with the fact that, during the eighteenth century, new forms of central–local interaction developed, which gave local authorities a greater degree of autonomy than in most continental states. See the detailed and nuanced article by J. Innes, 'The domestic face of the military-fiscal state: government and society in eighteenth-century Britain', in L. Stone, ed., *An imperial state at war: Britain from 1689 to 1815* (London, 1994), pp. 96–127.

[46] J. Innes, 'Politics and morals: the Reformation of Manners movement in later eighteenth-century England', in Hellmuth, ed., *Transformation of political culture*, pp. 57–118, esp. 65.

Parliament, a redistribution of electoral boundaries, and an expansion of the suffrage were, indeed, called for by almost all reforming and radical movements in the second half of the eighteenth century.[47] As a result of different constitutional conditions, there was, of course, no equivalent to this debate on political reform in Germany at this time. None the less, this debate is important for the comparison we are attempting to draw here because one of its integral constituents was the demand for economical reform, that is, the abolition of what William Cobbett called 'Old Corruption'. In my opinion this phenomenon allows us to draw a comparison, even if it is indirect.

Old Corruption was the archaic side of the English state; the other side of this Janus-faced figure was the administrative, fiscal, and military apparatus of great power and sophistication that John Brewer has shown us. Old Corruption involved practices which, at least in the larger German territories, had largely been eliminated by this time. They would have made any upright Prussian Kriegs- und Domänenrat (War and Domain Councillor) shudder if he had become aware of them.[48] Government offices degenerated into sinecures in various different forms. There were well-paid offices which were not associated with any duties; in other cases, office-holders drew emoluments from an office, but the actual work was done by others who were fobbed off with a fraction of the income from the office. Reversions (the right of succession to an office or place of emolument after the death or retirement of a holder) allowed high government officials to provide their kinsmen with office. Whether they were qualified for the job counted for little. There were other practices which contemporary critics condemned: pensions, government contracts, and church preferment were showered on those who proved themselves to be loyal supporters of the government of the day. Places and rotten boroughs allowed ministers and proprietors to pack the House of Commons with MPs who were willing tools of those who had brought them into Parliament.

Such 'corrupt' practices made critical contemporaries see the British state as a degenerate and parasitic monster which consumed vast sums of tax revenues and had become a vehicle of personal enrichment. Criticisms of this sort had already been voiced during the first half of the eighteenth century, in the context of the country opposition of the 1730s, for example.[49] But the

---

[47] For the most recent overview see Frank O'Gorman, *The long eighteenth century: British political and social history, 1688–1832* (London, 1997), pp. 221ff., and H. T. Dickinson, *The politics of the people in eighteenth-century Britain* (London, 1994), pp. 221ff.

[48] The following account of practices stigmatized as 'corrupt' by contemporary critics is indebted to P. Harling, *The waning of 'Old Corruption': the politics of economical reform in Britain, 1779–1846* (Oxford, 1996), p. 3.

[49] On this see H. T. Dickinson, *Liberty and property: political ideology in eighteenth-century Britain* (London, 1977), pp. 169ff., and J. G. A. Pocock, *The Machiavellian Moment: Florentine political thought and the Atlantic republican tradition* (Princeton, 1975), pp. 462ff.

extra-parliamentary reform movement of the 1760s and 1770s gave this criticism a new quality. Thanks to Wilkes and the Associaters, the idea that the British state was parasitical, wasted taxes, and shamelessly enriched a small elite, entered the British collective consciousness in an unprecedented way.[50] And the disastrous outcome of the American Revolutionary War for the motherland only strengthened this tendency. Military failures, a growing state debt, and the resulting rise in taxes revived 'country' criticism of the corrupt British state. In the early 1780s the Association movement and metropolitan radicals demanded the end of practices which in their eyes were corrupt.[51] The call for parliamentary reform was not least the result of a desire to put an end to ministerial greed and, in contemporary jargon, 'extravagance'.

Criticism voiced inside and outside Parliament in the early 1780s was not without effect.[52] It led to a number of reform measures and steps. From 1780, for example, the Rockingham whigs made serious attempts to make the machinery of state more efficient, and at the same time to reduce the cost of running it. The Establishment Act of 1782 abolished 130 'inefficient offices', and for a number of offices casual emoluments were replaced by regular salaries. Moreover, on North's initiative, the Commission for Examining the Public Accounts was established in 1780. Convinced that government should be as cheap as possible, and disturbed at the dramatically rising costs generated by the central bureaucracy during the American Revolutionary War, the commissioners made a number of radical and comprehensive reform proposals. If they had been realized, they would have wiped out the system of 'Old Corruption'. But this did not happen. Pitt, who had come to power in 1784, accepted only a limited number of the commissioners' suggestions. No more than three of their numerous proposals were put into practice, and one of these was the proposal to appoint another commission to look into fee-taking in all the public departments. But this commission suffered a similar fate to that of the Commission for Examining the Public Accounts. It stopped work in 1789, after examining only ten of the twenty-four offices originally identified for inspection. The practical effect of its work was minimal. 'Clearly', writes John Breihan, 'Pitt's treatment of the commission and its reports represented a lost opportunity for significant

---

[50] On this see J. Brewer, *Party, ideology and popular politics at the accession of George III* (Cambridge, 1976), pp. 249ff.

[51] The fact that propaganda sometimes deliberately exaggerated matters is made clear by I. Christie in 'Economical reform and the "Influence of the Crown"', in idem, *Myth and reality in late-eighteenth-century British politics and other papers* (London, 1970), pp. 296–310.

[52] On the following see esp. Harling, *The waning of 'Old Corruption'*, pp. 31ff. See also H. Roseveare, *The Treasury, 1660–1870: the foundations of control* (London, 1973), pp. 61ff; and J. Cannon, *Parliamentary reform, 1640–1832* (Cambridge, 1980), pp. 72ff.

administrative reform.'[53] This lack of commitment to reforming the administrative sector is all the more surprising because Pitt, by contrast, pursued the restructuring of the national budget with great vigour.

We can only speculate, as John Ehrmann, John Breihan, John Torrance, and W. D. Rubinstein,[54] among others, have done, as to why Pitt did not drive on the process of administrative reform and act against the system of Old Corruption with greater energy, or why this system proved to be so durable. But this is not interesting in our context. More important is the fact that all the economical reforms of the 1780s and 1790s were piecemeal. In other words: all attempts to restrain the Leviathan failed. On the contrary, the war effort during the revolutionary wars allowed the system of Old Corruption to blossom anew. It has been noted that

> the shortcomings had become glaringly obvious in the late 1790s, when ministry's failure to make systematic administrative improvements conveyed the impression that the wartime state was multiplying the opportunities for government insiders to feed off of the public revenue. . . It was in large part neglect of thorough administrative reform that led to the wartime growth of the Old Corruption critique.[55]

Why is the failure of administrative reforms important in our context? The reason is simple. Because of these administrative deficits, Leviathan remained an important object of reform attempts and actual reforms. Or to be more precise, the experiences of the eighteenth century meant that the aim of reform was a minimal state. And indeed, during the first half of the nineteenth century Britain embarked on the path to the minimalist mid-Victorian state, leaving the fiscal-military state of the eighteenth century behind. The end of the Napoleonic wars marked the beginning of the dismantling or modernization of the British state apparatus, which up to that time had concentrated on one main task: maintaining its formidable war machine. Philip Harling and Peter Mandler have recently retraced this path.[56] They demonstrate that economical reform did not arise simply out of the logic of intra-bureaucratic rationality, but that this process was also set in motion by political pressure from outside. Harling and Mandler write, among other things, that 'the primary motor . . . was the widespread

---

[53] J. R. Breihan, 'William Pitt and the Commission on Fees, 1785–1801', *Historical Journal*, 27 (1984), pp. 59–91, esp. 74–5.

[54] John Ehrmann, *The younger Pitt*, vol. I: *The years of acclaim* (London, 1969), pp. 239ff.: Breihan, 'William Pitt and the Commission on Fees, 1785–1801'; John Torrance, 'Social class and bureaucratic innovation: the Commissioners for Examining the Public Accounts, 1780–1787', *Past and Present*, 78 (1978), pp. 56–81; W. D. Rubinstein, 'The end of "Old Corruption" in Britain, 1780–1860', *Past and Present*, 101 (1983), pp. 55–86.

[55] Harling, *Waning of 'Old Corruption'*, p. 58.

[56] P. Harling and P. Mandler, 'From "fiscal-military" state to laissez-faire state, 1760–1850', *Journal of British Studies*, 32 (1993), pp. 44–70.

conviction that the British war machine was unacceptably expensive and wasteful and that it acted as a broker for parasitical interests — contractors, sinecurists, speculative investors, and the like — who robbed the "productive" classes of their hard-earned money.'[57] To formulate the minimal state as the aim of reform was all the easier, as during the eighteenth century the British state had taken on a much narrower range of tasks than its German counterparts. The characteristic features of this minimalist state, as they were developed in the first half of the nineteenth century, included 'cheap government, or low expenditures compared to other European states', 'good government, or the general acceptance and adaptation of rational standards of administrative efficiency', and '*laissez-faire*, or a reluctance . . . to interfere with property rights and market relations'.[58]

What can we conclude from all this? In my view, the following conclusions can be drawn. In response to the different experiences of Britain and the German territories during the eighteenth century, different reform profiles emerged. In the case of Britain, because of the experience of Old Corruption, reform to some extent meant minimizing the state. In the German case, reform was often synonymous with state intervention. Reform was frequently thought of only as reform from above. The Prussian reforms and those undertaken by the Confederation of the Rhine changed nothing in this respect.[59] The question now remains as to which of these two reform models was the more successful in the long term. If we look at this problem from a present-day perspective, at a time which has declared war on Leviathan, the answer seems clear. But if we look at it from the perspective of the nineteenth century with the challenges it faced in the fields of educational and social policy, then I am no longer so sure.

---

[57] Ibid., p. 66.

[58] Harling, *Waning of 'Old Corruption'*, p. 9.

[59] It may be that this trend was muted in the period that followed. On this see D. Langewiesche, ' "Reform" und "Restauration". Versuch einer Bilanz — Offene Fragen', in H.-P. Ullmann and C. Zimmermann, eds, *Restaurationssystem und Reformpolitik. Süddeutschland und Preußen im Vergleich* (Munich, 1996), pp. 269–72.

The Whigs, the People, and Reform

L. G. MITCHELL

CONTINENTAL EUROPE HAD NO WHIGGERY. It was a matter of regret both for anglophiles everywhere and for the Whig Party in England. The latter generously, but condescendingly, issued instructions on the workings of constitutional government to Spaniards and Italians, but such lessons were never well taken. They even created the term 'French Whig' for such men as Lafayette and Louis Philippe. Unfortunately, these candidates, too, failed the test. Lafayette was a general before he was a politician, while Louis Philippe relapsed quickly into press censorship and the bloody suppression of riot. Europe, of course, had aristocrats of a reforming temperament. As the friends and advisers of autocrats, they advocated change, and sometimes succeeded in promoting it. But this was not whiggery. The whigs saw reform coming from below, from a body they dubbed 'the people', not from the benevolence of kings and emperors. The whig mission, historically defined, was to lead the people in their aspirations, to make contact with them, and to give practicality to their hopes. This was whiggery, and it was specifically English.

Anglophiles in Europe wistfully regretted their loss. Madame de Staël, in *De l'Angleterre*, noted that it was 'la haute aristocratie d'Angleterre qui sert de barrière à l'autorité royale. Il est vrai que l'opposition est de plus libérale dans ses principes que les ministres: il suffit de combattre le pouvoir pour retremper son esprit et son âme'.[1] She was delighted by Erskine's claim that he personally chatted to every elector in the Westminster constituency, exclaiming 'tant il y a de rapports politiques entre le bourgeois et les hommes du premier rang'.[2] The Duc de Broglie was even more flattering:

> L'aristocratie Anglaise honore l'humanité; c'est un imposant phénonène dans le monde et dans l'histoire; associée de tout temps aux intérêts du peuple, elle n'a jamais cessé de revendiquer les droits du moindre citoyen, aussi courageu- sement que les siens propres; elle a ouverte la route à la nation marche

[1] Mme de Stael, *De l'Angleterre*, ed. W. G. Hartog (London, 1907), p. 56.
[2] Ibid., p. 58.

Proceedings of the British Academy, **100**, 25–41. © The British Academy 1999.

aujourd'hui; elle a couru les mêmes chances, défendu la même course, combatta le même combat. Depuis cent cinquante ans que la victoire est gagnée, elle n'a ni devié ni dégénéré.[3]

Whigs naturally assumed that such testimonials were not offered to the English aristocracy as a whole, but were rather intended for them. It was they, after all, who alone met all the conditions set out in de Broglie's encomium.

Unfortunately, the compliment could not be returned. Instead, whig writers had to point to the dire consequences resulting from an absence of whiggery in Europe.[4] In their extensive writings on French history, for example, it became a cliché to record the sad fact that the French aristocracy had not behaved well. Lord John Russell typically observed about eighteenth-century France that 'when the people, raised by commerce and agriculture to importance, asked for the blessing of a free government, they had no leaders among the great proprietors of the land, to whose honesty and wisdom they could confide their cause'.[5] As a result, the French Revolution, when it came, degenerated into violence and instability. Whiggery, a natural, moderating influence, was missing. Fox and his friends tried to supply the deficiency by writing directly to Barnave, Lafayette and others, but their advice was ignored. There was nothing between king and people, and so inevitably liberty and equality drowned in blood. Bagehot put the point even more bluntly: 'If France had more men of free will, quiet composure, with a suspicion of enormous principle, and a taste for moderate improvement; if a Whig party, in a word, were possible in France, France would be free'.[6]

If the French could not rise to whiggery, there was even less to hope for from the Germans, whose every instinct seemed to be for autocratic government. When whig administrations, in the 1830s, had trouble with William IV, it was attributed to the fact that he, 'like all princes, especially Germans, [was] lofty and arbitrary in his notions of Government'.[7] By their nature, German aristocratic reformers looked for change through the agency of autocrats. It appeared that they could not countenance notions of the people or the representative institutions that might express them. When Frederick William IV visited England in 1842, bringing with him a reputation for liberal values, the whig press naturally assumed that this implied changes

---

[3] *Edinburgh Review*, 87 (1826), p. 158.
[4] Ibid., 67 (1820), p. 35.
[5] Lord John Russell, *Memoir on the affairs of Europe from the Peace of Utrecht* (London, 1824), pp. 161–2; see also Sir J. Mackintosh, *Vindiciae Gallicae* in the *Miscellaneous works of the Rt Hon. Sir James Mackintosh* (London, 1846), III, p. 11.
[6] *National Review*, 1 (1855), p. 265.
[7] A. Kriegel, *The Holland House diaries* (London, 1977), p. 349.

offered by him to his subjects, and not a recognition of their rights. As a result, the best they could hope for was that he had come to London to see the English model at first hand, with the possibility of being converted to it.[8] As ever, the whigs were only too happy to offer themselves as tutors. As ever, they were condescending in every sense of the word.

The gap opened up between British and European politics by the existence of whiggery was recognized by both sides. In Europe, whiggery was either honoured or thought merely strange. Some writers struggled to find phrases that would make sense of it in their own political vocabularies. One writer could not improve on the strangled formula that whiggery was 'ni Monarchiste, ni Aristocrate, ni Démocrate. Il est, si je peux m'exprimer ainsi, Monarchi-Aristo-Démocrate: c'est en tempérant ces caractères qu'il en corrige les vices'.[9] Across the Channel, whigs graciously accepted these acknowledgements of their own distinctive qualities. According to them, the existence of whiggery gave reform movements in England a particular tone. They would be more measured and articulate; they would be well grounded in historical precedent and in the intellectual currents of the day; and, above all, they would have a permanent presence within the *pays légal*. Change in Europe came too suddenly through revolutions or too whimsically through the chance friendships of autocrats. In England, demands for it were an enduring feature of every parliamentary session. Unfortunately, history had not bequeathed whiggery to other European peoples.

The whigs were entirely comfortable with the idea that history had given them a special role. It had made them the natural arbiters of the pace and character of reform. In conjunction with 'the people', to whom they acted as mentors, they would regulate the whole process. In elaboration, this becomes the greatest cliché, perhaps, of whig writing in the period 1789–1830. Out of office almost by definition, whigs had the time and motive to write history and constitutional theory in great quantities. It was the hobby of Fox, Russell, Mackintosh and many lesser figures. These men talked of 'the people' endlessly, defining them as those whose intelligence and property gave them the right to a public voice. They preened themselves on the close relationship between whiggery and popular movements, and sadly reflected that such a model of politics could not be found elsewhere.

Popular movements under whig direction were, by definition, safe. Protest and demands for change would be channelled into the normal workings of the English constitution. Whigs therefore had no qualms about endowing 'the people' with all kinds of rights and, indeed, with the

---

[8] J. Paulmann, *Westfälische Forchungen* (1994) XLIV, p. 358.
[9] Anon., *Lettre familière d'un whig anglais* (London, 1791), pp. 5–6.

ability to legitimize government itself. Years before the French Revolution, Richard Watson told a Cambridge congregation that,

> the People are not made to swell the dignity of a Legislature, but the Legislature is every where established to promote the interest of the people . . . God forbid, that our Governors should at any time so far neglect their duties, as to make it necessary for the people to sit in judgement upon their conduct; for this verdict is usually written with the sword, and registered in blood.[10]

Watson's willingness to endow the people with rights up to and, apparently, including the right to resistance was echoed widely. Russell bluntly observed that, 'The Whigs look towards the people, whose welfare is the end and object of all government'.[11]

Such was the stuff of whig sermons, pamphlets and speeches. Russell's generation, in particular, had absorbed these nostrums through their very skin. Educated at Glasgow and Edinburgh universities, he and his contemporaries had heard such didacts as John Millar rehearse the point over and over again. In his influential *Historical view of the English government*, of 1787, he set out the whig creed:

> The whigs, . . . founded the power of the sovereign, and of all inferior magistrates and rulers, upon the principle of utility. They maintained, that as all government is intended for defending the natural rights of mankind, and for promoting the happiness of human society, every exertion of power in governors, inconsistent with that end, is illegal and criminal; and it is the height of absurdity to suppose, that, when an illegal and unwarrantable power is usurped, the people have no right to resist the exercise of it by punishing the usurper.[12]

Tory writers parodied this whig stance in doggerel. *Blackwood's Magazine* published a satirical poem, in 1840, which began,

> Twas echo'd on hustings, in hall and in bower
> Too long we've been slaves to the Crown:
> The PEOPLE, the source of legitimate power,
> In bumpers was pledged, though the wine might be sour,
> As the toast that alone would go down.[13]

Verses such as these stung, but they are in themselves evidence of how far a belief in a special relationship with the people had become part of whig self-identification.

Such an association was vital. The people left to themselves could become

---

[10] *Anecdotes of the life of Richard Watson, Bishop of Llandaff* (London, 1817), pp. 19–20.
[11] Lord John Russell, *An essay on the history of the English government and constitution* (London, 1823), pp. 180–1.
[12] W. C. Lehmann, *John Millar of Glasgow* (London, 1960), p. 352.
[13] *Blackwood's Magazine*, 47 (1840), pp. 792–3.

passionate and enthusiastic. Europe provided endless examples of what excesses the people could be driven to, if not guided and counselled. The whigs had the responsibility of 'filtering the turbid current of popular opinion through various modes of deliberation and counsel'.[14] They were duty-bound to prevent 'any collision between the King and people', both checking overmighty executives, but also 'intemperate innovation' from below.[15] Whigs carried the responsibility of searching the people out, of listening to just demands for change, of offering assistance. They were to manage and orchestrate reform.

To fall down on this duty carried terrible risks. The people, if unsupervised, might wander into inappropriate paths, led astray by any passing and plausible demagogue. The *Edinburgh Review*, in 1810, reminded Grey and the whig leadership of this point:

> If the Whigs are not supported by the people, they can have no support, and therefore, if the people are seduced away from them, they must go after them and bring them back; and are no more to be excused for leaving them to be corrupted by demagogues, than they would be for leaving them to be oppressed by tyrants.[16]

In a world of Spenceans, Hampden Clubs and Orator Hunt, it was more than ever necessary for the whigs to be busy. As Francis Baring observed, whigs 'in bad times keep alive the sacred flame of freedom, and when the people are roused, stand between the constitution and revolution, and go with the people, but not to extremities'.[17] It was, by historical and contemporary experience, the whig *raison d'etre*. This was so obvious to John Allen, who, as Librarian at Holland House, ate and drank at whig expense for the whole of his life, that he contemptuously noted that, should his masters ever lose touch with the people, they would diminish into 'a mere Aristocracy'.[18] In other words, they would simply become no better than their French or German cousins.

What some whigs feared in the early nineteenth century, if indeed fear was an element in their thinking about reform, was that the people were indeed drifting away from them. The awfulness of Peterloo led Grey into momentary self-doubt. He worriedly confided to Brougham that, 'Everything is tending and has been for some time tending, to a complete separation between the higher and lower orders of Society; a state of things which can only end in the destruction of liberty, or in a convulsion which may too

---

[14] Lord John Russell, *The causes of the French Revolution* (London, 1832), p. 197.
[15] Lord John Russell, *A letter to the Rt Hon. Lord Holland* (London, 1831), pp. 40–1. See also Henry Brougham in the *Edinburgh Review*, 85 (1825), p. 234.
[16] *Edinburgh Review*, 15 (1810), p. 514.
[17] Quoted in J. Leonhard, *Jahrbuch zur Liberalismusforschung*, Jan. 1996, p. 34.
[18] J. Allen to Sir C. Vaughan [1809], All Souls Coll., Oxford, Vaughan MSS. c9/3.

probably produce the same result'.[19] Whigs debated vigorously whether they should sponsor public meetings and petitioning movements, in order to undermine Burdett and Hunt. The younger members of the party were inclined to accuse their elders of too much complacency in this respect. But all were clear that, even if tactics could be a matter of disagreement, whig duty and objectives were unchanged. The people had to be met on their own ground.

Recent history suggested vigorously to the whigs that their immediate antecedents had more than fulfilled this obligation. The events of 1688 were still the model for the whigs of the late eighteenth and early nineteenth centuries, still the precedent to follow. It was the supreme example of whigs leading the political nation into constitutional and religious reform. All tory involvement in the establishment of William and Mary on the English throne disappeared into historical fog. Whigs of Russell's generation claimed 1688 as their own. Lord Albemarle, publishing Rockingham's memoirs in 1852 had no doubt of this:

> It need hardly be stated that it was to a small body of wealthy landed proprietors that the country is indebted for the Revolution of 1688; that it was *for* the people, and not by the people, that the great measure was accomplished; that both at the time, and afterwards, the nation at large were passive spectators of the struggles made and making in their behalf.[20]

It was a matter of self-congratulation for the whigs that the whole undertaking had not been 'effected by an indignant and enraged multitude, but was slowly prepared by the most virtuous and best informed amongst the higher and enlightened classes of the people'.[21] The passing of a century and more did nothing to diminish its value as a lesson to be learnt, and then put into practice. A whig pamphleteer of 1819 was still of the view that, 'The Revolution of 1688 is considered by all wise and eminent statesmen, and by the great mass of the people of this country, as an example of singular value and importance'.[22]

After 1688, examples multiplied in whig minds of occasions on which whigs had acted on behalf of the people, and increasingly in active collaboration with them. Whig history was always special pleading, and never more so than in this respect. Tory and radical historians were often aghast at whig claims, but the whigs themselves never doubted. After 1688 came the great crises of the eighteenth century. Richard Watson was proud of the fact that

[19] Grey to Brougham, 25 Aug. 1819: H. Brougham, *The life and times of Henry, Lord Brougham* (Edinburgh, 1871), II, pp. 342–3.
[20] Lord Albemarle, *Memoirs of the Marquess of Rockingham and his contemporaries* (London, 1852), II, pp. 92–3.
[21] Anon., *A short defence of the whigs* (London, 1819), p. 4.
[22] Ibid, pp. 2–3.

John Wilkes, while criminal in his manipulation of a 'senseless popularity beneath the notice of genuine Whiggism', was yet recognized by the whigs as the champion of a just cause.[23] It was a matter of distinction that whigs had been prominent in movements to relieve religious dissidents and to emancipate slaves. In America, in India, even in Poland and Corsica, whigs had spoken and written in support of popular causes.

Above all, their performance in the 1790s was worthy of all praise. Whigs of the early nineteenth century never tired of intoning the glories of the martyrology of those years. According to this myth, the people, by petition and organization, had tried in these years to call for change. Pitt's government responded with all the brutality of the law. In response, whigs did what they could to help the victimized. Thomas Erskine defended Hardy and Tooke in their trial free of charge. Fox, Sheridan, and others gave character references for Arthur O'Connor. Fox also had supper with Muir and Palmer in the hulks on the evening before their transportation to Australia. Whigs saved the lives of some radical leaders and symbolically showed solidarity with others. Famously, in 1798, Fox joined Tooke and other radicals at a dinner where the famous, or infamous, toast of 'Our Sovereign Lord the People' was given.

All this came at a cost. Whig association with radicals allowed their opponents to accuse them of being irresponsible revolutionaries, and, in their kind remarks about Americans and Frenchmen, unnaturally un-English. Fox and many of his followers had little or no experience of government. Their careers were frosted. Whig doctors could not find patients, nor whig lawyers briefs. They were sometimes at loggerheads with their families, and sometimes disinherited. Yet they never abandoned the duty to talk to radicals and to suggest amendment. In the next generation, the Hollands made a point of inviting Burdett and Hazlitt to dinner. Such invitations were not always accepted, but at least they were persistently offered. According to whig hagiography, the party paid dearly for its contacts with the people and its representatives, but never allowed this to divert it from its well-defined mission. Typically, in 1795, the Whig Club passed a declaration which bravely reaffirmed that, 'The Constitution of Great Britain is established on the consent and affection of the People, and can only rest, with dignity and safety, on those genuine foundations of all social authority'.[24] There was courage here, as well as historical calculation.

After all, contact with the people was not simply a matter of speeches and philosophizing. There was also stink, public insobriety and familiarities that

---

[23] *Anecdotes of the life of Richard Watson, Bishop of Llandaff*, p. 34.
[24] *Declaration and form of association recommended by the Whig Club* (London, 1795), p. 2.

shocked foreign visitors. Sometimes, whigs complained that they were asked
to put up with a great deal for very little recompense. When Holland
protested about the radicals' 'ingratitude & distrust towards the Whigs',[25]
he was merely rehearsing a theme that permeated the writings of his party.
Yet they persevered. The people at election times took whigs away from their
palaces in the West End of London and marooned them in small country
towns. The Bessboroughs, for example, enjoyed great influence in St Albans
if they chose to keep it up, but the social cost was high. Hertfordshire is not
too far from Piccadilly, but Lady Bessborough's letters suggest a gulf that
went beyond mere geography:

> My brother sent to me to beg I would come here to do civilities for him, but
> more to attend a morning ball and visit some freeholders' wives, whom he
> wanted to please. Conceive being dress'd out as fine as I could at eleven o'clock
> in the morning, squeez'd into a hot assembly room at the Angel Inn, cramming
> fifty old Aldermen and their wives with hot rolls and butter, while John and
> Fred danced with the Misses, playing at fourpenny Commerce and tradille, and
> then visiting all about the gay town of St Albans. Can you boast of any thing to
> surpass this?[26]

Whig men were manhandled by the people, and whig women kissed the
people's lips. The Duchess of Devonshire and Lady Caroline Lamb drank
with the people, and outdrank the people, in alehouses. They were jostled
and freely addressed. When Lady Granville was confronted by a man who
asked after her husband's health with the words, 'G. d—n you, how is
Granville today?', she had to admit that, 'it is difficult to meet this sort of fire
and spirit in conversation with any degree of success'.[27]

Inevitably, cartoonists took full advantage of the spectacle. There was an
irresistible fascination in watching people, whose every instinct was for social
exclusion, mingling with the crowd because history had given them a duty to
do so. At the same time that whiggery rolled out more and more social
barbed wire, in terms of dress, accent and style of living, to ward off
intruders, they not only trumpeted the rights of the people, but also engaged
in mutual backslapping. The humour in the situation was all too obvious,
and not least to the whigs themselves. In December 1829, Sydney Smith, for
example, wrote to Lord Bathurst as follows:

> My next door neighbour is dead, so much the better for he was a perfect
> devil — but he has left his estate . . . to a little linen draper in a very small town

[25] British Library (BL) Add. MSS 51738, f. 22, Holland to Caroline Fox, 3 Nov. 1806.

[26] Lady Bessborough to G. Leveson Gower [1794]: *Lord Granville Leveson Gower* (London, 1916), I, pp. 98–9.

[27] Lady H. Granville to Lady G. Morpeth, 11 Oct. 1811: F. Leveson Gower, *The letters of Harriet, Countess Granville* (London, 1894), I, p. 23.

in Dorsetshire; and my merchant of linen has 8 grown up sons all brought up to low professions, and they are all coming to live here. What can this be but a visitation of Providence for my Whig principles? This is indeed a severe dose of the People.[28]

Nevertheless, Melbourne, in the difficult years 1830–4, regularly contacted Burdett and Place to ask them to keep their followers within bounds. Negotiations were no doubt helped by the fact that Place had once been his tailor. Allegedly, Melbourne still owed him money. There was much to be wondered at when social Brahmins actually encountered the people they idolized in print and oratory, but such meetings nevertheless took place. They seemed to have few European parallels.

In fact, whigs were historically condemned to take the people seriously. Ancestor worship was an integral part of their creed. They surrounded themselves with the iconography of great, historical missions, in which their families had taken leading parts. As a French admirer was instructed:

> L'histoire déposait en sa faveur. Dans leurs chartres et actes publics, ils voyoient, non les *titres* et *preuves* de leur liberté…mais ils voyoient les démarcations du Gouvernement légitime tracées par la valeur et la prudence …Le généreux courage, qui s'étoit toujours sévi contre la tyrannie, les animoit. Le sang dont il avait arrosé la plaine et l'échafaud ne s'effaçoit pas.[29]

Contemporary politics became the vindication of martyred ancestors. In writing a biography of William, Lord Russell, Lord John Russell acknowledged that, 'it cannot fail to be gratifying to the feelings of a descendant of Lord Russell to record the actions of so worthy an ancestor'.[30] So prominent was this family in the securing of English liberties that a birth was a matter of great rejoicing, not only in a personal sense, but also because 'the manufacture of Russells is a public and important concern'.[31] Beside the Russells always stood the Cavendishes, with a pedigree no less dramatic, that was recorded in a poem entitled *Chatsworth*:

> A line illustrious, thy retreats have known,
> In whom the HERO, STATESMAN, PATRIOT shone,
> Whose Virtue, Wisdom, Honour, Genius, Birth,
> Display'd their great hereditary worth.
> These are the rays which so conspicuous shine,
> And shed their glory, o'er great DEVON'S line.
> By these alone, distinguish'd we can see,
> The titled Slave, from the Nobility:
> Such are the barriers plac'd by Reason's hand,

[28] A. Bell, *Sydney Smith* (Oxford, 1980), p. 150.
[29] Anon., *Lettre familière d'un whig anglais*, pp. 15–16.
[30] Lord John Russell, *The life of William Lord Russell* (London, 1820), preface.
[31] H. Mackey, *Wit and whiggery* (Washington, 1979), p. 25.

From Anarchy to guard their native land,
When tyrant Pow'r, or fierce tumultuous Rage,
Would stain with war and blood th' historic page.[32]

Lesser whigs, with no historical endowments, nevertheless claimed the past in other ways. Erskine christened his son Hampden,[33] and was not alone in doing this. After Fox's death in 1806, more boys were given the names Charles James than was perhaps strictly necessary. Toasts at Whig Club and Fox dinners never failed to link the diners with their political ancestors. All whig epitaphs placed the honorand in a long line of heroes who had defended the rights of the people against tyrants. It was an apostolic succession older than the Christian. Chatsworth's garden was adorned by busts of Aristeides and Socrates, as well as Fox and the fifth Duke of Devonshire. Visitors to Holkham in Norfolk were similarly instructed about the owner's place in history. Four panels decorate a magnificent lobby. They depict the deaths of Socrates and Germanicus, the entry of Cosimo di Medici into Florence, and the signing of Magna Carta at Runnymede. In the last, the figure of King John has the face of William IV, while those of the barons standing around have the features of the members of the 1830 government. No words could more eloquently express the whig trusteeship of reform and constitutional change.

The opponents of the whigs were breathless with indignation at their claims that they had, for centuries, taken the hand of the people in the cause of reform and constitutional propriety. Pittites and tories allowed whigs a history, but not one that they would have relished. Socrates and Aristeides disappeared from view. Instead, a spoof play published in *Fraser's Magazine* had three witches giving political instruction to Lord John Russell. Chanting the slogan,

The monster of discord with faction is big
Which is christened Reform by its father, the Whig

they then conjured up the shades of Tiberius Gracchus, Catiline, Bonaparte and Oliver Cromwell by the way of offering models of behaviour. To make the point more firmly, they then turned Russell into Cromwell, as cartoonists had Fox in the previous generation.[34] Whig association with the people was nothing but ambition mounted on popularity. Sometimes the ruse succeeded, and a Bonaparte or Cromwell could build arbitrary government in the people's name. Sometimes it failed, and the Gracchii would then be torn apart by the people whose claims they trumpeted. To anti-whig writers, the whole spectacle was unedifying and unnatural.

[32] Anon., *Chatsworth: a poem* (London, n.d.), p. 20.
[33] Bodleian Library (Bod. Lib.), Oxford, MS. Eng. Misc., e 888 f. 40.
[34] *Fraser's Magazine*, 3 (1831), p. 496.

Disraeli was not alone in accusing the whigs of being so free with their favours that they effectively had put themselves outside the nation. They were beyond legitimate, political consideration. This patronage of demagogues was to be set alongside their friendship for Irish and American rebels and for French revolutionaries. By perverse instinct, they had 'tried to hoist the tricolour and to cover their haughty brows with a red cap'.[35] As a natural minority within politics, whigs had desperately searched out allies anywhere. Mongrel-coupling was their inevitable fate. According to *Blackwood's*, in 1825,

> Ever since the days of Fox, our Whig and other friends of the 'liberal system' have been addressing themselves principally and almost exclusively to the lower orders. They have passed by the better classes — the educated people — in scorn and have called upon the poor and the ignorant — the *uneducated people* — to decide on the most intricate constitutional questions, and the most complicated matters of general policy.[36]

The Reform Bill of 1832 was a case in point. Only an alliance with radicals would give them a parliamentary majority. Reform was the price of such an alliance, and so the whigs became reformers. As Disraeli bluntly put it: 'in the present instance they became sincerely parliamentary reformers, for by Parliamentary reform they could alone subsist'.[37]

It was an horrendous spectacle to tory eyes. Whiggery's excursions into the gutter, its unrestrained *nostalgie de la boue*, left it besmirched and defiled. David Robinson, one of the most effective anti-whig propagandists of the early nineteenth century, made this point often:

> That man, be he the most rigid of Tories, must have a heart formed of very strange materials, who can now look at Whiggism, and not compassionate its wretchedness. The blooming damsel who shone forth in so much fascinating loveliness in 1688, sacrificed her virtue in the French Revolution, and her subsequent adventures and present condition prove that she had drunk the cup of misery which seduction offers, even to the very dregs. She fell successively to the blandishments of Buonaparte, of the Radicals, of the Liberals, of the Carbonari, of the Benthamites, of any sooty body, and she is now sunk so low as to be rejected by all.[38]

Such writers characterized the new government of 1830 as the whig coalition with Captain Swing.[39] The whig association with the people was bogus from beginning to end. It did not spring from a genuine or well-intentioned wish to promote change, but rather from a wish to end years of proscription at any

---

[35] B. Disraeli, *The Runnymede letters* (London, 1936), II, p. 46.
[36] *Blackwood's Magazine*, 17 (1825), p. 534.
[37] Disraeli, *Runnymede*.
[38] *Blackwood's Magazine*, 16 (1824), p. 540.
[39] Ibid., 30 (1831), pp. 962–3.

price, even that of handing over power to the worst kind of demagogues and populists.

What made matters even worse, in tory eyes, was the sheer incongruity of whigs and radicals side by side. Whiggery was a caste system of great depth and complexity, and yet it caroused with the gutter. Tories bitterly noted that:

> aristocratic feelings ... in the Whigs ... created an anomaly, and involved, if ever traced fairly up to their source, two contradictory and hostile principles. A proud and exclusive temper, a demeanour somewhat haughty and reserved, a devotion to the interests of particular families, a great deference to the accident of birth, were scarcely reconcilable with that extreme attachment to the spirit and practice of the democratic parts of our government which they so loudly proclaimed.[40]

At the same time that whigs commented adversely on the low social origins of a Canning or Peel, they were apparently happy to consort with the rabble. For tories, this eclecticism was bewildering and more than a little unfair. It also created doubt about the whig definition of 'the people'. They claimed that the term referred to the country's intelligence and property, but could this be believed if they also disparaged the middle classes and chose to spend their evenings in taverns?

Tories trying to make sense of this behaviour could only grind their teeth at the stupidity of it. Whigs seemed incapable of understanding that, following the line they did, they must in the end bring about their own demise. The people must inevitably destroy aristocracy sooner or later. In private, they talked 'the most haughty and conservative language', and expatiated on 'the imminent danger to the holders of property', but in public all was different:

> listen to these Whig aristocrats on the hustings, or at public meetings; you will hear nothing but the necessity of yielding to public opinion, the growing importance and vast intelligence of the people, the irresistible weight of their voice, the paramount sway which they have acquired in the Constitution.[41]

The absurd incongruity of it all was staggering. According to the tories, whigs were quite right to see fellow-feeling in Lafayettes and Talleyrands, aristocrats who had made a lively contribution to the destruction of the system that had nourished them. It was matter for the novelist as well as the politician. Trollope, in *Phineas Finn*, was moved to describe 'as gallant a phalanx of Whig peers as ever were got together to fight against the instincts of their own order in compliance with the instincts of those below them'.[42]

---

[40] Sir J. Walsh, *On the present balance of parties in the state* (London, 1832), p. 22.
[41] *Blackwood's Magazine*, 35 (1834), p. 79.
[42] A. Trollope, *Phineas Finn*, ch. 10.

Some tories credited whigs with the belief that they could regulate the pace of change, and indeed that they could apply the brake if it went too far or too fast, but this was self-deception. W. C. Roscoe angrily referred to 'the childish way in which the Whigs say they can give a large impetus to democratic tendencies and stop them when they choose'. It made him 'long to whip them like foolish little boys'.[43] The penetrating intelligence of Tocqueville had reached the same conclusion, if in a more measured way. By 1835, he thought that the people had the whigs by the throat:

> For a century and a half the Whigs have played with the British Constitution, they believe that the game can continue, but the machine is worn and should be handled with discretion. They have talked of equality and freedom at a time when the people had a vague instinct, not a clear practical idea of these two things; they used it to come to power, and then left society almost in the state in which they found it. This experience of the past deceives them, and they believe they can do the same thing in a century when these same conceptions of freedom and liberty have taken clear shape in the idea of certain laws. After all the *Whigs* are only a fragment of the aristocratic party; they have long used democracy as a tool, but the tool has become stronger than the hand that guides it.[44]

On this analysis, whig cooperation with the people was only sustainable while popular demands lacked clarity and self-consciousness. Once these qualities were in place, whiggery was redundant. Poignantly, Lord John Russell must have entertained a similar opinion when he privately confessed to a close friend that he feared that the Reform Bill would destroy the Whig Party.[45]

There was much truth in the tory description of the whig cavortings with the people. It was indeed a strange spectacle, and whiggery would have no place in a democratic future. But to argue only this is to miss the essential point. Even if whig values were at a discount by 1850 or 1886 or 1914, they had, in the crucial years between 1760 and 1832, been of supreme importance. English radicalism, had, to some extent, been influenced in its tactics and views by the mere existence of whiggery. The English radical always had friends, real or pretended, at the very heart of the political elite. He had no reason to feel marginalized, or that his cause would not receive a parliamentary hearing. Counterfactually, if no whig party had existed, it is surely possible to argue that a straight fight between Orator Hunt and Lord Eldon, or even Robert Peel and Francis Burdett, would have been altogether much

---

[43] W. C. Roscoe to R. H. Hutton, 1859: Anon., *Poems and essays by the late William Caldwell Roscoe* (London, 1860), p. 64.

[44] J. Mayer, *Journeys to England and Ireland* (London, 1958), p. 80.

[45] Lord John Russell to Melbourne, 9 Sept. 1837: Public Record Office (PRO), Russell MSS., 30/22/2F XC 10466, f. 73.

less decorous. It is no disgrace in a party to have once done good service, but then to be made extinct by a change in the political climate. When the moment came, whigs exited gracefully.

Mischievously, from a whig viewpoint, radicals too often echoed some or all of these tory criticisms. Being unpleasant about whigs was an essential aspect of the phenomenon known as tory radicalism. Though whigs and radicals had, by 1830, at least fifty years of co-operation in lobbying and voting, the latter rarely showed the gratitude the former expected. In 1836, J. S. Mill brutally concluded that whigs 'were accepted by the Reformers as leaders because they offered themselves, and because there was nobody else'.[46] Clearly, whigs were useful in the sense of providing money and expertise, but there was always a feeling among radicals that they should be kept at arm's length. No radical, according to Hazlitt, should become 'a dangler after lords', and all of them should beware of 'the painted booths of the Whig Aristocracy'.[47] He himself sedulously declined dinner invitations for fear of contamination.

By 1841, after the experience of the Grey and Melbourne governments, many radicals gave whiggery up as an ally from whom real results could be expected, but this sense of distance was being expressed by the *Westminster Review* as early as 1824. James Mill there noted that,

> vague phrases, though of no service to the people, are admirably suited to the purpose of the Whigs; which is, to please the people, just as far as is consistent with not alarming the aristocracy. A well-turned rhetorical sentence asserting popular supremacy, is expected to be grateful to the ears of many among the people ... But if they require anything tangible — if they ask <u>what they are to get</u> by this boasted sovereignty, it calls them radicals and democrats, who wish for the annihilation of property, and the subversion of the social order.[48]

Alongside instances of whig helpfulness were memories of whig hauteur. In the 1790s, Horne Tooke was defended against Pittite persecution, but he was rejected as a running mate for Fox in the Westminster election of 1796. Melbourne was fond of Brougham and made him one of the executors of his will, but none of that led him to think him a fit member of a cabinet. The self-abasement required as the price of whig friendship was often too hard to learn.

Like so many tory critics, radicals accused the whigs of using them to win power only. Once in office, they forgot all radical claims, and settled down to some serious patronage-grazing. Sir William Molesworth observed that although the whigs 'had professed the most Radical doctrines and given the most democratic votes', and although they 'had been placed in power by

---

[46] Leonhard, *Liberalismusforschung*, p. 37.
[47] W. Henley, *The collected works of William Hazlitt* (London, 1902), VII, p. 376.
[48] *Westminster Review*, 1 (1824), p. 506.

the cry of union of reformers', they had almost immediately restricted politics to the distribution of 'emoluments'.[49] Joseph Parkes, fuming at the inactivity of the Melbourne government, denounced the whigs as 'an unnatural party standing between the People and the Tory aristocracy — chiefly for the pecuniary value of the offices and the vanity of power. Their hearse is ordered'.[50] Radical figures born within whiggery, like Grey's son-in-law Durham, were neutralized by being sent off to St Petersburg or Ontario. Radical leaders born outside the caste had not the slightest chance of ever being accepted within it. It seemed that whig words were welcoming and offered much. Whig government produced little or nothing.

Like tory critics again, therefore, radical writers accused the whigs of turning hypocrisy into art. They spoke of the rights of the people, but could be shocked by any low-born pretension. In 1820, a certain Dick Spooner announced his intention of standing for Warwickshire. The news sent the Lyttelton family into panic. A Birmingham manufacturer might possibly be accepted as the representative of a borough constituency, but it was out of the question that such a man should offer himself for a county seat. This was 'Brummidjam impudence'. It raised the possibility that the traditional knights of the shire were to be overtaken by men with 'plated spurs'.[51] The whig offer to help and guide the people was made on the understanding that the people should not take initiatives themselves. This did not necessarily cast doubt on the sincerity of the whigs in wishing to help, but these were terms that radicals and reformers found unacceptable. Roebuck, in 1835, believed that 'reform would never go boldly forward until the Whigs had been pushed back among the Tories, since, after all, they were but a modified offshoot of the Tories'.[52] Accordingly, radicals joined tories in denouncing whiggery as deceitful and only ambitious for office. To both groups, politics would have been so much less fuzzy if whiggery had not existed. But it did exist, and it had to be taken account of. Its presence gave British politics a unique dimension.

Reform in the 1830s, therefore, had a special character, because it was under whig management. Tocqueville, trying to describe the nature of change in England, was reduced to discussing political moods. The whigs, he wrote, 'have instincts rather than definite opinions in favour of reform; they let themselves be carried along without resistance by the spirit of the age which goes that way . . . they keep marching day by day without knowing too much

---

[49] Ibid., 26 (1837), p. 153.

[50] J. Parkes to F. Place, 2 Jan. 1836, quoted in W. E. S. Thomas, *The philosophic radicals* (Oxford, 1979), p. 289.

[51] W. H. Lyttelton to Lady S. Lyttelton, 16 Oct. 1820: H. Wyndham, *The correspondence of Sarah Spencer, Lady Lyttelton* (London, 1912), p. 230.

[52] Mayer, *Journeys*, p. 84.

about where the road they follow will end'.[53] What he should have gone on to say was that these 'instincts' were the product of a particular history, and not chance or random products of a particular situation. For decades, whigs had claimed to lead the people. The idea had become part of their self-identification, and it carried them along in the Reform Bill debates. Many cabinet ministers were the most reluctant of reformers, but they justified their votes by reference to prescription. Grey asserted that reform must come because it was in accordance with 'the wants and wishes of the people'.[54] Sir James Mackintosh urged his fellow whigs to 'do now what our forefathers, though rudely, aimed at doing, by calling into the national councils every rising element in the body politic'.[55] Melbourne, who personally disliked change of any kind, was always moved, paradoxically, by vague feelings that the people desired this or that, which factor, in his mind, decided any matter.[56] He was far from being alone in following a line of politics that directly contradicted his own preferences. History dictated them. When Grey retired, in July 1834, Samuel Rogers properly put his career into historical focus:

> Grey, thou hast served, and well, the sacred cause
> That Hampden, Sydney died for. Thou hast stood
> Scorning all thought of Self, from first to last
> Among the foremost in that glorious field.[57]

The Reform Bill debates rehearsed long-standing themes. Tories continued to marvel at whigs acting against their own instincts and interests. Radicals continued to complain that whig sympathy was never genuine, and never enough. It seemed, they insisted, that the whigs, 'in making their party professions of identity with the people ... were afraid of being taken by the people at their word'.[58] No account of 1832 was more grudging than Sir William Molesworth's. The whigs

> had long been excluded from office, and had connected themselves most intimately with the people, they frequently gave utterance to the most liberal opinions, and for a considerable period had advocated a reform in Parliament: to the amazement of all, to the regret of many of them, by a strange combination of events, they found that their demand was complied with.[59]

There is much truth in this description, but Molesworth should have added that, given every qualification he might make, reform did take place and under whig patronage.

---

[53] Ibid., p. 85.
[54] E. A. Wasson, *Journal of British Studies*, 24 (1985), p. 460.
[55] Mackintosh, *Vindiciae Gallicae*, III, p. 549.
[56] *Parl. Hist.*, 7 (1831), pp. 1177–86.
[57] P. W. Clayden, *Samuel Rogers and his contemporaries* (London, 1889), II, p. 101.
[58] *New Monthly Magazine*, 32 (1831), p. 160.
[59] *Westminster Review*, 26 (1837), p. 157.

In August 1810, Lord John Russell, who had largely grown up at Holland House, was yet again given a lesson in whiggery by Lord Holland himself. He was told that it was 'essential in a good Whig' that he should have 'a certain disposition to Reform of Parliament and no alarm at it if the present mode be found to be inadequate to ensure the confidence and enforce the will of the people'.[60] Forty years later, Bagehot took up the idea that whiggery was 'a disposition':

> In truth Whiggism is not a creed, it is a character. Perhaps as long as there have been certain men of a cool, moderate resolute firmness, not gifted with high imagination, little prone to enthusiastic sentiment, heedless of large theories and speculations, careless of dreamy scepticism; with a clear view of the next step, and a wise intention to act on it; with a strong conviction that the elements of knowledge are true, and a steady belief that the present world can, and should be, quietly improved. These are the Whigs.[61]

No doubt, men of this disposition could be found in every European country. Unfortunately, the predisposition to foster change had not been channelled, by historical convenience, into association with the people. Too often they had, instead, promoted their aims as the friends and servants of autocrats. Whiggery, by contrast, detested a single focus of power. Rulers were to be feared more than the people, who thereby became allies. Whiggery, as a disposition, contributed greatly to the character of reform, and determined its shape and nature. Whigs expressed this purpose with a pleasing lack of self-consciousness. In 1796, Joseph Jekyll reported to Lord Lansdowne that Erskine was correcting and polishing addresses coming out of Thelwall's meetings. He went on proudly to approve this behaviour, because, by it, 'we shall quench their revolutionary Projects — by moulding and moderating them to general political Purposes'.[62]

---

[60] Holland to Lord John Russell, 13 Aug. 1810: R. Russell, *The early correspondence of Lord John Russell* (London, 1913), I, p. 137.

[61] *National Review*, 1, (1855) p. 262.

[62] J. Jekyll to Lord Lansdowne, 14 Nov. 1796, Bod. Lib. MS Film 2004, f. 76.

Legal Reforms:
Changing the Law in Germany in
the *Ancien Régime* and in the *Vormärz*

DIETHELM KLIPPEL

IF WE CONSIDER the notions of law and of reform and their relation to each other, our first reaction might be influenced by rather sceptical thoughts. To a certain extent, it always was and still is the task of the law to uphold the status quo. As far as this is the case, putting together 'law' and 'reforms' might even be seen as a contradiction in itself. On the other hand, the law is subject to change, and these changes can be effected by deliberate acts. Morever, any reforms are usually accomplished by the law, or, to put it in more general terms, by instruments which the law provides or which have legal effects.[1] In this sense, any reform is a legal reform and a legal change. For the subject of my paper, this would open up the whole panorama of reforms in Germany in the eighteenth and the first half of the nineteenth century.

The scope of my paper has to be more modest. I will not look at law reforms in the sense of a book published in London in 1901, which considers the changes in all branches of the law in the nineteenth century, from criminal law, public and private international law, labour law, real property and so on, to joint stock and limited liability companies.[2] I will deal with the

---

[1] For the history of the notion 'reform', see Eike Wolgast, 'Reform, Reformation', in Otto Brunner, Werner Conze and Reinhart Koselleck, eds, *Geschichtliche Grundbegriffe. Historisches Lexikon zur politisch-sozialen Sprache in Deutschland* (8 vols, Stuttgart, 1975–97), v, pp. 313–60; the relation between enlightened absolutism and reforms is discussed in H. M. Scott, ed., *Enlightened absolutism: reform and reformers in later eighteenth-century Europe* (Ann Arbor, 1990); cf. also the useful overview by Walter Demel, *Vom aufgeklärten Reformstaat zum bürokratischen Staatsabsolutismus* (Munich, 1993), and Günter Birtsch, 'Aufgeklärter Absolutismus oder Reformabsolutismus?', *Aufklärung*, 9 (1996), pp. 101–9; Eberhard Weis, ed., *Reformen im rheinbündischen Deutschland* (Munich, 1984).
[2] *A century of law reforms: twelve lectures on the changes in the law of England during the nineteenth century* (London, 1901).

Proceedings of the British Academy, **100**, 43–59. © The British Academy 1999.

changes in legislation and in its concept, in other words, with legislative reforms, with projects for reforms and with the theory of legislation. Still, the history of legislation remains a vast area, so I shall concentrate on some parts of it. My main point will be that, on the whole, the legal reform projects of enlightened absolutism in Germany were destined to fail, whereas the reform legislation of the German states in the first half of the nineteenth century was more successful.

My paper will have four parts. To begin with it will briefly outline the developments which are usually regarded as important for the history of legislation in Germany in the eighteenth and nineteenth centuries. Then the focus will be on some fundamental concepts and aims of legislation and reforms in the era of enlightened absolutism. The third section will deal with the question of how the ambitions of the reform programme of enlightened absolutism relate to the German states' reality. The fourth and final part will look at legislation and its theory in the German states in the first part of the nineteenth century.

The traditional view: the two phases of the history of codification in Germany

In the history of legislation and of the theory of legislation in Germany in the eighteenth and nineteenth centuries, as one would find them, for instance, in textbooks on legal history, two developments are usually considered to be important.[3] The first one comprises the four decades around 1800 and is commonly, yet misleadingly, referred to as the era of natural law codifications (*Naturrechtskodifikationen*). It is seen as a European phenomenon, the most important and influential results of which are supposed to be the Prussian 'Allgemeines Landrecht' of 1794, the Austrian civil code of 1811–12 (*Allgemeines Bürgerliches Gesetzbuch*) and the French codifications. In terms of Germany, one might describe the projects and results of this movement towards codifying the law as the legislative efforts of enlightened absolutism and of the age of reforms. Both the history of the codes themselves and the political and legal theory upon which they were based are covered relatively

---

[3] See R. C. van Caenegem, *An historical introduction to private law* (Cambridge, 1992); Friedrich Ebel, *Rechtsgeschichte. Ein Lehrbuch* (Heidelberg, 1993), II; Wilhelm Ebel, *Geschichte der Gesetzgebung in Deutschland* (2nd edn, Göttingen, 1958; reprinted with supplements, Göttingen, 1988); Ulrich Eisenhardt, *Deutsche Rechtsgeschichte* (2nd edn, Munich, 1995); Hans Hatten-hauer, *Europäische Rechtsgeschichte* (Heidelberg, 1992); Karl Kroeschell, *Deutsche Rechtsgeschichte* (2nd edn, Wiesbaden, 1993), III; Adolf Laufs, *Rechtsentwicklungen in Deutschland* (5th edn, Berlin/New York, 1996); O. F. Robinson, T. D. Fergus and W. M. Gordon, *An introduction to European legal history* (2nd edn, Edinburgh, 1987); Hans Schlosser, *Grundzüge der Neueren Privatrechtsgeschichte* (8th edn, Heidelberg, 1996); Uwe Wesel, *Geschichte des Rechts. Von den Frühformen bis zum Vertrag von Maastricht* (Munich, 1997).

comprehensively by scholarly literature.[4] However, there is considerable controversy about the political aims which enlightened rulers in Germany pursued with planning or — in Prussia — actually putting into force new codifications.

The second crucial development is usually seen to be the vast legislation by the second German empire after its foundation in 1871. In fact, the many codes enacted during that period have moulded even the German legal system of today; quite a number of them are still in force, though they have been altered to a greater or lesser degree since then. Legislative efforts before 1871, for instance by the German Union (*Deutscher Bund*), are usually regarded as mere predecessors of the legislation of the German empire.

This view of the history of legislation in Germany seems to be corroborated by the result of one of the most famous controversies in German legal history.[5] In 1814, Anton Friedrich Justus Thibaut, professor of law at the University of Heidelberg, had argued in favour of a civil code for Germany.[6] His Berlin colleague, Friedrich Carl von Savigny, opposed this view and pleaded that Roman law should retain its central position.[7] As a German civil code did not come into force before 1900, it seemed that Savigny and the historical school of law had effectively prevented legislative efforts for codifications for more than half a century.

Yet the whole view seems to neglect other and perhaps more important perspectives. The concept of 'natural law codes' is misleading as it suggests that the codes mostly embodied the principles and teachings of the textbooks and writings of the natural law of that time. Moreover, it seems to underline the common characteristics rather than the vast differences between the Prussian code on the one hand and more modern ones like the French codes and the Austrian civil code on the other. Apart from this, the focus on a few however important codes does prevent us realizing the importance of many other statutes and to see the whole scope of the legislative activities and aims of the German states of that time. As to the period up to the founding of the 'Norddeutscher Bund' and the second German empire, the considerable and successful legislative activities of the German states up to that time are not

---

[4] See the useful bibliography in Laufs, *Rechtsentwicklungen*, 145–8, 159–61; Helmut Coing, ed., *Handbuch der Quellen und Literatur der neueren europäischen Privatrechtsgeschichte* (Munich, 1982), III(i), entry on France by Ernst Holthöfer, pp. 863–1068; for Austria see note 18, for Prussia note 35.

[5] For a thorough and scholarly analysis of the Thibaut–Savigny controversy, see Joachim Rückert, *Jurisprudenz und Politik bei Friedrich Carl von Savigny* (Ebelsbach, 1984), pp. 160–93.

[6] Anton Friedrich Justus Thibaut, *Ueber die Nothwendigkeit eines allgemeinen bürgerlichen Rechts für Deutschland* (Heidelberg, 1814).

[7] Friedrich Carl von Savigny, *Vom Beruf unserer Zeit für Gesetzgebung und Rechtswissenschaft* (Heidelberg, 1814); an English translation by Abraham Hayward was published in 1831: *Of the vocation of our age for legislation and jurisprudence* (London, 1831).

taken into account. Recent research indicates that it might be this legislation which adapted German law to the social, economic, and political needs of that time.[8]

Legislation and reforms in the era of enlightened absolutism

1 In the course of the eighteenth century, the governments of many German states, and likewise many intellectuals, thought of reforming the existing law. But what was the existing law, or, more precisely, which were the sources from which the law was drawn? In the German context, there usually is no simple answer to this question, as it might be that dozens of quite different sources have to be considered, depending on which territory, town or even village the question would be asked for. To give a somewhat simplified answer one could say that, on the whole, Roman law applied since the so-called reception of the Roman law or rather since the spreading of academically trained lawyers since the twelfth century. In addition to that, there were statutes of the German empire and of the German princes and townships as well as medieval precedents, law-books (*Rechtsbücher*) — i.e. private compilations like the *Sachsenspiegel* — and customary laws, to mention but a few other sources. In theory, the more specific sources prevailed over Roman law; but, in practice, it might be difficult to prove that a specific customary law really existed in a village, and lawyers trained in Roman law certainly tended to apply their skills and their knowledge of Roman law, which they had learned at the law faculty of a university, even to legal sources of quite different origins.

But if the sources — not to mention the contents — of the law were heterogeneous in this way, the question arises what the concept of reforming the law was, who would be the competent person or body to change the law, and what changes were to be brought about?

2 In 1747, two lecturers at the Prussian University of Halle, the brothers and doctors Gustav Bernhard Beckmann and Ott David Heinrich Beck-

---

[8] See Rolf Grawert, 'Gesetzgebung im Wirkungszusammenhang konstitutioneller Regierung', in *Gesetzgebung als Faktor der Staatsentwicklung* (Berlin, 1984), pp. 113–60; Coing, ed., *Handbuch der Quellen und Literatur der neueren europäischen Privatrechtsgeschichte* III(ii), pp. 1403–561 (entries by Barbara Dölemeyer on several German states), pp. 1626–773 (Stephan Buchholz); in III(i), see also the introductory essays by Helmut Coing ('Allgemeine Züge der privatrechtlichen Gesetzgebung im 19. Jahrhundert'), pp. 3–16, and Dieter Grimm ('Die verfassungsrechtlichen Grundlagen der Privatrechtsgesetzgebung'), pp. 17–173; as to the criminal law of that time, see the reprinting project *Kodifikationsgeschichte Strafrecht* (Goldbach, 1988–), ed. and with introductory essays by Werner Schubert *et al.*; Rainer Schröder, 'Die Strafgesetzgebung in Deutschland in der ersten Hälfte des 19. Jahrhunderts', in *Die Bedeutung der Wörter. Festschrift für Sten Gagnér* (Munich, 1991), pp. 403–20.

mann, dealt with some of these problems in a pamphlet called *Thoughts on reforming the law*.[9] Reforming the law, they pointed out, has two meanings: firstly, to change the law and statutes of a state, and secondly, to change the way to teach them at a university. They emphasize that it is a *ius majestaticum*, the exclusive right of the ruler of a state, to legislate and to change the law by legislation; therefore, they point out, it cannot be up to his subjects to legislate or even to come near to it by teaching a new law. If academic lawyers want to reform the law, they are restricted to changing the manner of teaching it, but they are not allowed to meddle with its contents.

Though the direct purpose of the pamphlet was to attack the law professor Daniel Nettelbladt,[10] a colleague of theirs in Halle, we can use it as a starting point to get some answers to our questions, since the brothers Beckmann represent the mainstream of political theory dealing with legal reforms at the time.

First of all, the question of reforming the law was clearly deemed worth treating in the middle of the eighteenth century. Changes in the law were to be effected by legislation. As the Beckmanns wrote in the eighteenth century and not in the Middle Ages, this is not surprising. But who is to be the legislator?

The authors presuppose that the ruler of a territory in Germany had the right to legislate. Legally speaking, this was not self-evident at all, as this right was supposed to be the most important part of sovereignty.[11] Up to the end of the German empire, it was highly controversial among German lawyers and political theorists as to who in the empire was sovereign — the emperor, or the emperor together with the imperial estates (*Reichsstände*), or the rulers of the many German monarchies and republics (e.g. *Reichsstädte*), or these rulers together with their estates (*Landstände*) respectively.[12] Nevertheless, in the eighteenth century, the legislative power is usually attributed to the rulers of the many German territories, and they certainly exercised this right, which was usually considered as encompassing the right to give general laws and to provide for single cases by legislation, as well as the right to

---

[9] Gustav Bernhard Beckmann and Ott David Heinrich Beckmann, *Gedancken vom Reformiren des Rechts. Womit sie ihre instehende Winter-Vorlesungen anzeigen* (Halle, 1747).

[10] This becomes obvious when reading the anonymously published answer to the Beckmanns' pamphlet, *Schreiben eines guten Freundes von Halle an einen andern nach Jena, nebst einigen Anmerckungen über die Gedancken der Herren Beckmänner vom Reformiren des Rechts* (Jena, 1747).

[11] See Helmut Quaritsch, *Staat und Souveränität, Die Grundlagen* (Frankfurt, 1970), I, especially pp. 343 ff.; Helmut Quaritsch, *Souveränität. Entstehung und Entwicklung des Begriffs in Frankreich und Deutschland vom 13. Jh. bis 1806* (Berlin/Munich, 1986).

[12] See Diethelm Klippel, 'Staat und Souveränität VI–VIII', in Brunner, Conze and Koselleck, eds, *Geschichtliche Grundbegriffe*, VI, pp. 115–20.

interpret the laws authentically, to change them, to repeal them generally or in a particular case (*Dispens*), and to grant privileges.[13]

3 But what, then, were the goals of law reforms by legislation? This question can be answered by looking at a contemporary English translation of one of the first comprehensive reform projects, the Prussian *Project des Corporis Juris Fridericiani*. Two parts of the planned three parts were published in German in 1749 and 1751. Section 10 of the introduction summarizes what the reform was thought to be about; it neatly and concisely puts together the aims of the legislative reforms of an enlightened absolutist government:[14]

> In order to remedy so many abuses, we have caused compose a body of law for our dominions, founded on certain and rational principles; in which we have indeed taken the Roman law for a foundation, in so far as its general principles appeared drawn from natural reason, and we have preserved the names and terms of art, to which so many judges, and even the subjects are already accustomed. But we have excluded all the subtilties [sic] of the Roman laws, and every thing not applicable to the constitution of our dominions. We have especially had it in view, to reduce the whole work to the form of a clear and distinct system; and we have caused publish it in the German language, that our subjects may themselves be able to read it, and occasionally to have recourse to it. We have introduced into it, under proper rubrics, all the edicts concerning judicatures, without treating here of those which regard the police, military affairs, and the like.

Here, we find all the well-known ingredients which are typical for enlightened absolutist law reforms: the author aims at replacing the function of Roman law by a codification which, nevertheless, is based on Roman law to a great extent. The code's purpose is to simplify and unify the law; it is to be clear and easily understandable, therefore, it is to be written and published in German.

Elsewhere, the Bavarian codes dated around 1750 and an Austrian draft, the *Codex Theresianus*, from 1766, are early examples of the states' efforts to codify their law or parts of it. In the case of Prussia and Austria, there is no need to recall the further history of these efforts: they resulted in the Prussian

---

[13] E.g. Ludwig Julius Friedrich Höpfner, *Naturrecht des einzelnen Menschen, der Gesellschaften der Völker* (2nd edn, Gießen, 1783), pp. 164 f.; Carl Anton Freiherr von Martini, *Lehrbegriff des Natur-, Staats- und Völkerrechts*, III, *Allgemeines Staatsrecht* (Vienna, 1783), pp. 49 f.; Ludwig Gottfried Madihn, *Grundsätze des Naturrechts zum Gebrauch seiner Vorlesungen*, II (Frankfurt a. d. Oder, 1795), pp. 77 f. Cf. Heinz Mohnhaupt, 'Potestas legislatoria und Gesetzesbegriff im Ancien Régime', *Ius commune*, 4 (1972), pp. 188–239.

[14] I quote from the English translation: *The Frederician Code; or, a body of law for the dominions of the king of Prussia. Founded on reason, and the constitutions of the country* (2 vols, Edinburgh, 1761), I, p. 10–11. The English translation was based upon a French edition.

Allgemeines Landrecht of 1794 and the Austrian general civil code of 1811. But these three comparatively big states were by no means the only ones which addressed themselves to the task of legal reforms. On the contrary, in the eighteenth century, nearly every German state considered drafting a codification. Further examples about which Barbara Dölemeyer has collected new material are Baden, Hanover, Hessen-Darmstadt, Hessen-Kassel, Mecklenburg, and Saxony.[15] Some authors, like Karl Theodor von Dalberg in 1787 or the Dean of the Faculty of Law of the University of Freiburg as late as in 1803, even demanded that the German empire draft and put into force a general code.[16]

All the examples display the same pattern.[17] As a first step, a compilation consisting of Roman law and the law of the land was considered; in this process, Roman law was to be cleared of discrepancies and academic controversies. In some states this was all that happened. As a second step a complete code of law was planned, in some cases later on influenced by the developments in Prussia. Even the theory underlying the projects and the thoughts about the aims of legislation were more or less the same as in Prussia.

Ambitions and reality

The authors of various eighteenth-century texts justifying plans to reform the law pointed out that the existing unclear and complex laws were the reason for unnecessary and costly litigation.[18] This indicates that the states possessed ulterior motives for revising the law. In fact, the planning of codes was part of what might be called an entire programme of reforms in contemporary German states. It is well known that we speak of 'enlightened' or 'reformist' absolutism, because such reforms are seen as characteristic for most governments in the second half of the eighteenth century.[19]

---

[15] Barbara Dölemeyer, 'Kodifikationspläne in deutschen Territorien des 18. Jahrhunderts', in Barbara Dölemeyer and Diethelm Klippel, eds, *Gesetz und Gesetzgebung im Europa der Frühen Neuzeit* (Berlin, 1998), pp. 201–23.

[16] Ibid.

[17] See Dölemeyer, 'Kodifikationspläne'; Werner Ogris, 'Aufklärung, Naturrecht und Rechtsreform in der Habsburgermonarchie', *Aufklärung*, 3 (1988), pp. 29–51; Wilhelm Brauneder, 'Vernünftiges Recht als überregionales Recht: Die Rechtsvereinheitlichung der österreichischen Zivilrechtskodifikationen 1786–1797–1811', in Reiner Schulze, ed., *Europäische Rechts- und Verfassungsgeschichte. Ergebnisse und Perspektiven der Forschung* (Berlin, 1991), pp. 121–37.

[18] *The Frederician Code*, I, p. 8; Georg Friedrich Lamprecht, *Versuch eines vollständigen Systems der Staatslehre* (Berlin, 1784), p. 203.

[19] The various views of 'aufgeklärter Absolutismus' and 'Reformabsolutismus' are discussed by Demel, *Vom aufgeklärten Reformstaat*, pp. 61 ff. and in Scott, ed., *Enlightened absolutism*.

1 I would like to illustrate this with the case of Hessen-Darmstadt.[20] When Landgrave Ludwig IX assumed power in 1768, he inherited a debt of enormous proportions: almost 4 million Gulden was owed to around 150 creditors, threatening to precipitate direct rule on the part of the Holy Roman Emperor, bringing an end to the rule of the house of Hessen-Darmstadt. In 1772 Ludwig IX appointed the famous Friedrich Karl von Moser chancellor and president of council. Moser tried to reconstruct the declining Hessian economy through reform; sequestration was avoided by financial settlements concluded in 1772 and 1779. Among those measures that he sought to introduce were reforms to the administration and to the judiciary, which involved among other things the introduction of a new form of remuneration to judges, the creation of a court of appeal, the inauguration of a commission charged with the collation of information on prevailing economic and social conditions, and also the foundation of a journal, the *Hessen-Darmstädtische privilegirte Landeszeitung*; Moser succeeded in getting the writer and poet Matthias Claudius as an editor. Administrative reform required, not least of all, suitably qualified experts, and Moser expected that these would be created by thorough cameralistic training rather than by relying on the state's existing elites. This training was going to be provided by the Economic Faculty of the state's university, the University of Gießen; therefore, a fifth faculty, the Economic Faculty, was founded in 1777. However, the faculty existed for eight years only.[21]

It is not surprising that the plan to create a code, the *Codex Ludovicianus* formed part of this programme in Hessen,[22] as it was realized that the quality of the law and of the staff putting it into practice influenced the amount of litigation and the economy in general. Consequently, the law and the judiciary could not be neglected.

The motivations and pitfalls of reform in the smaller and medium-sized states of the German empire have been outlined by Eberhard Weis:[23] the aim

---

[20] For the following, cf. Jürgen Rainer Wolf, 'Hessen-Darmstadt und seine Landgrafen in der Zeit des Barock, Absolutimus und der Aufklärung (1650–1803)', in Uwe Schultz, ed., *Die Geschichte Hessens* (Stuttgart, 1983), pp. 121 ff., 130 f.; Karl Witzel, *Friedrich Carl von Moser. Ein Beitrag zur hessen-darmstädtischen Finanz- und Wirtschaftsgeschichte am Ausgang des 18. Jahrhunderts* (Darmstadt, 1929); Hans Heinrich Kaufmann, *Friedrich Carl von Moser als Politiker und Publizist (vornehmlich in den Jahren 1750–1770)* (Darmstadt, 1931); Angela Stirken, *Der Herr und der Diener. Friedrich Carl von Moser und das Beamtentum seiner Zeit* (Bonn, 1984).

[21] Diethelm Klippel, 'Johann August Schlettwein and the Economic Faculty at the University of Gießen', *History of Political Thought*, 15 (1994), pp. 203–27.

[22] Dölemeyer, 'Kodifikationspläne', p. 203.

[23] Eberhard Weis, 'Der aufgeklärte Absolutismus in den mittleren und kleinen deutschen Staaten', *Zeitschrift für bayerische Landesgeschichte*, 42 (1979), pp. 31 ff., also in idem, *Deutschland und Frankreich um 1800* (Munich, 1990); cf. Charles Ingrao, 'The smaller German states', in Scott, ed., *Enlightened absolutism*, pp. 221–43.

was to strengthen the state by increasing its revenues; but the realization of this aim was prevented by constitutional and social structures of the corporatist state in which the estates (the *Stände*) played a central or important role, by a fragmented and/or small territory with an equally fragmented sovereignty, both of which impeded the implementation of an independent economic policy, and by the lack of an efficient, well-educated administration. This might well be true for the larger states as well.[24]

2   Before turning to the question of success or failure of the reforms, I would like to look briefly at the blueprints for the reforms, the underlying political theory of enlightened absolutism: it is the 'law of nature' of that time. In Germany, numerous textbooks and treaties on natural law and universal public law — *ius publicum universale*, that part of natural law concerned specifically with the state — legitimated the absolutist ambitions of the princes as well as the reforming activities of enlightened absolutism.[25]

This may be illustrated by the theory of the purpose of the state.[26] In the natural law of enlightened absolutism, *Glückseligkeit* — happiness — both of the state as a whole and of its subjects, was frequently regarded as the chief end of all the state's activities. This led to a vast extension of the concerns of the state, as it was regarded as the task of the state to achieve even the happiness of the individuals, who, therefore, were not supposed to be free or independent in their pursuit of happiness. Accordingly, the state had to legislate very comprehensively, as shown by a book on the theory of legislation, published anonymously in 1777: 'if they [i.e. the laws] do not regulate everything which can be regulated, if they do not put the whole of society into such an order that all its parts and their changes correspond with the common weal, then disorder will more or less prevail in them'.[27]

Contemporary textbooks of universal public law and *Polizeiwissenschaft* convey an image of what the state had to regulate by legislation. In addition

---

[24] See Demel, *Vom aufgeklärten Reformstaat*, pp. 73 ff., 77 f., 80 ff., 83 ff.; for Prussia, see T. C. W. Blanning, 'Frederick the Great and enlightened absolutism', in Scott, ed., *Enlightened Absolutism*, pp. 265–88; Eckhart Hellmuth, 'Der Staat des 18. Jahrhunderts: England und Preußen im Vergleich', *Aufklärung*, 9 (1996), pp. 5–24; the discrepancies between the plans of the enlightened absolutist reformers as regards schooling and their realization are described persuasively by Wolfgang Neugebauer, *Absolutistischer Staat und Schulwirklichkeit in Brandenburg-Preussen* (Berlin, 1985) and James Van Horn Melton, *Absolutism and the eighteenth-century origins of compulsory schooling in Prussia and Austria* (Cambridge, 1988).

[25] Diethelm Klippel, 'The true concept of liberty: political theory in Germany in the second half the eighteenth century', in Eckhart Hellmuth, ed., *The transformation of political culture: England and Germany in the late eighteenth century* (Oxford, 1990), pp. 447–66, especially 452–6.

[26] In the following, I rely on material and deliberations also used in Diethelm Klippel, 'Reasonable aims of civil society: concerns of the state in German political theory in the eighteenth and nineteenth century', in John Brewer and Eckhart Hellmuth, eds, *Rethinking Leviathan: the eighteenth-century state in Britain and Germany* (Oxford, forthcoming 1999).

[27] *Entwurf der allgemeinen Grundsätze der Gesetzgebung* (Frankfurt/Leipzig, 1777), pp. 117 f.

to war, taxation, and the administration of justice, it was the duty of the state to maintain '*gute Policey*'; '*gute Policey*' can be seen as the means to reach the final aim, i.e. *Glückseligkeit* as the purpose of the state. In this sense, a contemporary author defined *Polizei* as 'the sum of all endeavours to link the welfare of the individual directly with the *Glückseligkeit* of the whole. Its objects are the population, morality, skills, safety, comfort, nourishment, wealth, and honour'.[28] This opened up a vast area for the state's activities — and thus for legal reforms, starting with the economy and public health, and ending with morality, religion, the family, education, and other cultural aspects such as the arts.

One might ask where all this leaves the progressive concepts we usually associate with the Enlightenment, for instance natural rights, the abolition of torture and of the death penalty and others. On the whole, the discussion about all these topics fits well into the pattern outlined above. It was supposed to be in the interest of the state to find out what served its purpose and concerns best, and so the discussion of many subjects was encouraged by means of prize competitions run by academies, universities, societies, or by the state itself.[29] I am not concerned here with the dynamics public discourse could develop: of course, there were limits to what the state would tolerate. For instance, the Austrian government rejected the suggestion of a 'political code' which would have laid down, among other things, certain constitutional principles and perhaps even natural rights.[30] But, on the whole, enlightened discourse did not really trouble the enlightened absolutist state and its theory, as long as it did not question the absolutist rule.

3   Many German states actually put parts of their reform programme into practice or tried to do so. That raises the question of to what extent the law reforms were successful.

[28] Heinrich Gottfried Scheidemantel, *Das allgemeine Staatsrecht überhaupt und nach der Regierungsform* (Jena, 1775), p. 95. On the concept of '*gute Policey*' cf. Franz-Ludwig Knemeyer, 'Polizei', *Economy and Society*, 9 (1980), pp. 172–96; Peter Preu, *Polizeibegriff und Staatszwecklehre. Die Entwicklung des Polizeibegriffs durch die Rechts- und Staatswissenschaften des 18. Jahrhunderts* (Göttingen, 1983); Marc Raeff, *The well-ordered police state* (New Haven and London, 1983); Michael Stolleis, *Geschichte des öffentlichen Rechts in Deutschland* (2 vols, Munich, 1988 and 1992), I, pp. 334 ff., II, pp. 250 ff.; Hans Boldt, 'Geschichte der Polizei in Deutschland', in *Handbuch des Polizeirechts* (Munich, 1992), pp. 1 ff.

[29] Cf. the examples in: Hans-Heinrich Müller, *Akademie und Wirtschaft im 18. Jahrhundert. Agrarökonomische Preisaufgaben und Preisschriften der Preußischen Akademie der Wissenschaften im Zeitalter der Aufklärung* (Berlin, 1975); Rudolf Vierhaus ed., *Deutsche patriotische und gemeinnützige Gesellschaften* (Munich, 1980); Ulrich Im Hof, *Das gesellige Jahrhundert. Gesellschaft und Gesellschaften im Zeitalter der Aufklärung* (Munich, 1982). Indeed, after the publication of the first draft of the Prussian code (*Entwurf eines Allgemeinen Gesetzbuchs für die Preußischen Staaten*, Berlin, 1784–8), the public was asked to criticize the draft, and prizes were offered for the best contributions (*Monita*): see Andreas Schwennicke, *Die Entstehung der Einleitung des Preußischen Allgemeinen Landrechts von 1794* (Frankfurt a.M., 1993), pp. 29 ff.

[30] Ogris, 'Aufklärung, Naturrecht und Rechtsreform in der Habsburgermonarchie', p. 36.

There can be no doubt that they succeeded in some regards, for example the abolition of torture, or the enactment of minor but nevertheless important codes such as, for instance, procedural codes.[31] But I would like to argue that, contrary to widely accepted views, parts of the reform programme were bound to fail, and in fact did fail.

To start with, the mere scope of the reform programme is enough to render one sceptical. Even modern states with efficient administrations would find it difficult to fulfil the many goals of enlightened absolutism. In eighteenth-century German states there simply was no efficient, well-trained bureaucracy; on the contrary, one of the aims of the reform programme was to create an efficient body of civil servants, so that, at its best, this process had just started.[32]

Secondly, the intended reforms, and indeed many of the successful reforms, conflicted with the constitutional rights of the estates and corporations. Many aims of enlightened absolutism implied a massive infringement of these rights. This could create a dilemma: either the estates turned hostile to reforms, or reforms had to be watered down by taking into account the existing rights. In spite of bold theoretical ambitions, absolutism never really overcame these obstacles.[33] Still, sometimes the estates contributed to the reform policy.[34]

Thirdly, leaving economic reforms aside, there is also much evidence to suggest that the idea of having a universal code of law as represented by the Prussian *Allgemeines Landrecht* of 1794 is not a good argument for the success of enlightened absolutism, though this has hardly ever been questioned so far.[35] For a start, the *Allgemeines Landrecht* was only ever intended

---

[31] As to Prussia, new procedural codes were enacted in 1781 and 1793, and a *Hypothekenordnung* in 1783.

[32] See Wilhelm Bleek, *Von der Kameralausbildung zum Juristenprivileg. Studium, Prüfung und Ausbildung der höheren Beamten des allgemeinen Verwaltungsdienstes in Deutschland im 18. und 19. Jahrhundert* (Berlin, 1972); Bernd Wunder, *Geschichte der Bürokratie in Deutschland* (Frankfurt a.M., 1986).

[33] For the role of the estates in Prussia, see Peter Baumgart, 'Zur Geschichte der kurmärkischen Stände im 17. und 18. Jahrhundert', in Dietrich Gerhard, ed., *Ständische Vertretungen in Europa im 17. und 18. Jahrhundert* (Göttingen, 1969); esp. for their contribution to drafting the Prussian code: Günter Birtsch, 'Gesetzgebung und Repräsentation im späten Absolutismus. Die Mitwirkung der preußischen Provinzialstände bei der Entstehung des Allgemeinen Landrechts', *Historische Zeitschrift*, 208 (1969), pp. 265–94; Schwennicke, *Die Entstehung*, pp. 34 ff.

[34] Demel, *Vom aufgeklärten Reformstaat*, pp. 67 f.

[35] A number of books published on the occasion of the Prussian code's 200th anniversary provide a good impression about older and recent research and about scholarly controversies: Günter Birtsch and Dietmar Willoweit, eds, *Reformabsolutismus und ständische Gesellschaft. 200 Jahre preußisches Allgemeines Landrecht* (Berlin, 1998); Barbara Dölemeyer and Heinz Mohnhaupt, eds, *200 Jahre Allgemeines Landrecht für die preußischen Staaten. Wirkungsgeschichte und internationaler Kontext* (Frankfurt a.M., 1995); Friedrich Ebel, ed., *Gemeinwohl — Freiheit — Vernunft — Rechtsstaat. 200 Jahre Allgemeines Landrecht für die Preußischen Staaten* (Berlin, 1995); Gerd Kleinheyer, *Das Allgemeine Landrecht für die Preußischen Staaten vom 1. Juni 1794*

to be subsidiary law. As such, it replaced Roman law in some parts of the law, such as for instance private law. But Roman law maintained its leading role as the most important field even at Prussian universities, whereas lectures on the Prussian *Allgemeines Landrecht* were rarely given. Moreover, the notion of drafting a code which completely covered the fields of law it dealt with and which was so clear that it needed no interpretation soon turned out to be an illusion despite the nearly 20,000 sections of the code. Proof for this can be found in many successful periodicals which satisfied the needs of Prussian lawyers to be informed about legislation changing the *Landrecht*, about questions of interpretation and about interesting cases.[36] Moreover, the code was soon out of step with contemporary ideas about the methods and contents of legislation. A comparison between the *Allgemeines Landrecht* and the French codes can demonstrate this clearly. Still, some of the contents of the code were sensible legal innovations or proved to be useful in the nineteenth century; so, in this respect, the values of the code should not be underestimated.

But the assertions that the Prussian *Allgemeines Landrecht* guaranteed civil liberties or civil liberties of a kind, that it fulfilled the functions of a written constitution or that it really intended to further the rule of law are, at their best, grossly exaggerated.[37] Research by, amongst others, Eckhart

(Heidelberg, 1995); Detlev Merten and Waldemar Schreckenberger, eds, *Kodifikation gestern und heute. Zum 200. Geburtstag des Allgemeinen Landrechts für die Preußischen Staaten* (Berlin, 1995); Jörg Wolff, ed., *Das preußische Allgemeine Landrecht. Politische, rechtliche und soziale Wechsel- und Fortwirkungen* (Heidelberg, 1995). See also Gerhard Dilcher, 'Die janusköpfige Kodifikation', *Zeitschrift für Europäisches Privatrecht*, 2 (1994), pp. 446–69.

[36] In addition to the *Annalen der Gesetzgebung und Rechtsgelehrsamkeit in den Preussischen Staaten*, ed. Ernst Ferdinand Klein (26 vols, 1788–1809), which, originally, were meant to inform about questions relating to legislation and to the drafting and the progress of the Prussian code, there were the following journals: *Beiträge zur Kenntniß der Justizverfassung und juristischen Literatur in den Preußischen Staaten*, ed. F. P. Eisenberg and L. Stengel (18 vols, 1796–1804); *Archiv des Preußischen Rechts*, ed. Karl Ludwig Amelang and K. August Gründler (3 vols, 1799–1800); *Neues Archiv der Preußischen Gesetzgebung und Rechtsgelehrsamkeit*, ed. Karl Ludwig Amelang (4 vols, 1800–5); *Allgemeine juristische Monatsschrift für die Preußischen Staaten*, ed. August von Hoff and H. F. Mathis (11 vols, 1805–11); *Jahrbücher für die Preußische Gesetzgebung, Rechtswissenschaft und Rechtsverwaltung*, ed. Karl Albert von Kamptz (66 vols, 1813–45). Before Klein's *Annalen*, only three short-lived journals specializing on the law of Prussia were published, see Joachim Kirchner, ed., *Bibliographie der Zeitschriften des deutschen Sprachgebiets* (Stuttgart, 1969), I, nos 2548, 2564 and 2568.

[37] The controversies related to these questions are discussed by Demel, *Vom aufgeklärten Reformstaat*, pp. 81 f.; Schwennicke, *Die Entstehung*, pp. 4 f., 71 ff., 297 ff.; Günter Birtsch, 'Zum konstitutionellen Charakter des preußischen Allgemeinen Landrechts von 1794', in *Politische Ideologien und nationalstaatliche Ordnung. Studien zur Geschichte des 19. und 20. Jahrhunderts. Festschrift für Theodor Schieder* (Munich/Vienna, 1968), pp. 97 ff.; Dietmar Willoweit, 'War das Königreich Preußen ein Rechtsstaat?', in *Staat, Kirche, Wissenschaft in einer pluralistischen Gesellschaft. Festschrift für Paul Mikat* (Berlin, 1989), pp. 451 ff.; Rudolf Vierhaus, 'Das Allgemeine Landrecht für die Preußischen Staaten als Verfassungsersatz?', *200 Jahre Allgemeines Landrecht für die preußischen Staaten*, pp. 1 ff.; see also above, note 35.

Hellmuth and Andreas Schwennicke has shown that the ideas of the authors of the code were not compatible with a concept of a civil society based on liberty and equality.[38] As far as those parts of the *Landrecht* are concerned in which some authors believe to have detected traces of the rule of law: these sections were shaped by objections expressed by the Prussian estates, which saw that the absolutist state intended to infringe upon their rights; these sections, therefore, maintain the status quo of the *ancien régime* against the interests of the enlightened absolutist state.[39] Moreover, the authors of the Prussian code never intended to guarantee civil or human rights in a modern liberal sense: the 'natural liberty' which is mentioned in two sections of the code is subject to requirements of the purpose of the state, the common good. In fact, contemporary German political theory was far more advanced than the code.[40]

Legislation in the *Vormärz*

1   The authoritative bibliography on German periodicals, Kirchner, lists 123 periodicals dealing with law that were published for the first time in the four decades around 1800. According to their titles, 40 of these were devoted to legislation and the law in a particular German state, whereas we find only four of that kind in the rest of the eighteenth century, i.e. up to 1780.[41]

The significance of these periodicals is not just apparent in their overall publication figures, but stressed further by the fact that more and more periodicals of this kind were produced as the nineteenth century progressed: only five of them were published between 1781 and 1790, another five between 1791 and 1800, but 16 in the first decade of the nineteenth century, fourteen in the years between 1811 and 1820 and fifteen between 1821 and 1830. Moreover, a lot of these periodicals lasted rather longer than other law journals of that time.

These numbers indicate that the periodicals fulfilled a certain demand. A look at the forewords and the tables of contents reveals what the journals could offer: First of all, they printed amendments to codes, other statutes and all kinds of subordinate legislation and official regulations. Moreover, they

---

[38] Eckhart Hellmuth, *Naturrechtsphilosophie und bürokratischer Werthorizont. Studien zur preußischen Geistes- und Sozialgeschichte des 18. Jahrhunderts* (Göttingen, 1985); Schwennicke, *Die Entstehung*; Thomas Finkenauer, 'Vom Allgemeinen Gesetzbuch zum Allgemeinen Landrecht — preußische Gesetzgebung in der Krise', *Zeitschrift für Rechtsgeschichte. Germanistische Abteilung*, 113 (1996), pp. 40–216, 127 ff.

[39] Schwennicke, *Die Entstehung*.

[40] Diethelm Klippel and Louis Pahlow, 'Freiheit und aufgeklärter Absolutismus. Das Allgemeine Landrecht in der Geschichte der Menschen- und Bürgerrechte', in Birtsch and Willoweit, eds, *Reformabsolutismus und ständische Gesellschaft*, pp. 215–53.

[41] Kirchner, ed., *Bibliographie der Zeitschriften*, I, 140–50.

published precedents, commentaries and essays about parts of the codes and statutes, reviews, statistics, and so on. In brief, they tried to inform about the increasing legislative activities of the German states and especially about problems regarding the interpretation and implementation of the codes and statutes.

Apart from the law journals, many German states began to print official gazettes (*Gesetz- und Verordnungsblätter*), in which they published statutes and important other official regulations. To give some examples: the 'Großherzoglich Badisches Staats- und Regierungs-Blatt' started in 1803, the 'Königlich-Baierisches Regierungsblatt' and the 'Gesetz-Sammlung für die Königlichen Preußischen Staaten' in 1806, the 'Sammlung der Gesetze, Verordnungen und Ausschreiben für das Königreich Hannover' and the 'Gesetzsammlung für das Königreich Sachsen' in 1818, the 'Großherzoglich Hessisches Regierungsblatt' in 1819. These were by no means comprehensive, so that there still was enough official material to be printed by the law journals. Together with these the gazettes successfully ensured that the state's statutes and orders were well publicized and distributed throughout the country — something which the states never had really achieved before.

2 Both the law journals and the official gazettes prove the state's continuing and even increasing interest in legislation. In fact, the German states saw the necessity to unify the law and to pass new codes in many fields of the law, because the Holy Roman Empire had ceased to exist, because nearly every state which continued to exist after that and after 1815 had acquired new territories, and because there could no longer be any doubt that they had become sovereign. The reasons for legislation which had been brought forward by enlightened absolutism — among others, the uncertainty and the particularization (*Rechtszersplitterung*) of the law — not only continued to exist but had become more pressing because of the political developments mentioned above.

It is not surprising, therefore, that the German states addressed themselves to the task of legislation and succeeded in modernizing both the law and the administration. The codes and statutes they enacted covered most fields of the law, ranging from criminal and procedural codes to industrial codes and trade laws. Most German states even tried to draft civil codes like the French civil code, but only Saxony succeeded in actually putting the *Sächsisches Bürgerliches Gesetzbuch* into force in 1865.[42] Consequently, in those states which had not got a code covering private law, Roman law in combination with local statutes remained in force up to 1900.[43] But, of

---

[42] See Christian Ahcin, *Zur Entstehung des Bürgerlichen Gesetzbuchs für das Königreich Sachsen von 1863/65* (Frankfurt a.M., 1996).
[43] For details, see *Deutsche Rechts- und Gerichtskarte. Mit einem Orientierungsheft* (Kassel, 1896), reprinted with an introduction and ed. Diethelm Klippel (Goldbach, 1996).

course, this does not mean that the comprehensive legislative efforts of the states did not succeed in other fields of the law.

Though not much of the outcome of these efforts has as yet been closely looked at by historians or legal historians, and though there are still a number of gaps in our knowledge of these developments, I would like to argue that efforts at legal reforms continued building on the reforms or the reforming ambitions of enlightened absolutism, though underpinned by a different political theory, and managed to make the German states adapt to the social, economic and political needs of the nineteenth century.

The theoretical basis, again, was provided by the treatises and textbooks on the 'law of nature', but by a natural law quite different from that which had justified enlightened absolutism. In the last decade of the eighteenth century German natural law had turned into a political theory of liberalism, taking up many ideas of English and French political theorists, though, as to their method, most authors followed Immanuel Kant.[44] They did not cease to point out and criticize the deplorable discrepancies between natural and positive law; they did not tire in stressing the superior validity of natural law and demanded that its rules should be observed by the state.

If, as a result, natural law positions should be realized in positive law, legislation could not but become the vital link between natural law theory and legal practice. Therefore, legislation and its theory formed a major part of natural law. New codes and statutes were regarded as a means to implement natural law ideas. This was one of the crucial aims of natural law at the end of the eighteenth and in the first half of the nineteenth century: to base legislation firmly on natural law ideas, that is, to put into practice the political ideas of liberalism. In 1837, Carl Friedrich Wilhelm Gerstäcker put it like this: the 'science of natural law' is 'the one and only source by which positive legislation can be criticized, the one and only source of good statutes'.[45]

If legislation was deemed to be the most important connecting link between natural and positive law, then it became necessary to look more closely at the contents and the form of the state's legislative activities. This was the specific task of the so-called science of legislation as part of natural law. Thus, in 1806, Karl Salomo Zachariä made it quite clear that, in his opinion, the science of legislation was to be 'the science of those principles

---

[44] Diethelm Klippel, *Politische Freiheit und Freiheitsrechte im deutschen Naturrecht des 18. Jahrhunderts* (Paderborn, 1976).

[45] Carl Friedrich Wilhelm Gerstäcker, *Systematische Darstellung der Gesetzgebungskunst sowohl nach ihren allgemeinen Prinzipien, als nach den, jedem ihrer Haupttheile, der Civil-, Criminal-, Polizei-, Prozeß-, Finanz-, Militair-, Kirchen- und Constitutions-Gesetzgebung eigenthümlichen Grundsätzen* (Frankfurt a.M., 1837), I, p. 154; similar views are expressed by Carl Dresler, *Ueber das Verhältniß des Rechts zum Gesetze* (Berlin, 1803), pp. 162 ff., 191 ff., 202 ff.; Karl Salomo Zachariä, *Die Wissenschaft der Gesetzgebung* (Leipzig, 1806), pp. 222 ff.

which guide the drafting and enacting of laws'.[46] It follows that virtually every question concerning legislation, about its contents, forms, and procedures, was being discussed in the science of legislation.[47]

3   Though there are many other examples, criminal law is perhaps one of the best to illustrate the connection between the codifications of the German states in the first half of the nineteenth century and the natural law theory of legislation as well as eighteenth-century authors. In the first decades of the nineteenth century, many German states thought of drafting a modern criminal code. Starting with the Bavarian code of 1813, nearly every German state then succeeded in putting one into force in the first half of the century.[48] Most of these codes were discussed thoroughly by the public; drafts were criticized from the point of view of natural criminal law and the science of legislation as well as from a practical point of view; some authors even wrote and published alternative drafts of their own.[49] In books and journals, the modern discussion about the purpose of criminal punishment and criminal law, which had started with Beccaria, continued, together with the discussion on capital punishment and on prison reform.[50] It even led to a new branch of psychology, criminal psychology, being founded, which was

---

[46] Zachariä, *Die Wissenschaft der Gesetzgebung*, p. 18; cf. Friedrich Purgold, *Die Gesetzgebungswissenschaft, in Entwicklung der für den Entwurf eines neuen, namentlich deutschen, Gesetzbuches sich ergebenden Grundsätze* (Darmstadt, 1840), p. 19: 'The science of legislation . . . shows how natural law [Vernunftrecht] develops into positive law'.

[47] Zachariä, *Die Wissenschaft der Gesetzgebung*, pp. 26 ff.; Gerstäcker, *Systematische Darstellung der Gesetzgebungskunst*, I, pp. 194, 210.

[48] See Hinrich Rüping, *Grundriß der Strafrechtsgeschichte* (2nd edn, Munich, 1991), pp. 79 f; Rainer Schröder, 'Die Strafgesetzgebung in Deutschland in der ersten Hälfte des 19. Jahrhunderts', in *Die Bedeutung der Wörter. Festschrift für Sten Gagnér* (Munich, 1991), pp. 403–20.

[49] To give just a few examples: Eduard Henke, *Beyträge zur Criminalgesetzgebung, in einer vergleichenden Uebersicht der neuesten Strafgesetz-Bücher und Entwürfe* (Regensburg, 1813); Karl Salomo Zachariä von Lingenthal, *Strafgesetzbuch. Entwurf. Mit einer Darstellung der Grundlagen des Entwurfes* (Heidelberg, 1826); a review by Carl Trummer of eight books on the code planned for Hanover, *Kritische Zeitschrift für Rechtswissenschaft*, vol. 3/3 (1827), pp. 367–462; Carl Josef Anton Mittermaier regularly published overviews on criminal legislation, e.g. 'Ueber die neuesten Fortschritte der Strafgesetzgebung', *Archiv des Criminalrechts. Neue Folge* (1837), pp. 537–60, (1838), pp. 1–35; Ignaz Beidtel, *Untersuchungen über einige Grundlagen der Strafgesetzgebung mit Rücksicht auf die neueren Entwürfe zu Strafgesetzbüchern und einige neue Strafgesetze* (Leipzig, 1840).

[50] Cf. Monika Frommel, *Präventionsmodelle in der deutschen Strafzweck-Diskussion. Beziehungen zwischen Rechtsphilosophie, Dogmatik, Rechtspolitik und Erfahrungswissenschaften* (Berlin, 1987); Martin Fleckenstein, *Die Todesstrafe im Werk von Carl Joseph Anton Mittermaier (1787–1867). Zur Entwicklungsgeschichte eines Werkbereichs und seiner Bedeutung für Theorie- und Methodenbildung* (Frankfurt a.M., 1992); Richard J. Evans, *Rituals of retribution: capital punishment in Germany, 1600–1987* (Oxford, 1996); Franz von Holtzendorff, ed., *Handbuch des Gefängnisswesens* (Hamburg, 1888); Hemma Fasoli, *Zum Strafverfahrensrecht und Gefängniswesen im 19. Jahrhundert. Der Jurist Ludwig von Jagemann (1805–1853). Seine Rolle in Deutschland unter Berücksichtigung der Entwicklungen in England, Frankreich und USA* (Kehl am Rhein, 1985).

sometimes thought of as being a part of natural law.[51] Its theories greatly influenced those sections of the criminal codes which dealt with psychological questions: for example, under which circumstances a person was free from criminal liability, such as for instance delinquents afflicted by certain mental disorders.[52] It seems that in the first part of the nineteenth century the seeds of the enlightened discourse in the eighteenth century ripened, at last, in the criminal codes.[53]

[51] Thus in the bibliography by Hermann Theodor Schletter, *Handbuch der juristischen Literatur in systematisch-chronologischer Ordnung, von der Mitte des vorigen Jahrhunderts bis zum Jahre 1840* (2nd edn, Grimma/Leipzig, 1851), no. 12639–743.
[52] Ylva Greve, 'Die Unzurechnungsfähigkeit in der Criminalpsychologie' in Michael Niehaus and Hans-Walter Schmidt-Hannisa, eds, *Unzurechnungsfähigkeiten* (Frankfurt a.M., 1998), pp. 107–32.
[53] More generally on the question of continuity between Enlightenment and the 'age of reforms': Rudolf Vierhaus, 'Aufklärung und Reformzeit. Kontinuitäten und Neuansätze in der deutschen Politik des späten 18. und beginnenden 19. Jahrhunderts', in Weils, ed., *Reformen im rheinbündischen Deutschland*, pp. 287–301.

The Prussian Reformers and their Impact on German History

HAGEN SCHULZE

I

NOTHING IN HISTORY IS SO UNCERTAIN as posthumous fame. On 26 November 1822, the Prussian chancellor of state, Karl August, prince of Hardenberg, died. Two and a half weeks later the *Vossische Zeitung* published a brief factual death-notice. It was only a few days later that a comment appeared in the form of an occasional poem of homage in French addressed to Frederick William III, which ended with the banal sentence: '*Le choix d'un grand ministre est l'éloge des rois.*' (The choice of a great minister is the panegyric of the kings.) What a change of time and mood during the few years which had passed since the reform period and the wars of liberation against Napoleon! Freiherr vom Stein, who had long since withdrawn embittered to his estate at Cappenberg, felt like a relic of times past: 'among a strange race, incomprehensible to us and we to it, isolated, without friends or joys'.[1] The age of Prussian reforms seemed to be definitely over, an episode comparable to the Confederation of the Rhine or the earlier reforms under Joseph II in Austria — partially successful in the short run, but in the long run without major consequences. The poet Ernst Moritz Arndt wrote that nowadays time buries its own creations so fast, that what happened yesterday is forgotten today.[2]

But then, after a generation, the legend began. The turning point lies in the years preceding the revolution of 1848. It was then that people began to remember the deeds of their ancestors, whose blood had been shed in vain during the campaigns of 1813 for the completion of the Prussian reforms, thwarted by the opposition of the nobility and the king. From this perspective, the struggle of 1848 appears as a continuation of the war of liberation,

[1] Stein to Gagern, 19 July 1824, in Freiherr vom Stein, *Briefe und amtl. Schriften*, adapted by E. Botzenhart, re-edited by W. Hubatsch (10 vols, Stuttgart, 1965), VI, p. 740.

[2] E. M. Arndt to G. A. Reimer, 6 Jan. 1826, in A. Dühr, ed., *Briefe* (2 vols, Darmstadt, 1973), II, p. 326.

Proceedings of the British Academy, **100**, 61–77. © The British Academy 1999.

both as a struggle for civil liberty and constitutional law as well as for national independence.

The legend of the lost paradise of civil liberty contrasts with the myth of Reform Prussia as the predecessor of Bismarck's state: Heinrich von Treitschke, the prophet of the *kleindeutsch* German state of 1871 (i.e. Germany without Austria), wrote:

> Only now did Prussia truly become the German state... The old, hard, belligerent Prussianism and the wealth of ideas of modern German education finally merged and did not separate again... In this period of suffering and self-contemplation all the political ideals came into being which the German nation is still trying to realize today.[3]

Half a century later, Max Weber evaluated the exemplary character of that period differently. Just as after 1806, so also after the First World War, according to Weber, Germany would be reborn out of the greatest humiliation: '110 years ago we showed the world that we — and only we — could be one of the great cultured peoples even under foreign domination. We will do this again! History, which has already given us a second youth, will grant us a third'.[4] The youth of that period, however, did not care for the ideals of the liberal university professor; they preferred those of the man from Braunau who also was dreaming of a revival. In the mid-1920s Adolf Hitler shouted:

> What a difference! The state of 1806 was a state that had sadly capitulated on all fronts, an unprecedented wretchedness of civic spirit dominated, and then, in 1813, a state emerged with a glowing hatred of foreign rule and with a patriotic spirit of sacrifice for its own people... What had really changed to make that possible? The people? No, in their innermost being they remained as before, it was only only their leadership that had passed into new hands[5]

Twenty years later the *Führer* led his people into the worst catastrophe of their history. Whereas in the western zones of post-war Germany the memory of the Stein and Hardenberg era had to succumb to the harsh verdict of the victors against Prussia as a whole, their memory was carefully cultivated in the eastern zone under Soviet influence. The reforms, which according to the dictum of Friedrich Engels marked 'the beginning of the bourgeois revolution in Prussia',[6] were interpreted in the German Democratic Republic as a precondition for the wars of liberation, which, as a 'national-democratic uprising' under the benevolent auspices of the Prussian–Russian alliance, was considered unreservedly as a positive feature of the

[3] H. von Treitschke, *Deutsche Geschichte im 19. Jahrhundert* (9th edn, 5 vols, Leipzig, 1913), I, pp. 269 f.
[4] M. Weber, *Max Weber. Ein Lebensbild* (Tübingen, 1926), p. 649.
[5] G.L. Weinberg, ed., *Hitlers zweite Buch* (Stuttgart, 1961), p. 145.
[6] F. Engels, 'Die Bewegung von 1847' in *Marx-Engels-Gesamtausgabe*, 1 Abt. (Glashütten im Taunus, 1970), VI, p. 391.

national heritage — an interpretation that has been used by the East German regime to reinforce its weak bases of legitimacy.[7] In the Federal Republic of Germany, on the other hand, interest in the Prussian reform movement continued to diminish until the present day. Often a certain helplessness could be observed in the evaluation of the Prussian reformers and their accomplishments, as became clear in the great exhibition about Prussia mounted in Berlin in 1981. The organizers were content to display a few portraits of the reformers and a few reform edicts without any commentary whatsoever.[8] The information about the period conveyed in modern German school books concentrates on the promise of civil liberty, and a constitution is in the foreground — the 'black-red-gold' aspect of the Prussian reforms, in other words. It is not without reason that the revolution of 1848 serves as the starting point for the only noteworthy work in German historiography on the subject since 1945 that presents the Prussian reforms in a wider historical context — Reinhart Koselleck's classic work *Preußen zwischen Reform und Revolution* (Prussia between reform and revolution).[9]

Indeed, this broad theme not only serves to establish political legitimacy and solidarity. Hardly noticed by the public at large, there has been an increasing tendency to fundamental criticism of the achievements of the Prussian reform movement, primarily in those circles of historians with sociological or economic orientation. In addition to inquiring into the failure of the reforms and the reasons, the question of the social and political costs has also been examined. An impoverished rural population was wiped out, while at the same time the old landed aristocracy had the opportunity, in alliance with the bourgeois land speculators, to transform itself into a new agrarian capitalistic class. As a result of the reforms, a ruling cartel of state bureaucrats and landed aristocracy emerged, which succeeded in suppressing liberal and democratic mass movements. When considered in this light, the reform era appears to be a turning point in German history, the time when Prussian Germany left the mainstream of Western democratic development in order to take a different and peculiarly German path, leading away from Western ideals of liberty and equality.[10] This approach, which has attempted

---

[7] F. Straube, ed., *Das Jahr 1813. Studien zur Geschichte und Wirkung der Befreiungskriege* (Berlin, 1962); P. Hoffmann et al., eds, *Der Befreiungskrieg 1813* (Berlin, 1967); J. Streisand, *Deutschland 1789–1815* (Berlin, 1977).

[8] Critique in H. Schulze, 'Preußen — Bilanz eines Versuchs', *Geschichte in Wissenschaft und Unterricht*, 11 (1981), pp. 649 ff.

[9] R. Koselleck, *Preußen zwischen Reform und Revolution. Allgemeines Landrecht, Verwaltung und soziale Bewegung von 1791 bis 1848* (Stuttgart, 1967).

[10] W. M. Simon, *The failure of the Prussian reform-movement, 1807–1819* (New York, 1955); H. Rosenberg, *Bureaucracy, aristocracy and autocracy: the Prussian experience, 1660–1815* (Cambridge, Mass., 1958); A. Gerschenkron, *Bread and democracy in Germany* (New York, 1966); D. S. Landes, *Der entfesselte Prometheus* (Köln, 1973).

to place the Stein-Hardenberg reforms in line with the disastrous *Sonderweg* (special German path), leads logically to Barrington Moore's thesis that the victims of National Socialism were also among the special costs of the Prussian reforms.[11]

It is not the accomplishments of the reformers which are uncertain; an abundance of documentary publications and detailed monographs inform us extensively, even if not yet sufficiently, of what really happened during the Prussian reform period. It is not the facts which are problematic, but rather the connections, the interpretation, and the consequences of these facts. Thus, I would like to attempt to find the answers to two questions: What is the basic character of the Prussian reforms if one strips them of the accidental, individual, and unsuitable trimmings and treats them as a whole? And what were the consequences for German history?

II

In an anonymous article that appeared in Heinrich v. Kleist's journal *Berliner Abendblätter* on 3 December 1810, one can read the following:

> The law is the great inner bond of a nation. It embraces it in ever tighter circles which ultimately terminate in a single, lucid point, in the king. All members of a society must agree, despite other differences of opinion, on their religious veneration for him... In the strong and general will to maintain this law or to perish with it rests nationality or patriotism.

The anonymous author, apparently a leading reform bureaucrat, was not talking about the metaphysics of the state, as the tone of the article might lead one to think, but about the edict on taxes and tariffs of 28 October 1810, by means of which Prussia was to make the transition to freedom of trade.[12]

The substance was as interesting as the tone. The problems involved were very serious: the undeniable necessity of increasing the revenue of the pauperized Prussian state in order to pay the debts of the Napoleonic era. The funds were to flow as a result of a new tax to be levied on trade, itself to be expanded by the new freedom of trade, from which everyone could now profit, if they paid the appropriate tax: 'the entrance ticket to a free economy'.[13] Here the reasons of simple economy prevailed, just as was the case with the edict of 9 October 1807, which emancipated the peasantry, and whose preamble consisted mainly of reflections on the 'principles of an orderly state economy'.[14] It was the same with Stein's municipal ordinance of

[11] B. Moore, *Soziale Ursprünge von Diktatur und Demokratie. Die Rolle der Grundbesitzer und Bauern bei der Entstehung der modernen Welt* (Frankfurt a. M., 1969), esp. pp. 577 ff.
[12] *Preußische Gesetz-Sammlung* (GS) (1810), pp. 79 ff.
[13] Koselleck, *Preußen*, p. 588.
[14] GS (1806–10), pp. 170 ff.

19 November 1808[15] — an especially urgent measure, because the state could not fulfil its financial obligations resulting from its guardianship of the cities.[16] It is true that the reforms of Stein of 1807 and 1808, unlike those of Hardenberg, were not embedded in a grand plan to renew the economy and state finances, but they served one great goal, as did the reorganization of government authorities and later the judicial, educational, and military reforms: namely, to increase the efficiency of the Prussian state in order to master the acute emergency.

This was not really a programme without precedent, for Prussia was not alone in Napoleonic Europe in this respect. The states of the Confederation of the Rhine also initiated reforms, in some respects sooner and more comprehensively. In fact, the Prussian reformers did not consider themselves to be an *avant-garde*: on the contrary, they were aware that they faced strong competition. In a letter to his wife written immediately after the Peace of Tilsit of 1807, the financial official Stägemann, one of the leading reform bureaucrats, wrote enviously that in Napoleon's kingdom of Westphalia 'all the privileges of the nobility have been done away with, and the Junkers are going to be treated just like the sons of the bourgeois or of peasants. That's not bad'.[17] It was the explicit intention of Napoleon to make model states out of Westphalia and Berg. They were to become not only the imperial bases of personnel recruitment and of power, but also attractive examples of the realization of the promises of the French Revolution — of liberty and equality for all citizens. At least with respect to the legal and administrative reforms, this was accomplished so well that after the wars of liberation the victorious Prussian state adopted essential elements of the Napoleonic code in its western provinces. But the great difference, and what still today accounts for the myth-inspiring potential of the Prussian reforms, and not of those of Napoleon in Germany, is not just that history loves the winner, but that the Stein-Hardenberg reforms, for all their acknowledged dependence on French and English models, had their own peculiar tone, their own pathos, their own substance, and — in contemporary parlance — their own spirit.

If one wants to discover the bases of the Prussian reform legislation, one will have to inquire beyond the actual lawmakers. Of course, the names Heinrich Friedrich Karl Reichsfreiherr vom und zum Stein and Karl August Graf von Hardenberg are inseparably linked, and rightly so, with the events.

[15] GS (1806–10), pp. 324 ff.

[16] J. Ziekursch, *Das Ergebnis der friderizianischen Städteverwaltung und die Städteordnung Steins, am Beispiel der schlesischen Städte dargestellt* (Jena, 1908).

[17] Stägemann to his wife, 21 Sept. 1807, in F. Rühl, ed., *Aus der Franzosenzeit. Ergänzungen zu den Briefen und Aktenstücken zur Geschichte Preußens unter Friedrich Wilhelm III. vorzugsweise aus dem Nachlaß F. A. von Stägemann* (Leipzig, 1904), pp. 39 f.

The edicts and laws which were passed during their terms of office as ministers bear their personal mark, and the intermezzo of Dohna-Altenstein's ministry of bureaucrats from 1808 to 1810 demonstrates that without an outstanding personality as minister, who could confront the king independently and without fear, the reform spirit petered out quickly.

Personalities were programmes, and the fact that Stein held conservative views, whereas Hardenberg was strongly influenced by the liberal, rational concepts of society of West European provenance, has led to the opinion that one should distinguish between two phases of the reforms, each of which is associated with the name of the leading statesman.[18] This impression is intensified by the strong personal dislike of the two men for each other, especially on the part of Stein. Whereas Hardenberg accused his famous predecessor of political naïvety in dealing with France and of a preference for ineffective collegialism in administration, Stein literally hated the chancellor of state, accused him of political opportunism, even of having affairs with women, and upon hearing the news of Hardenberg's death, he went so far as to congratulate 'the Prussian monarchy on this happy event'.[19]

But, despite this first impression, Stein and Hardenberg were not the only actors on the stage. Behind and beneath them was a collective partner, the Prussian reform bureaucracy, a group of state and financial councillors, war and domain councillors, chiefs of police and officers, who after the defeat were concentrated in East Prussia and exercised an essential control over the reconstruction process. The names Altenstein, Frey, Gruner, Hippel, Raumer, Scharnweber and Schön or Scharnhorst, Boyen and Gneisenau are representative of many others. But they, too, did not constitute a small, socially isolated elite, as the literature would sometimes lead one to think. They were part of a social stratum that had started to emerge in Prussia since the middle of the eighteenth century.

This stratum was socially quite heterogeneous. Its members included bureaucrats, protestant ministers, university and secondary school teachers, doctors and other high-level professionals. One thing united them all: they exercised their offices and professions, not on the basis of their social standing, but on the basis of their qualifications; and the proof of their qualifications was their academic education. The growing need of the absolutist state for a capable, trained intelligentsia from which to recruit its top officials contributed decisively to the creation of this social stratum. Since 1755 lawyers in Prussia had had to pass a state examination, and from 1770 such an examination was required for all high-ranking officials. And to render such an education possible, the state established educational institu-

---

[18] B. Vogel, 'Reformpolitik in Preußen 1807–1820', in H.-J. Puhle and H.-U. Wehler, eds, *Preußen im Rückblick* (Göttingen, 1980), pp. 202 ff.
[19] Stein to Merveldt, 6 Dec. 1822, in Freiherr vom Stein, *Briefe*, VI, p. 138.

tions which surpassed in number and quality those of most other European countries. A bourgeois career was thus possible, and it was much sought after. The poet Clemens von Brentano, not without good reason, ends his poem in which he lists all the troubles of youth, with the comforting lines:

> So geplackt und so geschunden
> Tritt man endlich in den Staat.
> Dieser heilet alle Wunden
> Und man wird Geheimer Rat.
> (So tormented and mistreated
> Finally one joins the state;
> It heals all wounds
> and one becomes a privy councillor.)

The service nobility, too, was forced to comply with bourgeois standards of education in order to attain higher posts in the administration. By virtue of the Prussian Land Law, this group was clearly privileged: it enjoyed tax exemption, was not obliged to perform military service and was subject directly to the jurisdiction of the royal courts. In this way an educated elite, comprising both nobles and commoners and existing outside the structure of the traditional estates, came into being, bound to the state and the crown more strongly than the upper bourgeoisie in France.

In this respect Prussia was more modern than the otherwise so exemplary France of the *ancien régime*. In France the constant feeling of being under-privileged and socially discriminated against created a revolutionary bourgeoisie. Such a feeling did not find fertile soil in Prussia. It is true that the Prussian bureaucratic and cultural bourgeoisie was pervaded by the universal ideas of the Age of Enlightenment. In particular, the fact of its not belonging to the corporate estate of the nobility was always a painful thorn. The untenability of the social and economic order of the eighteenth century, which so strongly negated the great idea of man's freeing himself from his 'self-induced state of immaturity' (Kant), was a commonly held view among these citizens, who had an insatiable hunger for reading and discussion. Therefore, almost all the intelligentsia of Prussia welcomed the French Revolution, but at the same time they were absolutely convinced that such an event did not need to take place in Prussia. Thus, the Prussian Foreign Minister Hertzberg found general consent when in a widely circulated speech delivered a few months after the outbreak of the French Revolution he categorically said that 'the Prussian government is not despotic'.[20] That it was not despotic was proved by a whole series of reforms before the Reform,

---

[20] 'Abhandlung über das dritte Jahr der Regierung Königs Friedrich Wilhelm II., um zu beweisen, daß die Preußische Regierung nicht despotisch ist, verlesen am 1. Oktober 1789', quoted in K. von Raumer, 'Zur Beurteilung der preußischen Reform', in *Geschichte in Wissenschaft und Unterricht*, 18 (1967), p. 344.

starting with the General Land Law of 1794, followed by the abolition of hereditary serfdom for domain peasants, and extending to the beginnings of the tax and tariff reforms upon Stein's appointment as finance and economics minister in 1804.

In this manner, the bond between the state and the functional bourgeoisie was as strong as ever, although the increasing ossification, the structural immobility, of the system dating back to Frederick the Great, was painfully felt. It is interesting to read the articles of Lieutenant Hermann von Boyen — the later reformer — published in the magazine *Bellona* in 1795, in which he demanded, true to the spirit of the times, the abolition of corporal punishment for Prussian soldiers, to witness only eleven years later how a military machine held together by the fear of inhuman punishment was defeated by the French citizen-soldiers. This feeling of banging one's head in vain against the unyielding walls of tradition and convention was common to thousands. In addition, there was the change of consciousness from the generation of Frederick the Great to that of 1800, promoted by the radical upheavals in America, France and throughout the European states-system. Having experienced terror and genocide in the name of all virtues of the Enlightenment, there was in particular a spiritual reaction, begun in the 'Storm and Stress' period, in which the independent individual sought to emancipate himself from the cold abstractions of enlightened reason. The twenty-year-old Alexander von der Marwitz, the brother of the leader of the Junker opposition to the Hardenberg reforms, and Rahel Lewin's closest friend, wrote:

> It is a peculiar and truly mystical time in which we live... What shows itself to the senses is weak, incapable, completely rotten. Yet streaks of lightning dash through our souls, premonitions appear, thoughts wander through time and show themselves, like ghosts in mystical moments, to the more profound minds. These thoughts signify a sudden transformation, a total revolution, where everything from the past will disappear like land swallowed by an earthquake, while the volcanos bring forth new land in the face of dreadful destruction.[21]

It was a generation that lived with a strong consciousness of a current crisis and a new age to come. In contrast to the previous generation, to which for example Hardenberg belonged, it had a world view that was not rational, but poetic; and the promise of the Enlightenment appeared to it as shallow and discredited. The creation of a state as a more perfect machine to make mankind happy was no longer considered a worthy goal, but the aim was rather the unity of all social strata, the grand harmony of the state and the people. These two generations, that of the fifty-year-olds and that of the

---

[21] Von der Marwitz to Rahel Levin, 2 Jun. 1811, in F. Kemp, ed., *Rahel Varnhagen Briefwechsel mit Alexander von der Marwitz* (Munich, 1966), p. 67.

thirty-year-olds, determined the political climate and the agenda after the catastrophic defeats of 1806 and 1807, when only rudimentary state institutions existed, and the authority of the estates, the powers of inertia and tradition, suddenly lost all influence. The hour of the educated bureaucracy had come, the hour for which it had had to wait so long, and the reforms were carried out in the spirit of this social group.

Despite the dejection after a defeat the like of which Prussia had never experienced before, the catastrophe was also seen as an opportunity to create something new. The theologian Friedrich Schleiermacher, who belonged to the circle around Stein and Humboldt and was to have a decisive influence in establishing the University of Berlin in 1810, wrote the following lines to a friend only a few weeks after the battle of Jena:

> Everything political which existed until now was generally speaking untenable, a hollow appearance. The separation of the individual from the state and the educated person from the masses was so great that neither the state nor the masses could acquire any significance. This state of affairs must be eliminated and only upon its ruins can truth establish itself. An all-encompassing regeneration is a necessity and will develop on the basis of these facts. One cannot discern yet how, but we want to take part in it.[22]

The mood among that educated elite was nearly revolutionary, but only nearly. Their loyalty to the king and to the state remained firm and unfaltering, and the means of bringing about the change were determined by the bureaucratic origins of the reformers: by the law. The anonymous reformer-bureaucrat, author of the article cited above, who demanded religious veneration of the law, corresponded fully to the revolutionary pathos of the time: in France it was 'the holy guillotine' which was the instrument of inexorable progress, in Prussia it was the 'holy law'.

There are other characteristics of the reformers' rhetoric which remind one of revolutionary models: for example, their talk of nationality created by the common will to uphold law. One immediately thinks of Rousseau's '*volonté générale*'. And our anonymous author continues: this nationality 'will prosper best in a state in which the freedom of its members is not limited more than is necessary and by the equal rights of the others and in which the laws increasingly shed any arbitrary element.'[23] To get rid of tyranny, to achieve general and equal civil liberty — that is nothing less than revolutionary, and that was intended. According to the military reformer Neithart von Gneisenau, the only means by which Prussia's former power could be regained was to reach into 'the arsenal of revolution'.[24] Thus it was planned

---

[22] Schleichermacher to Georg Reimer, 14 Nov.1806, in K. Griewank, ed., *Gold gab ich für Eisen* (Leipzig, 1939), p. 150.

[23] *Berliner Abendblätter*, 3 Dec. 1810, p. 73.

[24] Gneisenau to the king, June 1810, in K. Griewank, ed., *Ein Leben in Briefen* (Leipzig, 1939), p. 150.

to abolish the estates and to introduce compulsory military service, national representation, and national education, in addition to streamlining and modernizing the state institutions and the economy. The fear of the landed gentry, who tried to warn the king of the new age in a petition dated 9 May 1811, drafted by Ludwig von der Marwitz, was well founded: the state was now to be governed by strange principles, the old estate order was to be abandoned, all rightfully acquired privileges of the landed gentry were jeopardized. In short, the country had begun to be revolutionized.[25]

But if that was revolution, then it was very different from the revolutions experienced by America and France. It was not the nation which had declared itself sovereign, which had given itself a constitution and which had established the unity of the bourgeoisie, the state, and the people. For the older reformers, of whom Hardenberg can be considered typical, the real aim was the re-establishment and extension of state authority. And the French Revolution only served as a model by suggesting two ideas to the Prussian reformers: that a defeat like that of 1806 should never happen again, and secondly, at least for some of them, that Prussia too should produce its own version of Napoleon one day. The new state was being conceived with an unprecedented degree of concentration and authority. And when speaking of the nation, this nation was yet to be created: to be precise, it still existed only in the heads of a small, educated elite, which provided the support for the reforms. Furthermore, Prussia was a maze of provinces, each with its own legal system and administrative bodies, and even if one was successful in unifying the institutions and legal systems, state authority was still limited by the extensive feudal autonomy of the lower gentry in the countryside. The largest portion of the Prussian population lived as serfs on large estates; for them the state and the king were very remote. This particular problem could not be solved in the face of the furious opposition of the landed nobility. As a result, there were only two means available for strengthening the state: apart from the reform of the executive and administrative structures, people in the cities and in the countryside had to be emancipated. But this liberty did not mean political liberty as reflected in the American or French constitutions, but 'civic' liberty; not equal participation in the state, but rather personal liberty in the state; not the ideas of Rousseau, but those of Adam Smith, whose doctrines were very popular at the universities of Prussia and Hanover, and who stood as godfather to the reforms. 'True liberty' meant equal application of laws, free competition based on competence, security of property and of the individual, and the fair distribution of the burden. The good citizen, according to Smith, was the free 'economic' citizen, who

---

[25] Petition to the king, dated 9 May 1811, in W. Conze, ed., *Quellen zur Geschichte der Bauernbefreiung* (Göttingen, 1957), pp. 128 ff.

increased the wealth of the state while increasing his own. Thus liberty was a constitutive element of the state, not its restriction.

Unfortunately, however, this free citizen was still an ideal. In reality tremendous resistance was encountered, and not only on the part of the noble estates, from whom nothing else could have been expected, but precisely from those social strata whose emancipation was intended. While the landlords were organizing their resistance to the reform, the peasants of Middle and Upper Silesia revolted. They took the October edict's promise of emancipation seriously. The peasants did not wish to accept the fact that they still had to perform services for the landlord, especially since they now had to pay excise duties, just like the urban population. This was impossible for them to do, since they were being paid in kind.

The introduction of the municipal ordinance provoked bitter resistance from the citizenry of the East Elbian small towns, because their tax burden had increased. The introduction of freedom of trades naturally offended those craftsmen who feared that they would lose the economic security previously guaranteed by the guilds. The introduction of compulsory military service mobilized citizens previously exempt who, though demanding liberation from the obligations of the estates, suddenly saw themselves confronted with considerable personal costs and duties.

The unavoidable conclusion the reformers drew from this resistance was that the Prussian people were not yet ready to grow together into a nation of free citizens. What was needed was education: and who better suited for this task than the bureaucrats and professors, who had experienced personally the blessings of good education and culture in the form of higher social status. Not only the great reforms of the educational system, namely that of the universities by Wilhelm von Humboldt and that of the schools by Johann Wilhelm Süvern, but also the preparations for great reform projects, such as the municipal ordinance, which were intended to help the citizens practise self-administration and self-responsibility before their direct participation in regional or central administrative bodies, should be seen in this light.

In addition to the establishment of a liberal educator-state, the reformers had another consideration based on experience. Both Stein and Hardenberg planned the establishment of a national representation of Prussian citizens as the culminating point of their reforms, to serve as an overt symbol of the union of the Prussian provinces in a Prussian nation and thus of a united and centralized Prussia. In the Finance Edict of 27 October 1810, this constitutional promise was proclaimed.[26] But not only did the opposition of the old estates have to be overcome: what was more important was that the real pressure necessary to overcome this resistance was lacking. The bureaucracy,

[26] GS (1810), p. 25.

which was virtually the incarnation of the citizen-state, considered itself the legitimate representative of the state as a whole, so that from the point of view of the reform bureaucrats a national parliament was more of an annoyance. This was a logical conclusion, for the reforms had to be pushed through against the will and customs of the population. Also the example set by the regional parliaments in the states of the Confederation of the Rhine showed that reforming legislation, such as the abolition of tax privileges in the kingdom of Westphalia, always had to contend with the opposition of the representative bodies.[27] Of the two institutions in Prussia which competed with each other in claiming to represent the interests of the whole, the bureaucracy existed first. So the bureaucracy remained the constitutional core of Prussia.[28]

All in all, the Prussian reforms present a peculiarly vacillating picture, simultaneously revolutionary and conservative, just like the bourgeois-bureaucratic origins of its drafters. The language, the pathos, the unmistakably utopian features, an optimistic confidence in the possibility of being able to create a new society and a new state through legislative action were revolutionary. As Altenstein put it, the reformer does not take the core of the state 'as it is, but as it could be and transforms it according to his aims, which coincide with the highest aim of the whole... A new creation must be the result.'[29] Prussian bureaucracy as the creator, as 'the tool which selects the world government for the education of the human race', as Hardenberg put it at the end of the reform era[30] — this was comparable to the confidence in a self-evident world plan which inspired Robespierre or Napoleon.

The re-creation of the Prussian state, however, which enjoyed its successes despite all opposition, was also essentially nothing more than the triumph of the absolutist Prussian tradition. Centralization and rationalization of the state's authority, depriving the estates of their political prerogatives in favour of the monarchical head of state, extension of the state's monopoly of power to all regional, social, and cultural fields — for even the state's self-imposed restriction with regard to the self-administration of the communes and the universities often had to be implemented by means of unilateral decisions on the part of the state — and last but not least, an independent bureaucracy committed only to the state and the monarch and free of all influences emanating from the estates — all this corresponds to an

---

[27] B. Vogel, ' "Revolution von oben" — Der "deutsche Weg" in die bürgerliche Gesellschaft?', *Sozialwissenschaftliche Informationen für Unterricht und Studium*, 8 (1979), p. 72.

[28] E. Fraenke, *Deutschland und die westlichen Demokratien* (Stuttgart, 1964), pp. 23 ff.

[29] K. Freiherr vom Stein zum Altenstein, 'Über die Leitung des preußischen Staats, Denkschrift vom 11.9.1807', in G. Winter, *Die Reorganisation des preußischen Staates unter Stein und Hardenberg*, 1 Teil (2 vols, Leipzig, 1931), I, pp. 369, 462.

[30] Hardenberg, quoted in Koselleck, *Preußen*, p. 160.

absolutist programme and had long been part of the history of Brandenburg-Prussia. In addition, there was an unmistakably patriarchal touch, for Prussia never shed its character of being an enlarged East Elbian estate with the king as the chief landlord. Paternal concern for the well-being of the subjects was deemed to belong to the Christian and social duties of the ruler.[31] The aim of the reformers was not to do away with the king, although Frederick William III often stood in their way. It was to remove all obstacles between the people and the king. In this the older, enlightened-absolutist reformers assisted the younger, romantic-conservative ones, whose utopia of a free people in a wisely guided monarchy became the common property of the people by way of Grimms' fairy tales and the folk songs of Arnim and Brentano. In these we find only the king and the people. The free, industrious, mobile journeyman is bound to be lucky, and as the greatest reward he wins the hand of the fair-haired princess, with whom he had once tended geese.

III

This Janus-faced glance of the Prussian reformers into both the past and the future enabled men as different as Treitschke and Max Weber to look to them as their mentors. The effects of the reforms extended into many German historical traditions, into the black-white-red as well as into the black-red-gold, even into the red. The attempt of the reformers to bind revolution and tradition to each other, as well as the experience of later decades that a state and a society cannot be created on a drawing board by an enlightened elite, both lead to the problem of discerning the essence of the reforms, because after all the spirit of the times did not reveal itself in the offices of Prussian civil servants. The reforms essentially had consequences very different from those intended by statesmen like Stein or Hardenberg, and the cause lay not in the resistance of the old estates, but in the reforms themselves.

The great error of the reformers was their conviction that liberties granted by the state would lead the community of free citizens and the Prussian authoritarian state to the harmony of a stable nation-state, united internally and strong externally. In the event, however, in the ensuing period the Prussian state bureaucracy saw itself in the role of the sorcerer's apprentice, who could no longer master the spirits he had set free. In the process, the hope of modernizing the economy was realized: agriculture, for many decades to come the backbone of the Prussian economy, was put on

---

[31] R. M. Berdahl, 'Paternalismus als Herrschaftssystem', in Puhle and Wehler, eds, *Preußen*, pp. 123 ff.

steadier foundations by supporting not only the Junkers but many owners of large and medium-sized farms, which provided a tremendous impetus to the extension of cultivation and the increase in agrarian production. With the introduction of freedom of trade, freedom to establish residence, free property relationships, with the reform of the customs duties and taxes, prerequisites were created which later permitted the industrialization of Prussia to proceed more rapidly and effectively than in many other European countries, especially faster than in Austria. This, and not merely the superiority of Prussian weapons, ultimately led to the Prussian-induced *kleindeutsch* solution to the German question.

But the social costs were high. In the countryside the decline in the vast number of petty jobs and of landowning peasants resulted in a destitute rural proletariat. A similar development took place in the cities, for after the great depression of 1817 it became clear that it was just the social stratum which had expected the most from the introduction of freedom of trades, namely the journeymen, who were the helpless victims of market forces, for they now lacked the former protection of the guilds. There were now far more people involved in trade than the market needed. Thus, while the financially powerful owners of land or trading enterprises profited from the new conditions of trade, the situation of the great mass of the rural and urban population deteriorated. The social climate did not improve: on the contrary, dangerous tensions developed. Furthermore, the fact that the reformers made use of the 'arsenal of revolution' did not remain unpunished. One could not introduce compulsory military service, improve public education, manipulate public opinion to the point of rousing the masses to frenzy during the wars of liberation, and then expect the people to submit to the wise, educating measures of an enlightened bureaucratic elite. In addition to the growing social discontent between 1815 and 1848, the people became embittered about the broken promise of a constitution. They also turned against a state which, shocked by the radical tone of public opinion and filled with the fear of a repetition of the events in France of 1789, sharpened censorship and attempted to master demands for combining economic with political freedom by the application of police power. In this way state and the society were not brought together; rather they were driven apart. It was a process which was contrary to the intentions of the reformers, but it had been facilitated by their measures. In 1848 they paid the price.

It is of decisive importance for the political culture of Germany that the successor to Reform Prussia was not the parliamentary, democratic nation-state of the 1848 liberals, but Bismarck's *kleindeutsch* authoritarian state. The problems faced after the unification of the German empire were not so very different from those experienced after Jena and Tilsit. Again, it was a matter of internal stabilization of the state by integration imposed from above. Now the profound social and economic breaches, which had developed as a result of the industrial revolution and which had jeopardized the unification process, had to be repaired. The clash of interests between north and south, east and west, between the traditional parties and those believing in the new, revolutionary ideas of legitimacy, as well as between Protestantism and Catholicism, had to be reconciled. The bureaucratic educator-state intervened again to bring state and society together.

Not only was economic adjustment sought, when the interventionist state implemented protective tariffs and cartel laws, granted subsidies and became economically active in its own right, but another objective was the pacification of society through bureaucratic regulation, and this not only by way of legal repression — the *Kulturkampf*, the law against the socialists, for example — but also by transferring the social costs of industrialization to the state with the help of social legislation. In the statement of the reasons for the Industrial Injuries Insurance Law of 1881 one can read that it is the duty of a policy which maintains governmental authority to pursue the goal 'of also convincing the unpropertied classes of the population ... that the state is not simply a necessary, but also a benevolent institution.'[32]

It was the state which had put into effect what two generations of democrats had fought for since the promise of a constitution in 1810. The state granted the universal and equal right to elect representatives to the Reichstag. Bismarck acted here in the spirit of Hardenberg, who had aimed at a 'good' revolution, which he defined as 'democratic principles within a monarchy', as a prophylactic against the revolution from below.[33] Bismarck, the 'white revolutionary',[34] was mistrusted for this very reason by his noble colleagues just as much as the notorious 'Jacobin' Hardenberg, but there remained a decisive difference: the pathos was missing, the wide ethical horizon, the liberal utopia. The 'moral and spiritual strength' with which Freiherr vom Stein had attempted to counterbalance, as he himself put it, 'the relative weakness of the Prussian monarchy'[35] was done away with, pure *Realpolitik* took the place of moral responsibility. What remained was a bureaucratic authoritative educator-state, which, with the help of civil servants cured of their liberal origins, placed society under their guardianship in its own interest. This was no more successful at the end of the nineteenth century than it had been at the beginning, and Bismarck ultimately failed due

---

[32] Verhandlungen des Reichstags, 4, Legislaturperiode IV, Session 1881, vol. 3, p. 228.
[33] K. A. von Hardenberg, 'Rigaer Denkschrift, 12 Sep. 1807', in Winter, *Reorganisation des Preußischen Staates*, 1/I, p. 306.
[34] H. A. Kissinger, 'The white revolutionary, reflections on Bismarck', *Daedalus* (1968), pp. 888 ff.
[35] K. Freiherr vom Stein, 'Verfassungsdenkschrift für den Kronprinzen, 5 Nov. 1822', in Freiherr vom Stein, *Briefe*, 4, p. 118.

to the dynamics of uncontrollable social developments affecting the mass of the population.

But the habit of looking to the state to be the initiator of all change, to expect from the top the control and reconciliation of social conflicts, the suspicion that the people were not mature for democracy, all this had deeply penetrated the political consciousness of the Germans, and not only of the bourgeoisie. '*Der Feind, den wir am tiefsten hassen, das ist der Unverstand der Massen*' ('The enemy we hate the most is the ignorance of the masses') was not a motto hanging on the walls of Prussian offices, but is a line from the social democratic 'Workers' Marseillaise'. That even the Social Democratic Party, which was programmatically opposed to this state, reproduced down to the last detail in its own party structure the relationship between authority and bourgeoisie, proves how deep bureaucratic absolutism — now lacking the soothing oil of the liberal spirit of times gone by — had penetrated German society. Not least here we can identify the causes for the next failure of the black-red-gold experiment of the Germans — the Weimar Republic. The democratic parties lacked self-confidence and the will to power, the authoritarian bureaucracy served as a safe haven offering refuge from the trials and tribulations of the times. This had a profound effect, although a man like Brüning was even less able to master the social forces of the masses than Hardenberg or Bismarck.

IV

What remains today of that period? There remains a tradition and an experience. Fortunately, the tradition of the Prussian reform era again has two faces. What had become historically operative once more after 1945 was not only the old problem of the correct relationship between the state and the citizen, of opinion-making 'from below'. Precisely in those fields which were at the core of the previous reform — in the administration and the army — the ambivalence of the goals and the possibilities again became apparent. We have the principle of compulsory military service, taken directly from the 'arsenal of revolution' by Scharnhorst and his colleagues of the Military Reorganization Commission, which is linked to the problematic postulate of the citizen-soldier, who should be no different from what he is in a civilian life. We also have the municipal statutes of Freiherr vom Stein, which have survived in the local government constitutions of the Federal Republic of Germany. And it is extremely important for the political culture of post-war Germany that, after the total collapse of the German state in 1945, the democratic reconstruction in the western zones proceeded from the bottom, from the municipality — a late but clear confirmation of Stein's belief that the municipality is the primary ground for civic self-determination, without which a free state cannot come into being. In my opinion a lesson for Germany can be drawn from the above, namely, that those elements of the Stein-Hardenberg reforms should be resurrected in the collective German memory, which resulted not merely from the mastering of an emergency, but stemmed from the liberal imperative of a state that has received its legitimacy and its structure from below, from its citizens. To learn from history means to learn against history: the state is not above us, we are the state.

Reform in Britain and Prussia, 1797–1815: (Confessional) Fiscal-Military State and Military-Agrarian Complex*

'ONLY THOSE RESULTS', Hans-Ulrich Wehler argues, 'which pass the litmus test of comparison, that unsurpassable substitute for scientific experiment, can give reliable information about the transnational or national character of problems'.[1] At first sight, the period of intensified international competition triggered by the diplomatic revolutions of the 1790s,[2] and its domestic resonances, or lack of them, in Britain and Prussia, seems to provide a fruitful avenue for the comparative approach. Moreover, although there is no shortage of comparative work on Britain and Germany in the eighteenth and nineteenth centuries, the Revolutionary and especially the Napoleonic period has been largely neglected.[3]

* I would like to thank Anita Bunyan and Peter Spence for reading this paper and making very useful comments. I am also grateful to Boyd Hilton and Miles Taylor for some suggestions, not all of which could be incorporated.

[1] Hans-Ulrich Wehler, '"Deutscher Sonderweg" oder allgemeine Probleme des westlichen Kapitalismus', in idem, *Preußen ist wieder chic. Politik und Polemik in zwanzig Essays* (Frankfurt, 1983), p. 30: 'Nur diejenigen Ergebnisse, welche das scharfe Säurebad des Vergleichs, dieses einzigen, unübertrefflichen Ersatzes für das naturwissenschaftliche Experiment, überstehen, geben verläßliche Auskunft über den transnationalen oder nationalen Charakter von Problemen'.

[2] For the revolution in international relations in the 1790s see Paul Schroeder, *The transformation of European politics, 1763–1848* (Oxford, 1994); T. C. W. Blanning, *The origins of the French Revolutionary wars* (London, 1986); idem, *The French Revolutionary wars* (London, 1996); and idem, 'The French Revolution in Europe', in Colin Lucas, ed., *Rewriting the French Revolution* (Oxford, 1991), pp. 183–207. For its effects on Germany see Brendan Simms, *The struggle for mastery in Germany, 1780–1850* (Basingstoke, 1998).

[3] Eckhart Hellmuth, ed., *The transformation of political culture: England and Germany in the late eighteenth century* (Oxford, 1990); Eckhart Hellmuth, 'Der Staat des 18. Jahrhunderts. England und Preußen im Vergleich', *Aufklärung*, 9/1 (1996), pp. 5–24; John Breuilly, *Labour and liberalism in nineteenth-century Europe: essays in comparative history* (Manchester, 1992). Wolf D. Gruner, 'The British political, social and economic system and the decision for peace and war:

Proceedings of the British Academy, **100**, 79–100. © The British Academy 1999.

Yet, as Fabio Rugge has pointed out, it is easier to demand comparative history than to practise it.[4] For one thing, not only were the two polities politically, socially, and economically fundamentally distinct at the beginning of the conflict with Revolutionary and Napoleonic France, they also experienced radically different pressures throughout the twenty years before 1815. To name only the most obvious differences: Britain was a confessional but parliamentary state in the throes of a socio-economic revolution; Prussia was an absolutist and socio-economically pre-modern polity. Despite periodic invasion scares, and brief French forays into Ireland and Wales in 1797–8, Britain remained largely inviolate throughout the period; Prussia on the other hand suffered a total military collapse and remained under occupation for several years. In no sense, therefore, would a comparison between reform in Britain and Prussia constitute a scientific 'experiment' in the Wehlerite sense, carried out under laboratory conditions. Nevertheless, within the framework of these and other caveats, comparison between Britain and Prussia in the Napoleonic period is not merely possible, but useful, for it casts some light on how these two very different polities reacted to the challenge of French power after 1792.

The chief theoretical impulse behind this paper is the primacy of foreign policy, and its domestic consequences. These were first explored in depth by the German historian Otto Hintze, and more recently revived at the macro- and micro-levels by Tom Ertman, Brian Downing, and John Brewer.[5] For both states were in the first instance vehicles for the conduct of war, or at least the maintenance and projection of external power. If Britain was, in John Brewer's phrase, a 'fiscal-military state' designed to maximize British financial resources for the naval and colonial struggle with France, then Prussia, in Hanna Schissler's adaptation of Eisenhower's famous neologism,

reflections on Anglo-German relations, 1800–1939', *British Journal of International Studies*, 6 (1980), pp. 189–218, concentrates on the period after 1815. With the exception of Linda Colley's article, the centre of emphasis of Lawrence Stone, ed., *An imperial state at war: Britain from 1689 to 1815* (London and New York, 1994), is on the pre-1790s. The comparative train of thought explored in my thesis on Anglo-Prussian relations in the Napoleonic period: Brendan Simms, 'Anglo-Prussian relations, 1804–1806: the Napoleonic threat', unpublished PhD dissertation, University of Cambridge, 1992, was largely dropped for its publication in book form: idem, *The impact of Napoleon: Prussian high politics, foreign policy and the crisis of the executive, 1797–1806* (Cambridge, 1997). Some very general and tentative comparative perspectives were offered in idem, 'Fra *Land* e *Meer*. la Gran Bretagna, la Prussia e il problema del decisionismo (1806–1806)', *Ricerche di Storia Politica*, 6 (1991), pp. 5–34.

[4] Comments by Fabio Rugge in a paper given at the Settimane di Perfeziamento at Trani, September 1991.

[5] See Thomas Ertman, *Birth of the Leviathan: building states and regimes in medieval and early modern Europe* (Cambridge, 1997); Brian M. Downing, *The military revolution and political change: origins of democracy and autocracy in early modern Europe* (Princeton, 1992); John Brewer, *The sinews of power* (London, 1989), which contains a strong comparative element.

was a 'military-agrarian complex', in which social inequalities were determined by the unique cantonal system of recruitment.[6] After all, between 1750 and 1815 both powers were at war as often as they were at peace: in 1756–63, in 1776–83, in 1778–79, and more or less permanently after 1792. It is therefore hardly surprising that domestic change in the two polities was not just self-generated by endogenous forces, but a direct result of external pressures.[7]

Of course, a detailed comparison of reforms at every level would be impossible within the confines of a short article. There are whole areas such as the growth of nationalism, tactical military reforms, the development of the financial system (particularly income taxes), opposition to reform, and the semantics of 'reform' and 'revolution', which must be passed over. Instead, this article will look at four areas only: (1) the rhetoric and justification of reform; (2) the reform of the executive; (3) social and military reform; and (4) political reform, or lack of it, under the primacy of foreign policy. Wherever a comparative perspective was explicitly opened up by the protagonists themselves, the sources have been allowed to speak directly.

The rhetoric and justification of reform

The streamlining of society and economy in accordance with external demands had a long tradition in Prussia: this principle had underlain the seventeenth-century governing compromise between prince and estates in Brandenburg Prussia by which the nobility sacrificed their participatory political powers for greater control over their peasantry. Similarly, the enlightened reform absolutism of Frederick the Great had aimed to maximize Prussia's military and economic strength, largely by increasing the power of the nobility in army and administration. Until the 1790s, this system had underpinned Prussia's rise to great power status and appeared to be a resounding success. It was only after the defeats at the hands of Revolutionary France in 1792–3, that plans for a more thoroughgoing

---

[6] Hanna Schissler, 'The social and political power of the Prussian Junkers', in Ralph Gibson and Martin Blinkhorn, eds, *Landownership and power in modern Europe* (London, 1991), p. 103. The literature on reforming activity before 1806 is surveyed in Simms, *The impact of Napoleon*, pp. 115–36. A good recent overview of the period after 1807 is to be found in Bernd Sösemann, ed., *Gemeingeist und Bürgersinn. Die preußischen Reformen*, Forschungen zur brandenburgischen und preussischen Geschichte, Neue Folge, Beiheft 2 (Berlin, 1993). The most recent treatment of Hardenberg is Thomas Stamm-Kuhlmann, '"Man vertraue doch der Administration!" Staatsverständnis und Regierungshandeln des preußischen Staatskanzlers Karl August von Hardenberg', *Historische Zeitschrift* (*HZ*), 264 (1997), pp. 613–54.

[7] For Britain see Clive Emsley, 'The impact of war and military participation on Britain and France, 1792–1815', in Clive Emsley and James Walvin, eds., *Artisans, peasants and proletarians, 1760–1860* (London and Sydney, 1985), pp. 57–80.

reform of state and society began to gain any currency. But before 1806, the Prussian reform debate remained primarily focused on improving the chaotic executive and gradually rationalizing the social system.[8] Radical demands for total reform, 'renewal' and especially constitutional reform only followed the complete military collapse of the Prussian state at Auerstedt and Jena.

The Prussian reform movement has sometimes been referred to as a 'defensive modernization'.[9] This characterization is correct, in so far as it describes the need to defend the state against absorption by Napoleonic France. But it is misleading in so far as it implies an attempt to preserve the existing order of society against revolutionary threats from below.[10] In fact, the reformers saw domestic change firmly within the context of the primacy of foreign policy, as the internal imperative deriving from Prussia's exposed geopolitical position. Reform, therefore, was 'offensive modernization' designed to underpin the Hohenzollerns' attempt to reclaim their rightful position in the European pentarchy.[11] As the leading reformer and later chancellor, Karl August von Hardenberg observed in his famous Riga memorandum of 1807:

> There can be no independence without power; therefore Prussia must strive to regain power. Now more than ever she cannot remain immobile. She must enlarge herself, not just to make up for her losses, but in order to achieve territorial increases, otherwise she will sink, she will perish completely. The geographical situation of Prussia alone would be enough to ensure that. If she does not recover her strength, she will become the prey of her powerful neighbours.[12]

---

[8] Simms, *Impact of Napoleon*, pp. 328–9.

[9] See Hans-Ulrich Wehler, *Deutsche Gesellschaftsgeschichte. vol. I. Vom Feudalismus des Alten Reiches bis zur defensiven Modernisierung der Reformära, 1700–1815* (Munich, 1987); Barbara Vogel, *Allgemeine Gewerbefreiheit. Die Reformpolitik des preußischen Staatskanzlers Hardenberg (1810–20)* (Göttingen, 1983).

[10] Simms, Impact of Napoleon, pp. 115–27. Eike Wolgast, 'Reform, Reformation', in Otto Brunner, Werner Conze and Reinhart Koselleck, eds, *Geschichtliche Grundbegriffe. Historisches Lexikon zur politisch-sozialen Sprache in Deutschland* (9 vols, Stuttgart, 1984), v, sees the concept of reform during the Prussian reform era, pp. 345–6, purely in domestic terms.

[11] See Simms, *The struggle for mastery in Germany*, pp. 75–90.

[12] Des Ministers Freiherr von Hardenberg Denkschrift 'Über die Reorganisation des Preußischen Staats, Sept. 1807, Riga, in Georg Winter, ed., *Die Reorganisation des Preussischen Staates unter Stein und Hardenberg. vol. I. Vom Beginn des Kampfes gegen die Kabinettsregierung bis zum Wiedereintritt des Ministers vom Stein* (Leipzig, 1931), pp. 306–7: 'Ohne Macht ist keine Selbstständigkeit und Interdependenz, also muß Preußen streben, diese wieder zu erlangen. Still stehen kann es jetzt weniger als je. Es muß sich wieder vergrößern, nicht nur seinen Verlust decken, sondern noch mehr erwerben, oder es sinkt, es geht ganz unter. Die geographische Lage Preußens macht dieses gewiß. Es wird, erhebt es sich nicht, ein Raub seiner mächtigen Nachbarn werden... Vor allen Dingen muß es Kraft sammeln, das Innere in allen Zweigen wohl ordnen und planmäßig in Übereinstimmung bringen, auch sich ohne Zeitverlust wieder zum Kampf rüsten, soweit es die Mittel gestatten, besonders zu dem der Verteidigung.'

Hence, Hardenberg continued, 'Above all, Prussia must concentrate her strength, and organise and systematically co-ordinate all aspects of her internal affairs. Moreover, she must prepare herself for battle without delay, as far as means allow, preparing herself especially for defence'. This principle was echoed by Karl vom Stein zu Altenstein, another prominent reformer, and close associate of Hardenberg: 'The internal constitution [of the state] is largely determined by the role which the state may wish to play in foreign affairs, and this in turn is linked to the military potential permitted by the [internal] constitution'.[13] This is the context in which the reforming blueprint in Prussia is to be seen. The determination to tackle domestic inequalities — of which more presently — was driven by geopolitically based foreign-political priorities and not, primarily, by any abstract plan for societal modernization, or fear of internal revolution.

There was no corresponding reform blueprint in Britain. Here the fear of revolution from below was certainly greater, at least before 1800: the various Corresponding Societies in England and, of course, the emergence of the United Irishmen caused the authorities considerable concern.[14] But fear of domestic unrest was as likely to lead to repression as to pre-emptive reform. As in Prussia, the main impetus for reform came from the need to mobilize national resources in the struggle against France. As John Ehrman has recently pointed out, Pitt's domestic policies (especially his fiscal reforms, which will not be addressed here) were primarily intended to strengthen the 'home base'.[15] However, there seem to have been no fundamental govern-mental reform plans from Pitt, Dundas, or other prominent British politi-cians on the Prussian model. The closest one comes to a programmatic British blueprint for reform are the writings of the radical military reformer, the Earl of Selkirk, whose pamphlet of 1808 on national defence was widely publicized, and whose remarks bear a remarkable resemblance to the reforming programme in Prussia:

> Though Great Britain has not been immediately involved in the catastrophe of the continent, yet her policy cannot remain uninfluenced by so vast a change in

[13] 'Des Geheimen Oberfinanzrats von Altenstein Denkschrift 'Über die Leitung des Preußischen Staats an S. des Herrn Staatsministers Freiherrn von Hardenberg', 11 Sept. 1807, Riga, in Winter, ed., *Die Reorganisation des Preussischen Staates*, p. 412: 'Die innere Verfassung wird größtenteils durch den Standpunkt bestimmt, auf welcher sich der Staat in den äußeren Verhältnissen setzen kann, und dieses hängt wiederrum von der militärischen Kraftäußerung ab, welche die Verfassung erlaubt'.

[14] Paradigmatic: E. P. Thompson, *The making of the English working class* (Harmondsworth, 1963); Marianne Elliott, *Partners in revolution: the United Irishmen and France* (New Haven, 1989); Jim Smyth, *Men of no property: Irish radicals and popular politics in the late eighteenth century*, (London and Dublin, 1992).

[15] See John Ehrman, *The younger Pitt: the consuming struggle* (London, 1996), pp. 98–129 and passim.

all that surrounds her. To us, as well as to the nations of the continent, this must
be a new aera: our arrangements, internal as well as external, must be adapted
to our new circumstances. Britain has long maintained a rivalry against a
country containing more than double her population, and, in point of natural
advantages still more her superior. If, against so great a disproportion of
physical strength, we have been enabled hitherto to maintain an equal contest,
it is not to be entirely ascribed to the advantage of our insular situation. Our
inferiority in regular military force has not yet occasioned very imminent
danger to our national independence, because the great military powers of the
continent kept our adversary in awe, and prevented the full extention of her
strength against us. That check is now no more. We are deprived of all
extraneous support, while the force against which we have to contend, has
been increased beyond all bounds. If, therefore, we are to remain on the list of
nations, it must be by exertions unprecedented in the improvement of our
internal resources.[16]

The reference to the preponderance of France, the geopolitical nod towards
Britain's island status, and the need to maximize internal resources to
external ends: all this is reminiscent of reforming rhetoric in Prussia.

Reform of the executive

If one turns to specific areas of reform, however, the preoccupations were
rather different. In Prussia, reform of the supreme executive was a central
concern before 1806, and remained important after 1807. During the early
years of the French threat, Prussian foreign policy-making had been complicated by the retention of multiple, usually two but sometimes three,
foreign ministers, the *Kabinettsministerium*, each vying to displace the
other in the confidence of the king, Frederick William III.[17] The picture
was further complicated by the *Kabinett*, a body of ostensible secretaries who
doubled as intimate councillors of the king, and constituted something of a
shadow government, undermining the authority of the official ministry.
Moreover, the organization of the General Directory, the supreme domestic
administration of the kingdom, into regional and topical ministries, resulted
in much confusion and duplication of effort. It was never quite clear, for
example, whether a certain issue fell most properly within the purview of,
say, the East Prussian Department, or of the Justice Department; matters
were not helped by the existence of the Silesian ministry, which lay outside
the General Directory altogether.

By the early 1800s, a considerable reform debate had developed which
stressed the need for greater executive cohesion, generally through the

[16] The Earl of Selkirk, *On the necessity of a more effectual system of national defence and the
means of establishing the permanent security of the kingdom* (London, 1808), pp. 2–3.
[17] See Simms, *Impact of Napoleon*, passim.

creation of a monocratic foreign ministry within a council of ministers, which would replace the polycratic chaos — to borrow a term from the historiography of the Third Reich — of the *Generaldirektorium* and the *Kabinettsministerium*.[18] One of the royal military adjutants, Colonel Massenbach, demanded a 'central point from which all instructions radiate as if out of one focus'; Count Alvensleben, himself a longtime co-foreign minister, demanded 'more unity in the administration and simplification and rationalisation of the affairs of state'.[19] This debate culminated in the famous memoranda by Baron Stein, Hardenberg and Altenstein in the summer of 1806, in which they called for the elimination of the Kabinett, and the creation of a ministerial council.

Unsurprisingly, the campaign for a reform of the executive was resumed with a vengeance after the defeats of Auerstedt and Jena. In his memorandum of March 1807, Hardenberg called for 'Unity of principles, strength and consistency of execution', and for a 'council which unites the individual sections [of government] and those individuals who lead the sections... the purpose: unity and speed'.[20] That same month, Voß stressed that 'what the Prussian state lacks, and which is indispensable for a great monarchy, is the spirit of unity or a central authority, associated directly with the King, which unites all the administrative branches of the state'.[21] Similarly, Baron Stein in his famous Nassau memorandum of 1807, demanded 'the creation of a state council or a supreme authority directly responsible to the King, with publically-recognised and not covertly-arrogated authority, which would be the final reference point for the various administrative branches of the state'.[22] The thinking behind these demands was subsequently summed up the royal councillor, Johann Peter Ancillon, as follows: 'The less

---

[18] See Hans Hausherr, *Verwaltungseinheit und Ressorttrennung. Vom Ende des 17. bis zum Beginn des 19 Jh.* (Berlin/East, 1953), pp. 189–204.

[19] Cited in Simms, *Impact of Napoleon*, p. 133.

[20] 'Denkschrift Hardenbergs an König Friedrich Wilhelm III', 3. Mar. 1807, Memel, in Leopold von Ranke, ed., *Denkwürdigkeiten des Staatskanzlers Fürsten von Hardenberg* (Leipzig, 1877), v, p. 456: 'Einheit in den Grundsätzen, Kraft und Konsequenz in der Ausführung... Konseil, welches die einzelnen Partien vereinige, darin diejenigen Personen, welche sie führen... Zweck: Einheit und Schnelligkeit'. See also p. 449 and passim for similar wording.

[21] 'Denkschrift des Ministers von Voß', 10. Mar. 1807, Memel, in Winter, ed., *Die Reorganisation des Preussischen Staats*, p. 140: 'Geist der Einheit oder eine Zentral-vereinigungsbehörde aller einzelner Staatsverwaltungszweige, unmittelbar an die Person des Regenten geknüpft, ist das, was dem Preußischen Staat fehlt, und für eine große Monarchie unentbehrlich ist'.

[22] Des Ministers Freiherr vom Stein Denkschrift 'ber die zweckmäßige Bildung der obersten und der Provinzial-Finanz- und Polizeibehörden in der Preußischen Monarchie', Nassau [Nassau memorandum], June 1807, in Winter, ed., *Die Reorganisation des Preussischen Staats*, p. 190: 'Bildung eines Staatsrates oder einer unmittelbar unter dem Könige arbeitenden, mit anerkannter und nicht erschlichener Verantwortlichkeit versehenen obersten Behörde, die der endliche Vereinigungspunkt der verschiedenen Zweige der Staatsverwaltung ist'.

cumbersome the wheels [of the machinery of government], the more reliable
and smooth the functioning of the machine'.[23]

This programme was implemented in fits and starts after 1807. The
General Directory was abolished and replaced by five monocratic subject
ministries: foreign affairs, military affairs, finance, justice, and the interior.
Hardenberg's plan for a prime ministerial system — headed by himself —
was briefly tried but lapsed in 1808–10 during the co-ministry of Dohna and
Altenstein. It was only in 1810, with Hardenberg's return as chief minister,
which he remained until 1822, that the reform of the executive demanded
before 1806 was truly complete.

The contemporaneous British debate on the executive was no less
concerned to find the winning formula against France, but it was couched
in very different, rather less trenchant terms, and its preoccupations were
somewhat different. Partly, this was due to the fact that the old British system
of two Foreign Secretaries, one for the Northern Department and one for the
Southern Department — in effect a Prussian-style co-ministry — had already
been abandoned in favour of a monocratic Foreign Office in 1782;[24] the
organization of the British executive was thus more efficient to begin with.
But mainly the explanation lies in the evolutionary development of the
cabinet council as an instrument for co-ordinating the war effort against
France.[25] Whenever necessary, an inner cabinet was formed to ensure secrecy
and speed of execution. In the 1790s this famously included Pitt, Grenville,
and Dundas,[26] whereas the last few years of the war were dominated by the
triumvirate Castlereagh, Bathurst, and Liverpool. The characteristics of this
new body: prime-ministerial guidance, joint responsibility, mutual delibera-

---

[23] Johann Peter Ancillon, Geheimes Staatsarchiv Dahlem (GStA), Rep. 92 Ancillon 22,
*Fragmente enthaltend Vorschläge zur Verbesserung der Staatsverwaltung in Preußen o. d. (nach
1815)*, unfoliated. The document contains further references to need for 'Einheit' and to avoid
the 'langsamen und sogar schleppenden Gang der Geschäfte': 'Alles was die Regierung
vereinfachet bringt sie nicht allein ihren Zweck näher, sondern führt auch immer ein mehr
oder minder grosses Ersparnis herbei. Die Bewegung der Machine wird um so sicherer und
leichterer, je weniger es in derselben Räder giebt, und je einfacher das Räderwerk, um so weniger
kostspielig der ganze Mechanismus'.

[24] Charles Middleton, 'The early years of the old Foreign Office, 1782–1810', in *Proceedings of
the Consortium on Revolutionary Europe* (PCRE), pp. 92, 97. See also Charles Middleton, *The
administration of British foreign policy, 1782–1846* (Durham, N.C., 1977).

[25] See Charles Middleton, 'The impact of the American and French Revolutions on the British
constitution: a case study of the British cabinet', *PCRE* (1986), p. 317. See also Richard Willis,
'Cabinet politics and executive policy-making procedures, 1794–1801', *Albion*, 7; and Arthur
Aspinall, 'The cabinet council, 1783–1835', *Proceedings of the British Academy, London*, 38
(1952). But see also John Ehrman's words of caution on 'grey areas' of cabinet, *The younger Pitt*,
p. 451.

[26] See Michael Duffy, 'Pitt, Grenville and the control of British foreign policy in the 1790s', in
Jeremy Black, ed., *Knights errant and true Englishmen: British foreign policy, 1660–1800*
(Edinburgh, 1989), pp. 151–77.

tion and co-ordination with the king, were not so very different from the Prussian ministerial system which emerged after 1807 under different circumstances but in the face of similar, if more keenly felt pressures.

Social, religious, and military reforms

These reforms of the decision-making apparatus did not *per se* involve fundamental changes in society or politics. Yet in both states the French threat prompted a more radical debate on internal reform. In Prussia, the reformers argued that the international situation demanded, to quote the famous passage from Hardenberg's Riga memorandum [1807], 'a revolution in the good sense of the word... Democratic principles in a monarchical government: this seems to me the form of government most congenial to the spirit of the age'.[27] But this modernizing programme was in no sense a departure from the old Prussian primacy of foreign policy. Hardenberg went on to observe that 'Under different, but similar circumstances, yet in the context of a completely different *Zeitgeist*, the Great Elector Frederick William revolutionalized his state, after the unhappy epoch under George William, and thus laid the foundations of his subsequent greatness'.[28] This shows the essential continuities between seventeenth- and eighteenth-century Prussian reform absolutism and the reform era of the early nineteenth century.

The resulting catalogue of domestic reforms was intended to 'set free' the hidden strengths of Prussian society. The noble monopoly of the officer corps and the senior ranks of the administration must be broken: bourgeois talent should be encouraged. Restrictions on the purchase of estates should be lifted: this would create a free market in land. The hereditary bondage of the peasantry should be abolished: this would both encourage agricultural improvement and create a flexible labour force. Local government was restored to Prussian cities: this would provide cheap administration and help to bind town-dwellers closer to the state than hitherto. Naturally, the changes provoked furious opposition, largely from the threatened junker elites. As one ardent reformer, Theodor von Schön, noted bitterly in his diary, 'the old aristocrats love only themselves... In their view the state may perish but seigneurial power would survive'.[29]

---

[27] Hardenberg's Riga memorandum, in Winter, ed., *Die Reorganisation des Preussischen Staats*, p. 306: 'eine Revolution im guten Sinn... Demokratische Grundsätze in einer monarchischen Regierung: dieses scheint mir die angemessene Form für den gegenwärtigen Zeitgeist'.

[28] Ibid., p. 306: 'Unter anderen, aber ähnlichen Umständen, jedoch bei einem ganz verschiedenen Zeitgeist revolutionierte Kurfürst Friedrich Wilhelm der Große nach der unglücklichen Epoche unter Georg Wilhelm gleichfalls seinen Staat und legte den Grund zu seiner nachherigen Größe'.

[29] Cited in Gerrit Walther, *Niebuhr's Forschung* (Stuttgart, 1993), p. 237: 'die alten Aristocraten, diese lieben nur sich... Der Staat gehen, ihrer Ansicht unter, aber die Gutsherrschaft bliebe'.

Much of the reforming programme — such as the creation of monocratic
ministries and the abolition of feudal leftovers — was in more or less self-
conscious imitation of Revolutionary France.[30] But many reformers looked
to Britain for inspiration instead. Indeed, there was a long eighteenth-century
tradition of Anglophilia in Germany, which for all the increasing criticism
was still strong around 1800.[31] For example, Barthold Georg Niebuhr and
Ludwig Vincke were impressed by what they took to be the freedom-loving
spirit of English local self-government.[32] Vincke's *Darstellung der inneren
Verwaltung Großbritanniens* (account of the domestic administration of
Great Britain) was only published in 1815, but penned in 1807, immediately
after Jena; the foreword was written by Niebuhr.[33] They proposed, as Vincke
put it in a memorandum of 1808, to 'transfer British internal administration
to Prussian soil, customs and constitution, as far as it can be made
applicable', in particular the highly successful system of justice of the
peace.[34] But there were also cautious voices, such as that of Regierungsrat
Merckel, who warned against simply grafting British institutions onto the
Prussian body politic: 'Before one can learn to run, one must learn to walk
properly; and the internal constitution of England, which is the result of a
representative constitution which has been firmly in place for hundreds of
years, and is the product of a long-cherished sense of freedom, cannot simply
be transplanted to a soil where hereditary bondage still prevailed only a year

[30] See Max Lehmann, 'Die preußische Reform von 1808 und die Französische Revolution',
Preußische Jahrbücher, 132 (1908), pp. 211–29, but also Ernst von Meier, *Französische Einflüsse
auf die Staats- und Rechtsentwicklung Preußens im 19. Jahrhundert*, (2 vols, Leipzig, 1907–8).
[31] See Michael Maurer, *Aufklärung und Anglophilie in Deutschland* (Göttingen and Zurich,
1987).
[32] Walther, *Niebuhr's Forschung*, pp. 114, 475; see also B. G. Niebuhr, *Nachgelassene Schriften
nichtphilologischen Inhalts*, ed. Marcus Niebuhr (Hamburg, 1842). Such views have also been
attributed to Stein, but this is contested by Walther Hubatsch, *Der Freiherr vom Stein und
England* (Cologne, 1977), p. 39. See also Werner Gembruch, 'Zum England-Bild des Freiherrn
vom Stein', in Johanne Kunisch, ed., *Staat und Heer. Ausgewählte historische Studien zum ancien
regime, zur Französischen Revolution und zu den Befreiungskriegen*, Historische Forschungen, 40
(Berlin, 1990), especially p. 538.
[33] Ludwig von Vincke, *Darstellungen der inneren Verwaltung Großbritanniens*, ed. B. G. Niebuhr
(2nd edn, Berlin, 1848). On Vincke see now Hans-Joachim Behr and Jürgen Kloosterhuis, eds,
Ludwig Freiherr von Vincke. Ein historisches Profil zwischen Reform und Revolution in Preußen
(Münster, 1994).
[34] Vincke memorandum, 'Über die Organisation der Unterbehörden zunächst für die Polizei-
verwaltung', 4 Jun. 1808, Berlin, in Heinrich Scheel and Doris Schmidt, eds, *Das Reformminis-
terium Stein. Akten zur Verfassungs- und Verwalungsgeschichte aus den jahren 1807–8* (Berlin,
1966–8), II, pp. 588–9: 'die britische Verwaltung des Innern . . . auf preußischen Boden, Sitten
und Verfassung zu übertragen soweit solche anwendbar gemacht werden kann'.

ago, without obviously endangering internal order and peace';[35] similar reservations were expressed by Altenstein.[36]

Social and administrative reforms were not an end in themselves, they were part of a process of national mobilization directed against Napoleonic France. As one military reformer, Colonel von Borstell, put it: 'Surrounded as she is by powerful states, Prussia's exposed military-geographical position, which is secure only towards the Silesian border with Austria, confers on it the rank of a subordinate ally. Therefore, at the moment, the reassertion of great-power status can only be achieved through the most sustained mobilisation of all the resources of the state'; similar views were expressed by other prominent military reformers, such as Gneisenau.[37] Crucial to the release of latent societal strengths in Prussia was the development of a new model of military organization, the logical consequence not merely of Prussia's precarious external situation, but also of the dismantling of the traditional military-agrarian complex. Hitherto, the Prussian army had been based on a corporate division of functions between a privileged nobility, which dominated the officer corps, and the peasantry, which provided the rank and file; townspeople were largely exempted from recruitment.

The reformers now assaulted this system from two angles. First, they argued that the closure of the officer corps to non-noble candidates deprived the nation of a range of talents. 'Birth confers no monopoly on merit', Gneisenau observed in 1808, 'if one grants it too many rights, a multitude of resources [will] lie sleeping, undeveloped and unexploited in the bosom of the nation'.[38] Moreover, the powerful corporate ethos of the old system had led

---

[35] Bemerkungen des Regierungsrats Merckel 'Zu dem von des Herrn Staatsministers von Schroetter Exzellenz unterm 13. Oktober 1808 eingereichten Plane zur Einrichtung der Kreisverwaltungsbehörden mit Rücksicht auf die dazugehörenden Beilagen', 9 May 1809, Breslau, in Heinrich Scheel and Doris Schmidt, eds, *Von Stein zu Hardenberg. Dokumente aus dem Interimsministerium Altenstein/Dohna* (Berlin, 1986), p. 282: 'Um fertig zu laufen, muß man erst sicher gehen lernen; und die innere Verwaltung Englands als das Resultat einer Jahrhunderte sicher bestehenden Repräsentativ-Verfassung, das Produkt eines lang genährten Freiheitssinnes, kann ohne offenbare Gefahr für innere Ordnung und Ruhe unmöglich plötzlich auf einen Boden verpflanzt werden, an welchem noch vor einem Jahre Eigenbehörigkeit klebte'.

[36] Marginalia to 'Bemerkungen des Geheimen Oberfinanzrats von Staegemann zum Organisationsplan', after Nov. 1807, in Scheel and Schmidt, eds, *Stein*, I, p. 188.

[37] Memorandum attributed to Lieutenant Colonel von Borstell, 20 Sept. 1807, Treptow a. d. Rega, in Rudolf Vaupel, ed., *Die Reorganisation des Preussischen Staates unter Stein und Hardenberg. Teil II. Das Preussische Heer vom Tilsiter Frieden bis zur Befreiung 1807–1814* (Leipzig, 1938), p. 87: 'Umgeben von mächtigen Staaten scheint Preußens ausgedehnte geographisch-militärische Lage, welche nur von der schlesisch-österreichischen Grenze Sicherheit gewährt, ihm den Rang eines untergeordneten Bundesstaates anzuweisen. Die jetzige Repräsentation einer selbständigen oder starken Macht dürfte folglich nur mit der äußersten Anspannung aller Landeskräfte zu realisieren sein'; Gneisenau memorandum, pre-1807, ibid., p. 187.

[38] Gneisenau's article in the *Volksfreund*, 2 Jul. 1808, in Vaupel, ed., *Preussische Heer*, p. 490: 'Die Geburt gibt kein Monopol für Verdienste, räumt man dieser zu viele Rechte ein, so schlafen im Schoße einer Nation eine Menge Kräfte unentwickelt und unbenutzt'.

to widespread indifference towards the fate of army and dynasty. Just after the catastrophe, one military commentator spoke of 'the indifference of civilians towards the relations of the state with other states . . . it appeared all the same to them whether they were ruled by friend or foe'.[39] For this reason the reformers supported measures such as the abolition of corporal punishment. As Scharnhorst put it in 1808, 'One must make the army more attractive to the nation and remove its hateful elements'.[40] Secondly, agrarian reform, with its associated freedom of movement, rendered the old cantonal system, based on bonded peasant recruits, obsolete. Even the Jews were permitted, *de facto*, rather than officially, to join the struggle against Napoleon; due to the relatively small numbers involved this was of more symbolic than practical significance.[41] From now on, however, the principle was clear: 'All inhabitants of the state should be born defenders of same'.[42]

There were, however, considerable differences as to how the military mobilization of Prussia should best be achieved. Some advocated the direct adoption of the French system of general conscription, perhaps with some form of substitution; others feared the impact of conscription on Prussian society and economy. Vincke famously warned that conscription would be 'the grave of all culture, of academic pursuits and trade, of civil freedom and all human happiness'; similar concerns were expressed by Theodor von Schön.[43] There was also the problem of finance: the costs of the lost war and Napoleonic exactions meant that, in the short term at least, the Prussian regular army after 1807 had to be reduced rather than increased. This explains why Prussian military reformers took such a keen interest in British military organization, particularly the militia system. Thus the initial reports of the military investigative commission in 1807 envisaged the creation of a 'Reserve Army' comprising those who could not arm, clothe and train themselves at their own expense; like the British militia, it would not normally be deployed outside its home area.[44] As with the English Militia

---

[39] Major von Lossau, 'Gedanken über die militärische Organisation der preußischen Monarchie', 21 Mar. 1808, Treptow a. d. Rega, in Vaupel, ed., *Preussische Heer*, p. 333: 'eine Kälte der Zivileinwohner gegen die Verhältnisse des Staats zu andern Staaten . . . so schien es völlig gleich, ob Feind oder Freund im Land war'.

[40] Scharnhorst to Stein, 3 Jul. 1808, Königsberg, in Vaupel, ed., *Preussische Heer*, p. 500: 'Man muß der Nation den Soldatenstand angenehm machen, und das Verhaßte aus ihn entfernen'.

[41] See Horst Fischer, *Judentum, Staat und Heer in Preußen im frühen 19. Jahrhundert. Zur Geschichte der staatlichen Judenpolitik* (Tübingen, 1968), pp. 32–53.

[42] Immediatbericht der Militär-Reorganisationskommission, 31 Aug. 1807, Memel, in Vaupel, ed., *Preussische Heer*, p. 82 and passim.

[43] Vincke to Stein, 30 Sept. 1808, n.p., in Vaupel, ed., *Preussische Heer*, p. 599: 'das Grab aller Kultur, der Wissenschaften und Gewerbe, der bürgerlichen Freiheit und aller menschlichen Glückseligkeit'; Schön's notes, 4 Dec. 1807, Memel, ibid., pp. 201–202.

[44] Report of Militär Immediat-Kommission, 31 Aug. 1807, Memel, in Vaupel, ed., *Preussische Heer*, pp. 82–3.

and Volunteers, the Prussian Reserve Army was also allotted a domestic role: one report of the investigative commission remarked that 'When England armed her property-owners and householders, thoughts of revolt and internal revolution disappeared'.[45] And in 1814, around the time of the introduction of universal military service in Prussia, attention turned once again to British models, with Hardenberg even going so far as to request details from the Prussian representative in London: 'Our government needs exact information on the organisation and numbers of the English militia. I therefore ask you, monsieur, to send me all the ordonances which relate to this topic'.[46]

The link between the emancipation of hidden societal strengths and military mobilization, which so characterized the Prussian reform movement after 1807, had already been accepted by the British government in the 1790s. Once Holland had fallen, Britain was effectively encircled: she now had to muster all her resources to man the extended perimeter line against the threat of French invasion.[47] This was done in two ways. First of all, the traditional county militia formations were re-embodied at the outbreak of war, the levy was increased under the Quota Act of 1796, and in 1797 the system was extended to Scotland. Militia service involved a proportional ballot of able-bodied men — excluding those who had already joined the Volunteers — for three years' service. They could pay a fine or provide a substitute, if they were unable or unwilling to serve. Secondly and more spectacularly, the government attempted to tap the reserves of patriotism in civil society through the Volunteer Act of 1794: this created a largely self-funded home defence force of about 300,000 men by 1803. As J. E. Cookson has recently pointed out, the Volunteering phenomenon was not just about 'loyalism',[48] but also — and

---

[45] Report of Militär Immediat-Kommission, 15 Mar. 1808, in Vaupel, ed., *Preussische Heer*, p. 323: 'Als England seine Grundeigentümer und Hausbesitzer bewaffnete, veschwand der Gedanke an Revolte und innere Revolution'.

[46] Hardenberg to Greuhm, 2 Jun. 1814, Paris, GStA, Rep. 11:82, London 272, *Acta der Gesandschaft zu London betreffend der Organisation und Einrichtung der englischen Miliz*, unfoliated: 'Il importe à notre government d'avoir une connaissance exacte de l'organisation et l'état de la milice anglaise. Je vous charge en conséquence Monsieur, de me transmettre toutes les ordonances qui ont rapport à cet objet'; Boyen (Prussian minister of war) to Greuhm, 15 Aug. 1813, ibid. See also the printed document 'Return of the effective strength of the British Army in rank and file, at the under-mentioned periods, distinguishing cavalry, artillery, infantry and militia, and British from foreign and colonial troops', with handwritten comments on it by Jacobi (Prussian ambassador to London): 'Ce qu'on appelle ici *local militia*, la milice qui ne quitte pas la comté ou le district ou elle est lévée monte à 250 000 h[ommes]', in: GStA, 2.4.1 Abt. I 5219, unfoliated.

[47] Re 'encirclement' see J. E. Cookson, *The British armed nation, 1793–1815* (Oxford, 1997), pp. 38–41.

[48] J. R. Western, 'The Volunteer movement as an anti-revolutionary force', *English Historical Review*, 71 (1956), pp. 603–14; H. T. Dickinson, 'Popular loyalism in Britain in the 1790s', in Hellmuth, ed., *The transformation of political culture*, pp. 503–33.

perhaps primarily — about 'national defence patriotism'.[49] After all, the biggest initial surge in volunteering came in coastal counties, where the threat of French invasion was greatest.[50] External defence, not domestic repression was the key to Pitt's policy in the 1790s.

It was this same primacy of foreign policy which prompted the government to address the question of those excluded from the civil society of *ancien régime* Britain. For the traditional restrictions on the full deployment of the nation's resources were not socio-legal — as in Prussia before 1806 — but *confessional.* If Britain was a parliamentary fiscal-military state resting on a large degree of consensus, then it was also indisputably a state based on institutionalized religious inequality: Roman Catholics, especially, were excluded from political and military participation. By the end of the eighteenth century, reform-minded British statesmen recognized that some form of emancipation would be needed to mobilize Catholics, particularly Irish Catholics, in the struggle against France. Irish Catholics were, to quote one British statesman, 'a weapon of war as yet untried'.[51] Indeed, as Tom Bartlett has shown, the military demands of the international situation were crucial to British government support for Catholic emancipation.[52] The first Roman Catholic Relief Acts of 1778 and 1782 were passed during the American War; and it was the outbreak of war with Revolutionary France in 1793 that prompted the government to couple its Militia Bill with a Relief Act for Irish Catholics enabling them to serve in it. At first, the idea was to deploy Catholic militia forces in defence of Ireland against French invasion,[53] but this narrow conception soon gave way to the desire to use them overseas as well. As Pitt and Dundas argued, 'the present state of the world' (i.e. the war) and 'the present circumstances of this country and Europe' necessitated 'conciliating the Catholics as much as possible... and making of them an effectual body of support'.[54] Indeed, the Union of Ireland and Great Britain in 1800 was conceived as part of a broader programme to integrate Ireland and Irish Catholics into the war effort. Due to the opposition of the crown, however, Pitt was unable to deliver on Catholic emancipation.

---

[49] Cookson, *Armed nation*, p. 211. But see also Linda Colley, *Britons: forging the nation, 1707–1837* (London, 1994, 1st edn, New Haven, 1992), pp. 283–319.

[50] Cookson, *Armed nation*, p. 26.

[51] Thomas Bartlett, ' "A weapon of war as yet untried": Irish Catholics and the armed forces of the crown, 1760–1830', in T. G. Fraser and Keith Jeffery, eds, *Men, women, and war* (Dublin, 1993), pp. 66–85. Perhaps unsurprisingly, given the differing nature of the problem and the resulting disabilities, there does not seem to have been a military dimension to the problem of (Protestant) dissent: see Ursula Henriques, *Religious toleration in England, 1787–1833* (London, 1961).

[52] Thomas Bartlett, *The fall and rise of the Irish nation: the Catholic question, 1690–1830* (Dublin, 1992), p. 309.

[53] Ehrman, *The younger Pitt*, p. 159.

But by 1806–7, the triumph of French arms across the continent, and the perceived pressing need for more Irish Catholic recruitment, spurred the Ministry of All the Talents to make one supreme effort for emancipation. In December 1806, not long after the Prussian defeat at Jena, Lord Grenville — whose commitment to Roman Catholic emancipation admittedly long predated the need to mobilize the nation against France — spoke of the need of 'removing *all* restrictions on the employment of the King's catholic subjects indiscriminately . . . because the present times are felt to call for as much military exertion as the empire is capable of making',[55] a clear sign that — in this case — external considerations were being used to drive domestic policy. Four months later, the Earl of Moira argued that a further 100,000 men could be raised if Irish Catholics were recruited in the same proportion as the rest of Britain.[56] Once again, however, royal and parliamentary opposition proved fatal, and the issue of Catholic emancipation was not raised for the duration of the war.

In their different ways Catholic emancipation, volunteering and even the old militia system proved blind alleys for the war effort. Both forms of home defence organization, the Volunteers even more so than the militia, were hedged about with all kinds of restrictions. The Volunteers could not be deployed outside of their own county, let alone sent abroad, without their consent; and the same was largely true of the old militia. During the invasion scares of the 1790s and the early 1800s, this was less of a problem. But when it came to foreign expeditions, and especially with the revival of full-scale land warfare in the Peninsula after 1808, the need for a larger and more flexible regular army became inescapable. Indeed, there already existed a strong constituency for military reform within the British army and among certain politicians. For example, the Duke of York, the commander in chief, was an ardent 'Prussianist', who believed in the virtues of discipline and a large standing army.[57] On the political side, there was no greater critic of the voluntary system than William Windham, secretary of state for war in 1794–1801 and again in 1806–7. Britain, Windham observed to the House of Commons in 1806, was obsessed with 'substitutes for an army'.[58] 'If anything requires immediate use and is unfit to keep', he also remarked, 'it is an offer

---

[54] Cited in Bartlett, 'A weapon of war as yet untried', p. 43.

[55] Cited in Bartlett, *The fall and rise of the Irish nation*, p. 287.

[56] See Selkirk, *On the necessity of a more effectual system of national defence*, p. 113. See also the extracts from the *Morning Chronicle*, 8 Aug. 1808, cited in Peter Spence, *The birth of romantic radicalism: war, popular politics and English radical reformism, 1800–1815* (Aldershot, 1996), p. 65.

[57] See the discussion by Piers Mackesy, *British victory in Egypt, 1801: The end of Napoleon's conquest* (London, 1995), pp. 29–30.

[58] See William Windham, 'Motion relative to the military establishments of the country', *Hansard's parliamentary debates*, v, p. 655.

of voluntary service. It is more liable to spoil than mackeral itself'.[59] Or, as he put it in another analogy from the realm of nature, the Volunteers were merely 'painted cherries which none but simple birds would take for real fruit'.[60]

By contrast the Prussian army was widely admired — in the 1790s William Grenville described it as 'numerous, disciplined, ready and efficient' — and it was often seen as a model for Britain.[61] But there were considerable barriers to the creation of a large continental-style regular army in Britain: fear of standing armies had, after all, been a staple of opposition rhetoric since the early modern period. Many opposed the creation of an officer academy in 1801, as it was seen as a first step towards a standing army, and thus a 'danger to the constitution'; another critic objected to 'every thing that tended to Germanize the English army'.[62] Whereas British society grudgingly submitted to the arbitrary naval press gangs, straightforward conscription for army service overseas was unacceptable. Indeed, Windham candidly accepted the limitations this placed upon military organization. As he observed to the House of Commons in June 1804:

> If the danger to be guarded against were imminent, and...a levy were necessary immediately, unquestionably a compulsory proceeding to obtain that levy might be the most effectual. Measures of that sort are undoubtedly in their own nature the speediest and most certain in their operation. Nothing seems to be so sure and direct in a case where men are wanted, as to pass a law, by which men shall be forcibly taken. But here care is necessary, to consider the nature and condition of the country in which such powers are to be exercised. What is good for Russia or Prussia may not be good for Great Britain.[63]

In the end, Britain settled for a revised militia system. Castlereagh's Local Militia Act of 1808 maintained the principle of compulsory local county service, with substantial fines for non-attendance. This created a pool of trained men, from which the regular army could draw replacements, a measure which locally minded militia colonels had previously resisted. The Militia Interchange Act of 1811 enabled the rotation of regiments within the United Kingdom, and in particular released Catholic Irish regiments for service overseas. The Volunteers were allowed to run down. In principle, the act amounted to Napoleonic-style conscription, for local purposes, at least,

---

[59] Cited in Erin McCauley Renn, 'England faces invasion: the land forces, 1803–1805', *PCRE* (1974), p. 138.

[60] Cited in Clive Emsley, 'The Volunteer movement', in Alan Guy, ed., *The road to Waterloo: The British army and the struggle against Revolutionary and Napoleonic France, 1793–1815* (London, 1990), p. 47.

[61] Cited in Hartmut Gembries, 'Das Thema Preußen in der politischen Diskussion Englands zwischen 1792 und 1807', unpublished PhD dissertation, University of Freiburg, 1988, pp. 99, 168.

[62] Cited in Gembries, 'Das Thema Preußen', p. 101.

[63] *Hansard*, v, p. 495.

but as there were always enough (mostly Scottish and Irish) Volunteers, the system was never used to its full potential.[64]

Political reform

Another method of harnessing popular energies against Napoleon was political reform. In the Riga memorandum of 1807, Hardenberg had called for a Prussian national assembly in order to 'bring the nation into a closer relationship with the state administration to make people familiar with it and to interest them in it'.[65] A year later, Frederick William's decree of November 1808 called for a national representation; and in 1810, Hardenberg's Finance Edict was accompanied by a royal proclamation promising 'the nation an appropriately arranged representation, both in the provinces and for the whole'.[66] An assembly of (summoned) notables met in 1811, followed by the corporately elected provisional national representation of nobles, peasants and townspeople in 1812–13, and in 1814 by the short-lived 'interim representation'. The purpose of these assemblies was twofold. Their specific task was to advise on and support governement plans for fiscal reform. More generally, they were supposed to generate patriotic fervour for the final reckoning with Napoleon. In no sense was the national representation conceived by liberal reformers as a check on royal authority. As Mathew Levinger has persuasively argued, political reform was intended to 'enhance' royal power, not limit it. The Riga memorandum had explicitly stated that the national representation should be 'without compromising the monarchical constitution';[67] the Royal Edict of 1810 spoke only of 'counsel', not of control. This point was underlined by government-sponsored newspapers, such as the *Vaterlandsfreund*. The representation of the people, it argued in May 1809, 'should in no respect limit the power of the King, but merely advise, enlighten and guide'; 'his power should not be limited in any way by the representative body'.[68]

[64] This is the argument of Cookson, *Armed nation*, p. 87.

[65] Hardenberg's Riga memorandum, in Vaupel, ed., *Preussische Heer*, p. 318: 'Die Nation mit der Staatsverwaltung in nähere Verhältnisse zu bringen, sie mehr damit bekannt zu machen und dafür zu interessieren'.

[66] Cited in Mathew Levinger, 'Imagining a nation: the constitutional question in Prussia, 1806–1815', unpublished D.Phil. dissertation, University of Chicago, 1992, p. 134. See also Mathew Levinger, 'Hardenberg, Wittgenstein and the constitutional question in Prussia, 1815–1822', *German History*, 8 (1990), pp. 257–77.

[67] Hardenberg's Riga memorandum, in Vaupel, ed., *Preussische Heer*, p. 318: 'ohne Abbruch der monarchischen Verfassung'.

[68] *Der Vaterlandsfreund:* 'Über den Geist der neueren Staatsreformen', 10 May 1809, in Scheel and Schmidt, eds., *Von Stein zu Hardenberg*, p. 299: 'soll in keiner Hinsicht die Gewalt des Monarchen *beschränkend*, sondern bloß für seine *Kenntnis ratgebend, aufklärend und leitend sein*' (italics in original); ibid., 31 May 1809, p. 312: 'Seine Macht darf also durch die Repräsentation in nichts beschränkt werden'.

In particular, there was near-unanimity that the British model of parliamentary government was not applicable to Prussia.[69] Already, in 1796, one Prussian memorialist had observed that 'If the example of England sometimes demonstrates the benefit of a popular representation, which is only deliberative, it demonstrates still more the necessity that executive power be united in one hand, especially as far as a great power is concerned'.[70] In 1809 the *Vaterlandsfreund* criticized the British parliamentary system on the grounds not only that the franchise was too limited, but that 'the power of the King is too constrained by the representation of the people. The government is therefore obliged to use various, often immoral, means to secure a majority in Parliament'.[71] For this reason, it argued in a subsequent article, the new national representation 'ought not to have both consultative and legislative powers as in England, but should have consultative and advisory powers [only] ... It should not have the right to approve or reject [measures]'.[72] Shortly afterwards the conservative publicist Adam Müller observed that freedom of the press and British-style parliamentary government could not be introduced in Prussia:

> The example of England is completely inappropriate for the Prussian states. One cannot create large assemblies to deliberate on general government policy, even if they were merely to be granted a collective right of consultation, without greatly endangering the state ... It is obvious that in the current situation of the Prussian state, freedom of the press is quite impossible.[73]

[69] An exception would be Quast-Garz's memorandum of 28 Jun. 1812: see Levinger, 'Imagining a nation', p. 184.

[70] *Réflexions sur les motifs de la conduite des puissances de l'Europe et sur leurs intérêts rélativement à la Révolution de France*, 10 Nov. 1796, Berlin, paginated anonymous MSS, GStA, Rep.XI. 81 London 194, p. 36: 'Si l'exemple de l'Angleterre nous prouve quelquefois le bien résultant d'une réprésentation populaire, mais uniquement déliberante, il nous prouve encore plus souvent la nécessité que le pouvoir éxécutif soit réuni dans une seule main le besoin en est surtout demontré pour tout état considérable'.

[71] *Vaterlandsfreund* (anon), 10 May 1809, in Scheel and Schmidt, eds, *Ministerium Dohna-Altenstein*, p. 299: 'die Macht des Königs durch die Repräsentation zu eingeschränkt. Die Regierung ist dadurch genötigt, die Mehrheit im Parlamente durch verschiedene, oft unmoralische Mittel auf ihre Seite zu bringen, damit sie zu den Maßregeln der Regierung ihre Zustimmung gebe'.

[72] *Der Vaterlandsfreund* (anon), 31 May 1809, in Scheel and Schmidt, eds, *Von Stein zu Hardenberg*, p. 312: 'darf nicht berathschlagend und gesetzgebend zugleich sein wie in England, sondern *berathschlagend* und *ratgebend*. Sie hat nichts zu bewilligen, nichts zu verwerfen'.

[73] Adam Müller, memorandum for Frederick William III, 'Redaktion eines Preußischen Regierungsblattes unter dem Titel: Preußische Chronik oder Preußische Hof-und Nationalzeitung', 22 Sept. 1809, in Scheel and Schmidt, eds, *Von Stein zu Hardenberg*, p. 410: 'Das Beispiel von England paßt aber durchaus nicht für die Preußischen Staaten: Große, über die allgemeinen Maßregeln der Regierung delibierierende Körperschaften, wenn ihnen auch nur ein vereintes Votum consultativum einraumt wird, können ohne die äußerste Gefahr des Staats nicht errichtet werden ... Preßfreiheit ist der dermaligen Lage des Preußischen Staates, wie von selbst in den Augen springt, durchaus unzulässig'.

Even such a staunch reformer as Gneisenau was put off the British model by his visit to the country in 1809: 'In this country', he wrote to his wife in November 1809, 'the affairs of state are also conducted in such a woeful manner. Ignorant and rash figures are at the helm, and their ineptitude would surely lead to the destruction of this people as well, if it were not protected by its geographic location'.[74] Once again, this affirms the instinctive link that even Prussian reformers made between geopolitical pressures and the possibility of British-style parliamentary government.

Interestingly, the relative merits of the constitutional absolutist system was a subject often addressed in the Napoleonic period by two people best qualified to judge: the British ambassador to Berlin and the Prussian ambassador to London. They instinctively agreed that the greatest weakness of the British system was the retardative effect of representative structures. Thus Baron Jacobi in London observed that 'the administration of public affairs suffers greatly when ministers find themselves in the position of fearing the loss of their (parliamentary) seats [because] the means of maintaining oneself in parliament absorbs a large part of their attention'.[75] At around the same time, his counterpart in Berlin, Sir Francis Jackson, lamented Britain's tardiness in coming to Prussia's aid at Jena in the following terms: 'I speak of disadvantages that are I am afraid, inherent in our constitution, or at least form an unavoidable appendage to it'. British diplomats and ministers, he argued, always had to watch their domestic flank, which 'requires more time than if [they] could act upon every emergency [themselves], and independent of every consideration, above alluded to'.[76]

In Britain, political reform — that is franchise reform — during the Revolutionary and Napoleonic period on the continent was not sponsored by the government but demanded from below. For the first decade and a half after 1792, calls for broader political participation were coupled with opposition to the war.[77] But in 1803–6, with the breakdown of the Peace of Amiens and the collapse of the various continental coalitions, and especially after the beginning of the Peninsula War in 1808, this began to change. As Peter Spence has recently pointed out, a direct connection was now often made between political participation and the struggle against

---

[74] Gneisenau to his wife, 2 Nov. 1809, from England, in G. H. Pertz, *Das Leben des Feldmarschalls Grafen Neithardt von Gneisenau* (Berlin, 1864), I, p. 575: 'In diesem Lande werden die Regierungsangelegenheiten ebenfalls auf die erbärmlichste Art betrieben. Unwissende und leidenschaftliche Menschen stehen am Ruder, und durch ihre Ungeschicklichkeit müßte auch dieses Volk zu Grunde gehen, wenn solche nicht dessen geographische Lage schützte'.
[75] Jacobi dispatch, 12 April 1805, GStA, Rep.XI.73.179A, fo. 110.
[76] Cited in Lady Jackson, ed., *The diaries and letters of Sir G.J. Jackson, from the peace of Amiens to the battle of Talavera*, I, pp. 129–30.
[77] J. E. Cookson, *The friends of peace: anti-war liberalism in England, 1793–1815* (Cambridge, 1982).

France.[78] In 1806 the radical whig MP, Sir Francis Burdett, observed 'I begin to think that we have no choise but submission or revolution, & I believe our luxurious sheep-breeding gents would much prefer the former';[79] one is reminded of Schön's almost contemporaneous comment, cited earlier, that 'the old aristocrats love only themselves . . . In their view the state may perish but seigneurial power would survive'. Two years later, Burdett made the link between domestic change and external strength even clearer when he addressed a meeting in the following terms: 'Gentlemen, I say therefore, that in order to face this land from foreign subjugation, we must get rid of domestic oppression; we must have arms and reform'.[80] The veteran campaigner for franchise reform, John Cartwright, argued similarly in January 1809: 'naught remained to us but this alternative — either parliamentary reformation under George the Third, or national subjugation under Napoleon the first'.[81] Shortly afterwards he exclaimed in his tract 'Reasons for reformation' (1809): 'Hath warning upon warning been wanting to us? Have we not witnessed the catastrophes of Marengo, at Austerlitz, at Jena and at Fridland [sic], and found that no nation under an unreformed government, not even the strongest and least accessible [a clear reference to Britain's island location], can stand before the scourge that is abroad'.[82] Once again, the connection between geopolitics and representative government is made, but this time in Britain, and with radically different conclusions.

The link between external threat and political participation was made particularly forcefully in a reforming petition of the freeholders of Middlesex in January 1806, preserved in the Holland House papers:

> Gentlemen, Contemplating the experienced insufficiency of the two great Empires of *Russia* and *Austria*, even when combined, to contend with the energetic despot of *France*, seeing *Austria* broken and dismembered, that she may no more oppose the torrent of *French* ambition . . . ; while turning for defence and the means of defying the tyrant to our native *English* energies, we discover that the *military* branch of our constitution, that POWER of the collective counties in which every man from fifteen to sixty, in the days of our *Edwards* and our *Henries*, was, when necessity required, a soldier — that POWER which thus became the resistless SWORD OF THE STATE, has long been guilefully mislaid and kept out of sight; and that the *civil* branch of our Constitution, our Parliamentary Representation, which ought to be the perfect and impenetrable Buckler of our Defence, has become a mouldering ruin; and thus perceiving that he [Pitt], in whom for for twenty years past our country has placed her trust — he from whose hands death has recently struck

[78] Spence, *The birth of romantic radicalism*, p. 22.
[79] Cited in Spence, *The birth of romantic radicalism*, p. 35.
[80] Cited in Spence, *The birth of romantic radicalism*, pp. 61 2.
[81] Cited in Spence, *The birth of romantic radicalism*, p. 97.
[82] Spence, *The birth of romantic radicalism*, p. 139.

the reins of government, had not, during his long administration, either respected that SWORD, or repaired that BUCKLER;...we earnestly request you to call an early meeting of the freeholders at large for the following purposes; namely, First, To consider whether the administration of the Executive government of our country be or be not committed to men who are supporters of a system, by which the aggrandisment of *France* has uniformly been increased,...Secondly, To consider whether our country can be best defended by a Standing Army, assisted by Volunteer Corps, or by the proper military branch of our constitution, the POWER of the collective counties, properly regulated by law and by rules for military discipline. Thirdly, To consider of the propriety of requesting the Hon. Charles Grey, to renew, as soon as he shall find it convenient, his virtuous efforts towards obtaining for the people an efficient Representation in Parliament.[83]

There was thus a consituency, albeit a much more marginal one than in Prussia, which saw an intimate link between broader political participation and foreign affairs. At the same time, however, one should bear in mind that these radicals couched their military demands in terms of the ancient constitution: 'reform' meant — rhetorically at least — returning to a prior uncorrupted state.

Both Britain and Prussia reacted to the French threat with measures of domestic reform. Unlike Prussia, there was no fundamental governmental blueprint for radical change in Britain. Here reform tended to be more piecemeal, empirical, and disjointed; and in many ways the measures proposed were more explicitly linked to foreign-political exigencies. Nevertheless, there was willingness in both states to address traditional inequalities in the cause of increased national efficiency. In Britain, these inequalities were *confessional*, and so the drive for greater military mobilization was closely linked to the progress of Roman Catholic emancipation; this notwithstanding the fact that national mobilization could often also have a strongly sectarian, anti-Roman Catholic overtone.[84] In Prussia, the inequalities were *corporate* — that is socio-legal. The abolition of feudal residues, such as hereditary bondage and noble control of the officer corps, was an integral part of the military mobilization against Napoleon. In many ways, therefore, Roman Catholic emancipation was the *pendant* to the emancipation of the peasantry in Prussia. Broader political participation was another common aspect of the struggle with France. In Prussia, this was sponsored by a reforming elite within government; in Britain it was largely the preserve of a radical minority in parliament and a much larger movement outside Westminster. Both countries looked to the other for inspiration: Britain for an

---

[83] 'To John Austey and Thomas Smith, Esquires, Sherriffs of Middlesex', 25 Jan. 1806, in British Library (BL) Add MSS 51568, fos. 91–2.

[84] For which see Colley, *Britons*, passim.

efficient form of mass military organization, and Prussia for models of self-government. At the same time, however, both were clear about the limitations of such models: British politicians recognized the domestic constraints to the introduction of continental-style conscription, while Prussians believed their monarchy to be too geographically exposed to warrant an open parliamentary system.

As a result, in both countries reform met distinctly defined limits. The plans for a Prussian national representation were shelved after 1815, despite the monarchical promise of a constitution, not least because the old elites had used the interim assemblies to attack anti-feudal reforms. For this reason the Prussian reform period has been termed one of 'partial modernization', when political change failed to keep pace with socio-economic progress, thus contributing to the *Sonderweg*, a purportedly unique path of development which set Germany apart from Britain and France throughout the nineteenth century. Yet by the same criterion, British history during the Napoleonic period was equally characterized by partial modernization. Roman Catholic emancipation was not implemented until 1829, and franchise reform had to wait until shortly afterwards. The French threat was never quite powerful enough to persuade the king to agree to Catholic emancipation, or to force the government to widen the franchise.

In short, it may be undeniable that the reasons for the different British and Prussian paths of development were, as indicated at the outset of this paper, deeply embedded in the differing socio-political systems in Britain and Prussia at the start of the period. But they were also — and herein lies the value of the comparative perspective — directly related to the differing degrees of external pressure they experienced throughout the period, and to the differing domestic consequences resulting therefrom. In this respect, J.R. Seeley's famous dictum about the degree of internal freedom in a state being directly proportional to the strength of the pressure on its external borders needs to be revised. For in Britain such a basic traditional restraint on individual freedom as religious discrimination was retained not because of the French threat, but, objectively at least, *in spite* of it. In Prussia, on the other hand, those most concerned with Napoleonic domination were usually the most ardent reformers, determined to increase the amount of internal freedom necessary for, and compatible with, the recovery of great power status.

The English as Reformers:
Foreign Visitors' Impressions, 1750–1850

PAUL LANGFORD

THE KIND OF WRITING THAT DESCRIBES nations other than the writer's own is notoriously problematic as historical evidence: one reason, perhaps, why it holds such fascination for the 'postmodern' student of cultural studies, especially when gender and post-colonialism are in question. But it may be that the problem is even greater when the rich literature of European perceptions of other Europeans is considered. Let me give you one admittedly rather extreme but revealing example.

I am thinking of a book entitled *England und die Engländer* published in Germany in 1818.[1] This did not purport to be an original work, but a translation of a French publication, *L'Angleterre et les Anglais*, by the monarchist Joseph Antoine de Gourbillon in 1817. No matter, you may say, a French view of England is not less interesting than a German one, even if it loses some of its flavour in the translation. But Gourbillon's book was itself a translation of a work published in 1807 ostensibly by a Spaniard, though in an English version. The title had been *Letters from England: by Don Manuel Alvarez Espriella*. And here, if not before, you may well spot the irony. *Letters from England* is part of the *oeuvre* of the poet Robert Southey, not indeed the work of the mature, high-flying, high tory Southey, but none the less an idiosyncratic and satirical impression of his own countrymen. So Southey's self-distancing as a supposed Spanish visitor passes through two further filters, in the process losing countless nuances of perception and description. Not that only nuances were involved. Gourbillon generously inserted over a hundred pages of his own observations, on subjects that he believed Southey had strangely ignored, principally the vices and virtues of English women. To complicate matters further, incidentally, the same work was published in New York, with additions by an unnamed American

---

[1] Trans. J. A. Bergk (Leipzig, 1818).

Proceedings of the British Academy, **100**, 101–119. © The British Academy 1999.

editor.[2] Palimpsests of this kind are common enough in the history of letters, but it is difficult to gauge the effect that this one can have had on the ultimate end-user, for example the German reader who picked it up at Leipzig in 1818. And how can we make a judgement as historians about the processes of assessment and the intentions of the assessors in cases of this kind?

To go further and attempt sampling a hundred years of such foreign commentary on British life is a hazardous business, not least because the volume of commentary and the range of biases makes it hard to know how representative the opinions gathered are. However, casting caution to the winds, let me suggest a line of argument based on this evidence. To move from the mid-eighteenth century to the mid-nineteenth is to observe a shift not only in the accounts themselves but in the expectations that lay behind them. In the third quarter of the eighteenth century most literate foreigners came expecting to be impressed by Britain and its institutions. In the second quarter of the next century they came with much less easily classifiable expectations. The range of appraisals was greater, the difference of view sharper, and, by and large, the disposition to criticize more pronounced.

This shift bore heavily on the reputation of the British as reformers. In a period which figures as one of growing preoccupation with questions of reform, the contemporary view of outsiders was to say the least ambivalent. Reforms advocated or accomplished were often dismissed. And in contextualizing them the impression was given of a society that showed little interest in change. In the process some of the claims of continental Anglophiles were not only confounded but turned on their heads, transforming a nation of pragmatic revolutionaries into a nation of pusillanimous conservatives. This did not fit well with some more optimistic domestic judgements. Sir Richard Phillips, publishing his tour of the United Kingdom in 1828, described it as 'the most improved country that ever existed in the world'.[3] Such bombast would have seemed far more plausible in foreign eyes a century earlier.

One reappraisal concerned the ordinary people who would have had to provide the standard-bearers of reform and if necessary the infantry of revolution. Continental commentators were increasingly scathing about the revolutionary potential of plebeian Britons. Remarking on events in France and Belgium in 1830, Princess Lieven observed 'this sort of thing cannot do in England, because the masses (*canaille*) here are cowardly and the classes are courageous'.[4] The baron d'Haussez also impugned the courage of the English lower orders. 'Taken collectively, the populace of England is

---

[2] *Letters from England* (2nd US edn, 2 vols, New York, 1808).
[3] *A personal tour through the United Kingdom* (London, 1828), p. i.
[4] *Letters of Dorothea, Princess Lieven, during her residence in London, 1812–1834*, ed. Lionel G. Robinson (London, 1902), p. 372.

remarkable for its cowardice.'[5] By this time the orderliness of an English crowd was something to behold and its submissiveness in the face of constables armed with nothing but a stave or the new-fangled Peeler's truncheon astonishing.[6]

Their betters seemed all too ready to do duty on the streets in an emergency. In 1830–1, Fenimore Cooper was impressed by the flood of travellers returning from the continent to be at their posts in the event of revolution. The English gentry would not have abandoned Paris to the mob in 1792, he remarked.[7] The events of 1848 provided still stronger evidence. So did the seeming insouciance of the propertied classes in the presence of plebeian unrest. Theodor Fontane was amazed to witness a performance of *Coriolanus* at Sadler's Wells shortly after a working-class demonstration in Smithfield. Such an anti-mob play in such sensitive circumstances would have been thought most injudicious in absolutist Prussia.[8] All in all, Cavour's judgement of 1835, that the British were incapable of revolution, appeared a convincing one.[9] These are, of course, matters on which it was easy for outsiders to miss the subtleties. The veteran traveller J. G. Kohl was one of the few who tried to grasp them and perceived the brinkmanship that could occur in Britain on both sides of the class barrier. 'It is one of the most remarkable characteristics of the British constitution and of the national character, and one not sufficiently estimated by foreigners, that a course of agitation so nearly approaching to insurrection can be tolerated, without any serious mischief following.'[10]

Correct or not, these judgements contrasted with older images of the ordinary Englishman. He had been expected to be barbarously violent, brutally courageous and temperamentally insubordinate. His personal incivility, his beastly recreations and his mobbish tendencies all diverged from patterns of continental behaviour among the lower sort. To meet an Englishman on the streets of London, where most foreigners formed their opinion of the English lower orders, was to encounter a being quite unlike his equals elsewhere. The indignities and indeed injuries inflicted on visitors form one of the most dependable items in eighteenth-century accounts. So does the boisterous behaviour of an election mob. And it was easy to move from the particular to the general. The people formed a powder keg perpetually

---

[5] *Great Britain in 1833* (2 vols, London, 1833), I, pp. 280–1.

[6] Heinrich Meidinger, *Briefe von einer Reise durch England, Schottland und Irland im Frühjahr und Sommer 1820* (Stuttgart, 1821), p. 9; G. Crapelet, *Souvenirs de Londres en 1814 et 1816* (Paris, 1817), pp. 224–5.

[7] J. Fenimore Cooper, *England* (3 vols, 1837), II, p. 103.

[8] Rosemary Ashton, *Little Germany: exile and asylum in Victorian England* (Oxford, 1986), p. 249.

[9] *Souvenirs du Baron de Barante*, ed. Claude de Barante (8 vols, Paris, 1890–1901), IV, p. 180.

[10] Johann Georg Kohl, *Ireland* (London, 1843), p. 145.

ready to explode. Perhaps as a result, foreign opinion seems to have been less shocked than British opinion by the Gordon riots of 1780.

Underpinning such views was a dual assumption, largely a French assumption, I should perhaps add, that the British were barbarians by nature and libertarians on principle. The principle was as worrying as the nature. Under the *ancien régime*, English liberty was seen in France as a dangerous infection, just as later on, after the French Revolution, French equality was seen as a dangerous infection in Britain. Anglomaniacs were assailed on these grounds, as malevolent quacks bent on introducing an alien incubus into a healthy body politic. English liberty, not least of the kind associated with the internationally famous John Wilkes, was denounced for threatening to transform the French national character itself.[11]

The revised view that was arrived at by the early nineteenth century was very different, suggesting not merely subduing the mob of an earlier age, but turning its loyalties in new directions. Older depictions of the English showed them as natural republicans who had finally accepted monarchy only on terms they dictated themselves. From the execution of Charles I, through the expulsion of James II, and the sullen tolerance of successive revolution kings, William III, George I, George II, ran a consistent line that made it easy to contrast the pride of an English citizen with the servility of a French subject, not to say a German, Spanish, Italian, or Russian one. But there seemed little sign of this between the 1820s and 1850s. Perhaps the most telling episode, featuring in the recollections of those numerous travellers who descended on London after the Napoleonic wars, concerned the coronation of George IV. In English histories, this appears often as the nadir of monarchy, the humiliation of a British king by a mistreated queen and an alienated populace. But foreigners were startled by the evident popularity of the coronation. 'What of English liberty with all this fascination with royalty?' asked Édouard de Montulé. 'John Bull is humbled by his love of ceremony.' How had a northern and phlegmatic people come to acquire so Gascon a spirit, he wondered.[12] When the adulation extended even to foreign royalty, as in the reception accorded the allied sovereigns in 1814, similar surprise was in order.[13] The days seemed to have gone when, as in 1734 during the visit of the Prince of Orange, or in 1768 during that of the King of Denmark, the main interest of a royal tourist was to draw unfavourable contrasts with the British ruling house.

Evidence of servility was sought in all kinds of places, including the armed forces. Charles Dupin, who toured British military establishments

---

[11] *Gazette de Leyde*, 7 Aug. 1770.
[12] Édouard de Montulé, *Voyage en Angleterre et en Russie, pendant les années 1821, 1822 et 1823* (2 vols, Paris, 1825), I, pp. 246, 250.
[13] Crapelet, *Souvenirs de Londres en 1814 et 1816*, pp. 76 ff.

after the Napoleonic wars, was intrigued. 'Perhaps there is no army in Europe in which the distinction of rank is so strongly marked as among the British troops.' He thought the military consequences significant. A French soldier saluted only the officers of his own regiment. But in the British army a private obeyed any officer, and for that matter a corporal obeyed any sergeant. This was not the result of terror, he thought, despite the notoriously brutal code of discipline that obtained in the British forces. It was innate.[14]

Deference was not confined to respect for men of authority and standing. Eighteenth-century visitors had admired the independence of English servants, even if at times they had found it rather irritating. Their successors were as likely to find their meekness surprising. The American William Austin was particularly offended by the slavishness of English servants. He saw it as evidence of a nation that had had its chance of liberty in 1688 only to throw it away with predictable consequences for the national character. The English were traitors to their own history. 'They are utterly incapable of enjoying what their valor has so frequently accomplished.'[15] The fact that this servility was part of a commercial mentality, and that respectable young men would lower themselves to well-rewarded but menial tasks in London's most prestigious clubs and restaurants, merely proved how far the ancient pride of an Englishman could sink.[16]

The English obsession with rank and title dismayed many nineteenth-century Anglophiles. This was quite the reverse of earlier observations, which had stressed the Englishman's lack of interest in status. Voltaire had famously delighted in the prestige enjoyed by Sir Isaac Newton, a man of lowly origins whose celebrity could only have occurred in a country where rank counted for nothing and merit for everything. For Louis Simond, who came to London eighty years later, it was Newton's social apotheosis that was most distressing. 'The English do not say *Newton*, but *Sir Isaac Newton*. I cannot well express how much this *Monsieur le Chevalier* Newton shocks the ear of a foreigner.'[17] Others saw in this tendency a significant cast of mind. For the baron de Staël-Holstein England was 'a country eminently aristocratic. It is so by its institutions, opinions, and manners.' He thought habits of deference ingrained in all ranks of society, uniting them in a common sense of hierarchy. The respect that in a polite drawing room led the Younger Pitt to defer to a marquis of twenty or William Wilberforce to a

---

[14] Charles Dupin, *A tour through the naval and military establishments of Great Britain, in the years 1816–17–18–19 and 1820* (London, 1822), p. 106.

[15] *Letters from London: written during the years 1802 and 1803* (Boston, 1804), p. 86.

[16] *L'Angleterre et les Anglais, ou petit portrait d'une grande famille; copié et retouché par deux témoins oculaires*, transl. Joseph Antoine de Gourbillon and T. W. Dickinson (3 vols, Paris, 1817), III, pp. 280 ff.

[17] Louis Simond, *Journal of a tour and residence in Great Britain, during the years 1810 and 1811, by a French traveller* (2 vols, Edinburgh, 1815), I, p. 31.

fox-hunting baronet was the same that made the masses rush to see titled people.[18] He was not alone in being taken aback by the way blue blood took precedence over all considerations of age, sex, and frailty. 'I get awfully scandalized in England,' wrote Mary Clarke, the Paris-educated daughter of a Scottish Jacobite, 'when I see a whipper snapper of 20 above a respectable man of 80.'[19] Nor was this the custom only in the highest circles. Self-stratification was taken to be characteristic of all classes. In any social situation, it was noticed how different ranks sorted themselves out remarkably quickly.[20]

The ostentatiousness of English wealth and rank astonished even well-born visitors, as it had not during the eighteenth century. The duchesse de Dino, in England in 1830 as the wife of the French ambassador, was staggered by the extravagance of aristocratic life.[21] But more interesting still was the perception that British noblemen had grown insensitive to their own overblown opulence in a country that displayed numerous scenes of poverty. How, asked Victor Hennequin in 1844, could the British plebeian tolerate the immense aristocratic estates so offensively visible up and down the country, and this 'in the middle of the nineteenth century'.[22]

Centuries of parliamentary politics might have been expected to provide a counter-weight to such deference. But, as perceptive observers noted, the electoral system itself could work to strengthen aristocratic institutions. Mme d'Avot thought it revealing that the populace elected Burdett, not a man of the people but a country gentlemen. 'Everything finds its level in a free and constitutional government, and ends by partaking of stability.'[23] And why did popular election tumults produce so little disorder in the body politic? asked her countryman Haussez:

> The reason may be gathered in the predominance of the aristocratic principle in the midst of this democratic effervescence. These elections are not made by the people, but sold by them to the better classes of society, who buy them so dearly that they can only fall to the lot of those whose rank gives them a deeper interest in maintaining order and upholding the institutions of the country.[24]

Moreover the sheer irrationality of the electoral system, which contrived to grant power in some places to the urban scum while leaving the respectably

---

[18] A. de Staël-Holstein, *Letters on England* (London, 1825), pp. 104, 123, 131, 132.

[19] Marion Elmina Smith, *Une Anglaise intellectuelle en France sous la Restauration: Miss Mary Clarke* (Paris, 1927), p. 126.

[20] Christopher Mulvey, *Travel literature* (Cambridge, 1990), p. 150.

[21] *Souvenirs du baron de Barante*, IV, p. 10.

[22] Victor Hennequin, *Voyage en Angleterre et en Écosse* (Paris, 1844), pp. 300–1.

[23] Mme d'Avot, *Lettres sur l'Angleterre, ou deux années à Londres* (2nd edn, Paris, 1821), p. 175.

[24] Charles Le Mercher de Longpré, baron d' Haussez, *Great Britain in 1833* (2 vols, London, 1833), I, p. 167.

propertied in many others voteless, worked paradoxically to the advantage of aristocracy in giving potential middle-class reformers a horror of democratic forms.[25] In such a system small wonder that foreigners were impressed by the toryism of tory radicals and by the constraints that seemed to operate on other radical dogs, who, as Heine remarked of Cobbett, could not break away from their chain.[26] Giacomo Beltrami put the point about deep-seated habits of deference neatly. 'Every class in England is radically aristocratic', he wrote. 'Even the radicals in this respect are eminently aristocratic'.[27]

Other features of the political process might be interpreted in similar fashion. The English horror of centralization could be seen as the particularism of a landed aristocracy. Government would be the last thing to be rationalized in the world's greatest empire, as Léon Faucher noted when he discovered in 1838 that *The Times* had reported a rural uprising in Kent before the home secretary was told of it.[28] Perceptive foreign observers, such as Luigi Angiolini, argued that, in Britain, government was not about the imposition of public priorities on private practices, but the modelling of public institutions on private associations. Reform in such circumstances would have required a radical revision of the English approach to life, which was essentially based on the agreement of the club rather than the authority of the governor.[29]

Above all it was thought that a certain aristocratic spirit deprived authentic reformers of any prospect of success. What was at issue was an entire mentality. Prominent in this was the obsession with the formation of character rather than the moulding of mind. Since this was a growing preoccupation of educational reformers in all kinds of public and private schooling it fitted such analysis well. Some foreign critics tried hard to recognize the merits of character, and certainly thought it helped make Britain a formidable competitor in world markets and warfare. But the damage it did to intellectual rigour could not be gainsaid. Typical is the verdict of V. A. Huber on the university system. Huber devoted two gigantic volumes to close scrutiny of Oxford and Cambridge, and concluded with a rather backhanded compliment.

> Our own sincere conviction, founded, as it has been, upon the most conscientious investigation, and mature reflection; devoid also as it is of every prejudice or consideration foreign to the matter; is, that upon an average, and setting aside a few periods of very short duration, the immorality and folly at the

[25] *Journeys to England and Ireland*, trans. George Lawrence and K. P. Mayer, ed. J. P. Myer (London, 1958), p. 57.
[26] Heinrich Heine, *English fragments*, trans. Sarah Norris (Edinburgh, 1880), ch. 9.
[27] J.C. Beltrami, *A pilgrimage in Europe and America* (2 vols, London, 1828), I, pp. 353–4.
[28] *Études sur l'Angleterre* (2 vols, Brussels, 1845), I, p. 19.
[29] Luigi Angiolini, *Lettere sull'Inghilterra*, ed. Guido di Pino (Milan, 1844), p. 99.

English Universities is not greater than, considering the whole state of the nation, must be reasonably calculated on, as the price paid for the development of character.[30]

Huber underestimated the prospects of university reform and indeed provided useful ammunition for some of the reformers, including Newman, his translator's brother. But his judgement is revealing of the approach of many such painstaking critics of English institutions.

Anti-intellectualism was, of course, a common characterization of the English, supported very often by the thinnest and most impressionistic of evidence. The absence of a coherent body of enlightened men of science was a recurrent observation. Where was the Bureau d'Esprit of Paris or the formidable bureaucratic and academic elites of Germany? Savants there were, but they seemed to be distributed randomly through all classes, never bringing their combined force to bear.[31] This might sound a ludicrous characterization of British intellectual life, but it took more than the Scottish school of the eighteenth century or the political economists of the nineteenth to displace it. It represented not only a powerful strand in foreign perceptions but one that seemed to go well with an aristocratic system, in which status mattered more than systematic reflection. Some advantages were conceded. It could be pointed out that informed opinion in Britain was close to the opinion of the masses. In other societies intellectuals had invented languages and discourses that were philosophically superior but incomprehensible to the multitude.[32] Even so, the result was a refuge for dilletanti rather than a recipe for serious thought.

A common belief was that the empiricism of the English mind combined with the parochialism of the political process to deprive the idea of reform of most of its general interest. 'England is the country of details, of isolated facts; each parish has its administration, its usages, we might say almost its laws.'[33] Even questions that raised issues of principle were rarely treated as such. Listening to the debates on Catholic emancipation, Staël-Holstein was astonished by what he called 'this disposition of the English to confine all questions' within the sphere of the circumstances peculiar to England'.[34] Perhaps the most damning witness was von Raumer, whose unvarying goodwill and desire to find in England the embodiment of all that was best

---

[30] Victor Aimé Huber, *The English universities*, ed. Francis W. Newman (3 vols, London, 1843), II, pp. 313–14.

[31] Louis Dutens, *L'ami des étrangers qui voyagent en Angleterre* (Londres, 1787), p. 25.

[32] Lothar Bucher, *Der Parlamentarismus wie er ist* (3rd edn, Stuttgart, 1894), p. 10.

[33] Eugène Buret, *De la misère des classes laborieuses en Angleterre et en France* (2 vols, Paris, 1840) I, p. 147.

[34] De Staël-Holstein, *Letters on England*, pp. 33–4.

in ancient Germanic tradition finally baulked at the barrenness of adversarial politics on the British model. He found

> such rooted prejudices, that to a German and especially a Prussian, it is often impossible, at first, to understand the facts or the arguments he hears. So long as most Englishmen regard their own point of view as the sole, unalterably, and inviolably right, and that of their opponent as absolutely wrong, each party loses sight of that higher ground which overlooks both, and which it ought to be the aim of all civilization and all government to reach.[35]

Our assessment of von Raumer might be affected by his public statement that Frederick William III in the 1830s was 'the greatest and best Reformer in Europe'. However his earnestness is not in doubt.[36]

Others were less polite. Maurice Rubichon, who endured two long exiles in Britain, the first during the Revolutionary wars, the second after the fall of Charles X, thought that the aimlessness of English debate transcended even the famed national trait of taciturnity and reserve. The English were mere parotting schoolboys whose politics embraced no genuine reading or knowledge. The effect resembled clouds of smoke with no sparks. 'England may be the country of Europe in which least is said, yet it is that in which most ineptitudes are uttered.'[37] And most of all there was the crippling fact that all political change had to be shaped to meet the requirements of Parliament, whose members regarded rationality as the last thing to be considered and anything resembling an idea as suspect: in English ears the phrase 'foreign ideas' was almost a tautology. Prince Albert's adviser Stockmar was puzzled by what he called 'This English mania of making all political wisdom to consist in the art of satisfying Parliament.'[38] The baron Riesbeck was also disparaging about, 'Englishmen, who think that the essence of liberty consists in babbling, and giving vent in parliament to every species of ill-humour.'[39] Some favourite assumptions of eighteenth-century Anglophiles on such subjects were increasingly challenged. The famed power of the British press, for instance, did not impress everyone. Fontane remarked that 'the cleverest Englishmen if they are not politicians by profession and party members, are merely 100,000 echoes of the Times'.[40] His compatriot Niebuhr sought evidence of English enlightenment with scholarly scrupulousness but announced himself foiled. 'The praise which Jacobi accords to the

---

[35] Friedrich von Raumer, *England in 1835* (3 vols, London, 1836), I, p. 158.

[36] Ibid., p. 238.

[37] Maurice Rubichon, *De l'Angleterre* (London, 1811), pp. 138–40.

[38] *Memoirs of Baron Stockmar: by his son Baron E. Von Stockmar*, ed. F. Max Müller (2 vols, London, 1872), II, pp. 99, 450.

[39] *Travels through Germany, in a series of letters: written in German by the Baron Riesbeck*, transl. Rev. Mr Maty (3 vols, London, 1787), I, p. 52.

[40] Theodor Fontane, *Bilderbuch aus England*, ed. Friedrich Fontane (Berlin, 1938), 18 Oct. 1855.

philosophical spirit of the English nation is quite undeserved, and founded on ignorance.'[41]

Of course, some critics would never have been satisfied. Heine, for instance, was a genuine radical, though of a somewhat eccentric kind, and considered the pragmatic evolution of political rights in Britain as a distraction from the serious business of rebuilding humanity. Adjusting the form of the state could never revolutionize society.[42] But there were many others for whom reform in the English fashion looked too much like mere expediency, a succession of unavoidable concessions in which solid reasoning played no part. Lothar Bucher built one of the most devastating critiques of parliamentarianism on this reasoning. The British constitution was a rambling, ruinous edifice in which the simple beauty of its ancient Anglo-Saxon outline could barely be discerned. Every so-called reform merely complicated and weakened its structure. The Reform Act itself was no exception. Far from purifying politics it had merely created a new sump of corruption. Bucher was writing in 1856 when there was beginning to be talk of further reform. Would it result in fundamental reconstruction of the state, he asked. His answer was predictable. 'The past and the nature of the people speak against it.'[43]

Running through Bucher's argument was an assumption that this state of affairs resulted from centuries of aristocratic dominance. The English form of government was a gigantic conspiracy by the great to cheat the people of its ancient inheritance while pretending to serve it. Pragmatic, unsystematic reform was their weapon. Oligarchy depended on it. As the historian Bernard Sarrans put it, 'The science of aristocracies consists in avoiding the discussion of rights.'[44] It was evidently this that did much to explain the frivolity and prejudice that constituted so-called public opinion. The Swede Geijer was utterly baffled when he visited Britain in 1809 to find that the most controversial question of the day was the price of seats at Covent Garden Theatre. 'In all my life I have not heard or read so much about British freedom as in connection with this dispute.'[45] The notorious 'Old Price' riots resulted, of course. And an uneducated populace could not be expected even to applaud such reforms as were implemented. When Joseph-Alexis, Vicomte Walsh, whose Jacobite ancestors had once been banished from England, visited their homeland in 1829 at the time of Catholic emancipation,

---

[41] *The life and letters of Barthold George Niebuhr* (2 vols, London, 1852), I, p. 139.
[42] Nigel Reeves, *Heinrich Heine: poetry and politics* (Oxford, 1974), pp. 104–5.
[43] Bucher, *Der Parlamentarismus wie er ist*, pp. 273–4.
[44] B. Sarrans, *De la décadence de l'Angleterre et des intéréts dédératifs de la France* (Paris, 1840), p. 149.
[45] Erik Gustaf Geijer, *Impressions of England, 1809–10*, intr. Anton Blanck (London, 1932), p. 99.

expecting a newly enlightened climate of opinion, he found instead 'No Popery' scrawled on the walls.[46]

The literature in which Englishmen paraded the aristocratic nature of their own system is not the most quoted by historians, but for foreigners it was of understandable interest. Bulwer Lytton's *England and the English*, by a novelist as well known abroad as at home, was published in 1833, a year after the Reform Act. His central theme, aristocratic government in a commercial country, was employed to generate numerous examples of the way in which a society with a hugely vigorous middle class and notoriously independent plebeians could remain so securely aristocratic in its essentials. Partly this was the traditional faith in property, which invaded the language itself.

> The root of all our notions, as of all our laws, is to be found in the sentiment of property. It is *my* wife whom you shall not insult; it is *my* house that you shall not enter; it is *my* country that you shall not traduce; and, by a species of ultramondane appropriation, it is *my* God whom you shall not blaspheme!

And secondly there was the long-standing social mobility that permitted the humble to rise high, though only at the cost of others of their own estate. 'England has long possessed this singular constitution of society, — the spirit of democracy in the power of obtaining honours, and the genius of an aristocracy in the method by which they are acquired.'[47] The coping-stone to this intellectual edifice is usually attributed to Tocqueville, namely the remark that the English were more fearful of the insults of those below them than the oppression of those above them, but in various forms it was something of a commonplace of contemporary analysis, well expressed by Mill.[48] 'They do not dislike to have many people above them as long as they have some below them.'[49] An eighteenth-century traveller, Christopher Harvey, had put it still more simply, 'The common people even in England like to take orders, that they may become gentlemen'.[50] Or, in modern terms, this seemed the natural mentality of a society that had retained its essentially aristocratic institutions while commercializing its social relations.

The results could be viewed in quite different ways, of course. To a conservative statesman like Guizot it was remarkable how the British aristocracy had submitted to a succession of reforms that in effect conceded most of their independence of action in return for the privilege of retaining

---

[46] *Lettres sur l'Angleterre ou voyage dans la Grande-Bretagne en 1829* (Paris, 1830), pp. 33–7.
[47] *England and the English* (2 vols, New York, 1833), I, pp. 15–16, 21.
[48] Alexis de Tocqueville, *Democracy in America*, II (iii), ch. 2.
[49] Ashton, *Little Germany: exile and asylum in Victorian England*, p. 49.
[50] Christopher Hervey, *Letters from Portugal, Spain, Italy and Germany, in the years 1759, 1760, and 1761* (3 vols, London, 1785), III, p. 296.

their nominal role as leaders. The aristocracy, he observed, were now 'merely a governing class'. It is an intriguing insight and not without point, but others were less disposed to make distinctions between dominance on the one hand and mere rule on the other. For most the perception was that society itself, in accepting that continued leadership, had displayed its own inherently aristocratic cast of mind.[51]

That a society experiencing the most extraordinary economic turbulence could be profoundly aristocratic was no paradox. A whole school of French critics pointed out the logic that made England in essence a feudal state whose dynamics rendered industries so many feofs, and proletarians the new serfs. Here was a new and brutal class of employers, a manufacturing aristocracy alongside a landed aristocracy. The result was degrading to the human spirit: urban deprivation, child labour, demoralizing impoverishment worse than negroes endured. Appalled by what he called evidence even of racial degeneracy, the historian Michelet knew where to seek the sources when he was in England in 1834. 'Looking at the colossal chimneys of Leeds, Halifax, Liverpool, I said to myself. "Here are the towers of the new feudalism."'[52]

Moreover this system owed as much to commercial reformers as to died-in-the-wool conservatives. 'Behold humanity such as radicalism has made her' wrote the former minister of Charles X, d'Haussez.[53] Or, from a different perspective, that of Eugène Buret, England as an aristocratic society had misery, whereas egalitarian France had only poverty. The result was 'une voie sans issue' a society that could not be reformed but could only be abolished by revolution. France, by comparison, had every prospect of redemption by means of predictable economic reforms.[54]

Viewed from this perspective most of what passed for reform in the early nineteenth century was simply rearranging the chains of industrial oppression in order to bind them ever tighter. 'Here civilization works its miracles, and civilized man is turned back almost into a savage.'[55] The utter uselessness of the British bourgeoisie was a predictably common cause for dismissal. Two forces had sapped it of any promise in this respect, two forces that might have been expected to be in conflict but in England were part of one coherent system: religion and materialism. Engels probably had a closer acquaintance with this class than almost any foreign-born commentator of his day.

---

[51] François Guizot, *Memoirs of Sir Robert Peel* (London, 1857), pp. 370–1.
[52] *Sur les chemins de l'Europe* (Paris, 1893), p. 159.
[53] Le Mercher de Longpré, *Great Britain in 1833*, II, pp. 34, 43.
[54] Eugène Buret, *De la misère des classes laborieuses en Angleterre et en France* (2 vols, Paris, 1840), I, pp. 19–20, 59, 206–8, 237, 475, 485.
[55] Steven Marcus, *Engels, Manchester, and the working class* (London, 1974), p. 66.

> I have never seen a social class so deeply demoralized as the English middle classes, I have never seen a class so incurably corrupted by egotistic self-seeking, so inwardly corroded, or rendered so incapable of progress... For it, nothing exists in the world that does not solely exist for the sake of money — itself not excepted — for it lives for nothing except making money.[56]

Not least interesting about this famous judgement is the fact that it reflects a perception shared by many less articulate commentators and expressed long before systematic analysis by the Marxian school. The numbing materialism of the British bourgeoisie was a feature of a swelling body of commentary from at least the 1780s on.

Of course, not every view was pessimistic. But when visitors were impressed, what impressed them most was not necessarily the accumulation of demands for reform, the mounting of a case for rational improvement, or even the prudent concessiveness of the whig aristocracy. Rather they were struck by the characteristic idiosyncrasies of British society in so far as they served reforming causes.

Late eighteenth-century travellers were greatly taken with the quantity and quality of British benevolence. The leading role played by private individuals and public associations, with no help from the state and little from the church, marked this out as a uniquely caring society.[57] Visitors plainly came expecting to have their sensibility gratified. Even so, there were some discordant voices before the turn of the eighteenth and nineteenth centuries, and a substantial body of sceptics thereafter. A standard criticism was that, contrary to the proverb, charity did not begin at home. Numerous travellers were appalled by the state of the poor amidst stupendous wealth. If Bruce in Abyssinia or Park in Africa, observed Austin, had found conditions described by Colquhoun in London 'I will do the English the justice to believe they would instantly open subscriptions, and enterprise an expedition to their relief: yes, even to the source of the Nile.'[58]

Admiration at the disinterested philanthropy of the British often gave way to dismay at their vanity and egotism. It did not go unnoticed that charity depended heavily on the publicity that attended giving, and that charitable associations operated primarily as a self-imposed tax on snobbery rather than a spirit of selflessness. From the nobleman who could not endow his parish without emblazoning his virtues on the church wall, to the humble subscriber whose ambition was to dine once a year with the great and good, or see his name enrolled among them in the newspapers, the object was self-advertisement.[59] The patronizing and rather conveniently propertied

---

[56] Ibid., p. 231.
[57] Gabriel François Coyer, *Nouvelles observations sur l'Angleterre* (Paris, 1779), chs 6, 7.
[58] *Letters from London: written during the years 1802 and 1803*, p. 86.
[59] René-Martin Pillet, *L'Angleterre vue à Londres et dans ses provinces* (Paris, 1815), pp. 131–2.

assumptions of charitable institutions angered those familiar with a less self-interested system of church charity abroad, even if they rejected its spiritual foundations. Marat was shocked that letters of recommendation were necessary to get into hospital.[60] Spiker, the librarian to the king of Prussia, who dedicated his book on Britain to 'The friends of England', thought the practice of having better rooms for rich patients in lunatic asylums disgraceful — 'all should be equally good'.[61] And the insularity of English practice made it hard to see what lessons states with a different tradition could learn. British reformers seemed characteristically rooted in their national small-mindedness. Even John Howard, whose pioneering investigations were genuinely international, was accused of a xenophobic bias.[62]

Hypocrisy was detected and condemned by relatively impartial observers, such as Adolphe Blanqui. The British believed themselves the most benevolent nation on earth, yet this was a nation for whom animals were objects of cruel sports, a nation that invented hulks for prisoners of war, and a nation whose army was disciplined with punishments as bestial as those of Muscovy.[63] Subjected to criticism of this kind the proudest boasts of English reformers could be rendered empty indeed. Flora Tristan's grim catalogue of horrors in her *Promenades dans Londres* of 1842 took care to sabotage anything that looked in the least creditable. For her the British model of progress was 'the greatest obstacle to the advancement of Europe and the rest of the world'. Prison reformers were among those she systematically dismissed for their ameliorations. At Newgate she found 'they exhibit the systematic spirit which is peculiar to them in practising essays of benevolence at the expense of the unfortunate beings who crowd their prisons'.[64] Cold Bath Fields, supposedly a country mansion compared with Newgate, was notable in reality chiefly for its peculiar torture of the tread-wheel and the unproductive idleness it imposed on its inmates. Unsurprisingly, the fact that her countryman Marshal Soult had pronounced his satisfaction with the prison left her unimpressed. Millbank, one grade higher on the register of prison improvement, was remarkable for the refinement of its cellular organization, but without visible effects on its inmates. For Flora Tristan it was not necessary to see to condemn. She had been told that the slaves emancipated in the West Indies after fifty years of abolitionist campaigning had merely been 'turned into proletarians on the English model'. The

[60] Frances Acomb, *Anglophobia in France, 1763–1789: an essay in the history of constitutionalism and nationalism* (Durham, N.C., 1950), p. 42.

[61] Samuel Heinrich Spiker, *Travels through England, Wales, and Scotland, in the year 1816*, transl. (2 vols, London, 1820), I, p. 84.

[62] Pillet, *L'Angleterre vue à Londres*, p. 37.

[63] Adolphe Blanqui, *Voyage d'un jeune français en Angleterre et en Écosse pendant l'automne de 1823* (Paris, 1824), pp. 92–4.

[64] Le Mercher de Longpré, *Great Britain in 1833*, I, p. 11.

extreme hypocrisy of emancipation was characteristic of the English. As for the numerous new schools of which the British boasted, they were but a pale imitation of their French counterparts, and ludicrously obsessed with scriptural education.[65]

Ironically much of the evidence that was cited by those who refused to believe in the redeemability of the British was provided by the British themselves. Indeed it was in the nature of reform in the English fashion, building patiently on bricks of closely constructed factual evidence, accumulated by royal, parliamentary and public bodies of information gatherers, that it generated material not readily obtainable elsewhere, however short it was on philosophical principles. Some of the most hostile foreign treatments were dependent on such material. Ledru-Rollin's notorious *De la décadence de l'Angleterre*, which gave great offence in Britain, was in fact based on the findings of Henry Mayhew, originally published in the *Morning Chronicle*.[66] Ledru-Rollin provided much of this material in book form to a French audience before Mayhew himself produced it in a collected edition in London. If this was an indictment, it was certainly not fabricated by a foreigner. As the radical George Holyoake observed

> had the great Republican lawyer entitled his volume, "Extracts from the *Morning Chronicle*", or "England drawn by Henry Mayhew", or the "Fall of the English Foretold by Themselves", any one of these titles would have expressed the character of the work. But because the author employed another title, the public were entitled to take offence at the book.[67]

Rosemary Ashton has pointed out that official statistics and reports were often employed more by foreign exiles than by the English themselves.[68]

Self-exposure of this kind went back some decades before the age of blue books, and helped prepare the way for this growing belief that the more the British required reforming the less they were likely to be reformed. If there was a decisive moment it was in the 1770s, when the War of American Independence, a notable era of parliamentary eloquence and unprecedented international publicity for British politicians, combined to create novel conditions. Brissot claimed the credit for exploiting them, if credit is the right word, in that it was he who contributed so much to the success of the journal *Courrier de l'Europe*. He was an ironically appropriate figure for this purpose, having as a young man been induced by his enthusiasm for all things English to change his somewhat bogus title of Ouarville to Warville, in order to 'to give my name an English air', as he put it. The *Courrier*, he said,

---

[65] *The London journal of Flora Tristan*, trans. Jean Hawkes (London, 1982), pp. 10, 135–42, 160.
[66] Alexandre-Auguste Ledru-Rollin, *De la décadence de l'Angleterre*, (2 vols, Paris, 1850).
[67] George Jacob Holyoake, *Sixty years of an agitator's life* (2 vols, London, 1893), II, pp. 261–2.
[68] Ashton, *Little Germany*, p. 6.

made England known as it had never been known before, except through the distorting spectacles of a few travellers. 'Up to the moment of the publication of the *Courrier*, England had been truly a foreign land for the rest of Europe.'[69]

Brissot exaggerated the significance of the *Courrier*. It was by no means the first newspaper to report English events at length. A number of Dutch journals, read or reprinted across the continent, had done so for decades. What was new was the effective failure of the House of Commons to stop detailed reporting of parliamentary debates during the 1770s. There is no doubt that the *Courrier*, which seems to have been financed by both the British and French governments, each in the belief that it was thereby contributing to the downfall of the other, was well placed to carry the resulting debates far and wide.[70] The censors of absolute governments made no attempt to restrict the flow of information that was assumed to be disadvantageous only to the British government. The result was that when Burke, Sheridan and Fox trumpeted the faults of George III's government, they were unintentionally addressing an audience that dwelled as far afield as Rome, St Petersburg, and Copenhagen. The last great patriot opposition of the 1730s had signally failed to influence continental opinion in this way.

During the following decades, Anglomania was battered down by an unlikely alliance of assailants, not all of them on the radical or revolutionary left. These included men as far to the right as Joseph de Maistre, who believed that English contractualism had lured Frenchmen into abandoning their sacramental faith in monarchy,[71] and Bonapartists such as Joseph Fiévée and René-Martin Pillet, who considered that the luminaries of *ancien-régime* France had been corrupted by the British government into a propaganda campaign on its behalf.[72] But most of all, Anglomania suffered from its own success.[73] It was all too tempting for a new generation of commentators to write off their most celebrated predecessors — Voltaire, Montesquieu, Delolme, Archenholz, Gentz, as mere panegyrists of Britain.[74]

Admirers were precisely those whose conservatism made them the least impressive of champions in the eyes of liberal reformers. Charles de Rémusat

---

[69] *Mémoires de Brissot* (Paris, 1877), pp. 30, 118–19.

[70] Hélène Mespero-Clerc, 'Samuel Swinton, éditeur du Courier de l'Europe à Boulogne-su-Mer (1778–1783)', *Annales historiques de la Révolution française*, 57 (1985), pp. 527–31; N. A. M. Rodger, *The insatiable earl: a life of John Montagu, 4th earl of Sandwich* (London, 1993), p. 210.

[71] F. Holdsworth, *Joseph de Maistre et l'Angleterre* (Paris, 1935).

[72] Pillet, *L'Angleterre vue à Londres;* Joseph Fiévée, *Lettres sur l'Angleterre, et réflexions sur la philosophie du XVIIIe siècle* (Paris, 1802).

[73] Josephine Grieder, *Anglomania in France, 1740–1789: fact, fiction, and political discourse* (Geneva, 1985); Michael Maurer, *Aufklärung und Anglophilie in Deutschland* (Göttingen, 1987), ch. 12.

[74] *Londres et les Anglais par J.L. Ferri de St.-Constant* (4 vols, Paris, an. XII [1804]), IV, pp. 362–7.

was one such. He was a moderate royalist who made it his mission to revive that admiration for British institutions that had inspired the Anglomaniacs of Louis XV's reign. 'Once England was our study. We came in search of government here as we went to Italy in search of arts.'[75] But now the French had fatally fixed their attention on America, a much more dangerous guide. For the British had achieved reform without social conflict, preserving the essentially aristocratic nature of their society, averting the class conflict that revolution had unleashed on two continents, and adapting an ancient constitution painlessly to the requirements of change. Rémusat's ideal was an English government in a French society. Its outstanding boon was the abandonment of speculative principles. 'Every principle is identified with certain forms, attested by certain facts, which convert it into legal truth and historic truth.' This was more or less a list of the features of English government that others found objectionable, but Rémusat was nothing if not a friend of England. His essays on Bolingbroke, Horace Walpole, Junius, Burke, and Fox, revealed the depth of his knowledge of eighteenth-century English life, and his account of its philosophers his admiration of its modes of thought. Lamartine's more qualified admiration had a not dissimilar basis. Returning to England after twenty years' absence, in 1850, he was impressed by the effects of the intervening reforms. But he saw their essence as compromise and conciliation rather than genuine change, preserving intact the historic English triad of liberty, aristocracy, and monarchy. This 'socialisme conservateur', as he called it, was a treaty between rich and poor, not a new society of equality and justice.[76]

For some German reformers in search of a project that steered clear both of Jacobinism and Bonapartism it was the organic vitality of the British constitution as represented by the involvement of propertied people at every level of government that was so appealing. The state that Friedrich Vincke scrutinized on two fact-finding visits to Britain in 1800 and 1807 was one that needed no fundamental reform because it held within itself an ancient formula for self-renewal, defying central planning. The voluntary service of an aristocratic class naturally had considerable attraction for those who regarded bureaucracy and democracy as different but equal evils. Vincke described it as the true secret of what he called English 'Besonderheit'.[77]

There were others during the following decades who admired this spirit but they would not have been regarded as particularly liberal either in Britain or elsewhere. The ultimate accolade is perhaps the published and translated

---

[75] *L'Angleterre au dix-huitième siécle* (2 vols, Paris, 1856), I, p. 1.

[76] Robert Mattlé, *Lamartine voyageur* (Paris, 1936), pp. 281, 297.

[77] Friedrich Ludwig Wilhelm Philipp, [Freiherr von Vincke], *Darstellung der innern Verwaltung Grossbritanniens*, ed. B. G. Niebuhr (Berlin, 1815), p. 6.

account of the Saxon Carus, who visited England in 1844, and was delighted by the moral tone that absence of bureacracy helped generate.

> All this greatness, however, would be inconceivable, were it not that, in the general administration of the country, a certain elevated tone of simplicity prevails, which is as far remote as possible from what may be called the dillettantism of governing, which seeks for its renown in a multitude of petty regulations, and in a peculiarly artistical structure of the state machine. It strikes a stranger with astonishment when he hears how small a number of individuals compose the efficient force of the executive; with what simplicity and brevity the communications between the respective ministerial departments are made; how little verbal communication takes place, and how limited the number of the whole official staff is, which in Germany is so inordinately increased. There is, perhaps, no country in which, relatively speaking, the number of paid officials is so small as in England, and where the direction of the public affairs is conducted *on so elevated a scale*; and in this respect in particular, it must undoubtedly furnish an interesting object of study for the diplomatists and statesmen of all nations. I must still add, that it is this very elevated mode of conducting public affairs, which opens up the widest and richest field for the appearance of men of the highest talents and character.[78]

Perhaps the absence of bureaucrats was a matter on which diverse authorities could agree. Charles Cottu, who came to Britain to examine its legal system, consulted Samuel Romilly closely and yet found almost nothing that needed reforming, called this a nation governing itself without agents of government.[79] At any rate before the civil service reforms and Whitehall office-building of the mid-nineteenth century this was one of the most striking of all impressions. There was, after all, something very peculiar about a country in which the most important government building, Somerset House, was shared by Treasury clerks on the one hand and Fellows of the Royal Academy on the other, as Amédée Pichot observed. 'By thus crowding clerks and artists together, England sufficiently reveals the scarcity of her public buildings. Perhaps, however, the government offices in England dispense with that host of clerks who with us have nothing to do but to mend pens for our ministers.'[80] Again, the closest student of parliamentary reform, Duvergier de Hauranne, was more than anything else struck by the English success in minimizing the influence of executive government. For him, the glory of English reformers was their success from the time of Queen Anne up to the 1840s, when he was writing, in gradually curbing the power of ministers and

---

[78] C. G. Carus, *The King of Saxony's journey through England and Scotland in the year 1844*, transl. S. C. Davison (London, 1846), p. 36.

[79] *De l'administration de la justice criminelle en Angleterre, et de l'esprit du gouvernement anglais* (Paris, 1820), p. 220.

[80] Amédée Pichot, *Historical and literary tour of a foreigner in England and Scotland* (2 vols, London, 1825), I, p. 45.

office-holders in Parliament.[81] He might be forgiven for not predicting that precisely the reverse process would soon be under way.

There are, of course, other standpoints altogether, even more negligent of the theme of reform than those I have discussed. Harping on Britain as a bulwark of Burkeian stability during the Revolutionary wars was one such, creating a climate of opinion that was reluctant to look for evidence of reform and unlikely to find it. Friedrich Gentz was one of those for whom all other considerations were submerged by the requirement to fight the principles of the French Revolution to the death. Gentz not only defended Britain's role in European politics, but even glorified its seemingly cynical exploitation of continental wars to extend its commerce and colonies. Its ancient constitution and commercial supremacy were synonymous with European civilization. 'No enlightened European', he wrote, 'will be able to perceive England's prosperity without exclaiming with that dying patriot: *Esto perpetua!*'[82]

For Gentz the triumph of Britain was the taming of modernity. Once the English had been seen as unleashing it. But almost regardless of vantage point, this was certainly not the early nineteenth-century view, notwithstanding the innovation associated with industrialization. It is an interesting case of the way that political perceptions can overshadow all kinds of alternative impressions. For the foreigners who came, saw, and went home, Britain as a pillar of legitimacy and stability in a changing world seems to have had more evocative power than Britain as the leading edge of a new form of civilization. Or perhaps there was all the stronger sense of the underlying continuities of British life as a result. Many of those who wrote about Britain were more interested in its cultural message than any other, and themes such as rage for the Gothic, the obsession with heritage, the cult of everything old English, naturally made an impression on visitors more interested in Sir Walter Scott or the English country house than Lord Grey and Sir Robert Peel. Some of them connected such trends with the innate sense of hierarchy and the obsession with heredity that seemed characteristic of all classes in Britain. Self-conscious antiquity appeared to such travellers the most striking of all English characteristics. It evoked some of the most powerful of all tributes, including the ultimate masterpiece in the genre, Emerson's *English Traits* of 1852. Whether English or not, Britain needed reform: doubtless an interesting question to Britons. For many of the foreigners who chose to characterize them it was either beside the point or positively misleading.

---

[81] *De la réforme parlementaire and de la réforme électorale* (Paris, 1847).
[82] Paul F. Rieff, *Friedrich Gentz, an opponent of the French Revolution and Napoleon* (Urbana-Champaign, 1912), p. 81; Frederick Gentz, *On the state of Europe before and after the French Revolution; being an answer to the work entitled De l'état de la France à la fin de l'an VIII*, transl. from German by John Charles Herries (2nd edn, London, 1803), pp. 41–2.

Riding a Tiger:
Daniel O'Connell, Reform, and
Popular Politics in Ireland, 1800–1847

K. THEODORE HOPPEN

THE POLITICAL MOVEMENTS LED BY DANIEL O'CONNELL in early nineteenth-century Ireland encouraged a predominantly Catholic peasant population to adopt — or at least to acquiesce in — demands for liberal reform. Although neither the socio-economic conditions of contemporary Ireland nor, indeed, many of the cultural and organizational characteristics of Irish Catholicism were unique, this, in the European context of the time, was a highly unusual achievement. The context in which it proved possible for such a development to take place was Ireland's singular political condition as a subordinate and peripheral national entity within an increasingly liberal state. It was this combination of circumstances that proved crucial in allowing O'Connell to introduce a reformist programme to a society for which religion provided the fundamental basis of identity, not simply for a class or a community, but for something approaching the nation as such. The contrast with other parts of Catholic Europe makes the point. For example, Polish Catholicism, though also underpinning feelings of national identity, faced so autocratic and anti-liberal a state that reform projects never possessed the credibility of practical implementation, while Rhineland Catholics, though deeply resentful of their incorporation into Prussia after 1815, simply lacked the possibility of maintaining *national* distinctions between themselves and their new rulers.

This is all the more striking because, in many respects, the spiritual and organizational development of early nineteenth-century European Catholicism proved a very general phenomenon in which the Irish Catholic Church participated to the full. The same attempts were made, for example, in Ireland, Germany, and France, to adjust popular religious practices to the norms of an increasingly powerful ultramontanism. That close intermingling of the sacred and the profane so characteristic of late eighteenth- and early nineteenth-century rural Catholicism — enthusiasm for mass, disorganized,

Proceedings of the British Academy, **100**, 121–143. © The British Academy 1999.

and often wild pilgrimages, a belief in the efficacy of holy wells and fountains, morally relaxed celebrations of local feast days and of the seasonal passage rites of agricultural societies — was as energetically brought under close clerical control in Ireland as elsewhere.[1] Although such efforts were only slowly successful,[2] a kind of ultramontane *Gleichschaltung*, as regards belief, practice, and organization, undoubtedly took place throughout Europe as a whole. However, while the dominant political ethos of the official Catholic Church in continental countries remained generally conservative and anti-revolutionary, the Irish Church and its adherents were to follow a very different path. And if it was O'Connell who proved instrumental in helping to bring this about, the materials available for him to work upon, though complex and sometimes obscure, lacked neither malleability nor promise.

Whereas in those parts of France most resembling the economic, social, and religious circumstances of contemporary Ireland, many peasants and rural artisans moved decisively towards counter-revolution in the 1790s, in Ireland the revolutionary year of 1798 was marked by developments of an altogether more ambiguous kind. Although the *modus operandi* of violent resistance was similar in both countries, the aims and the enemies in view were not. Many of the scenes commonly witnessed during the Vendée rising of 1793 — such as large numbers of men gathering together 'with guns, forks, scythes, etc., all wearing white cockades and decorated with small square, cloth medals, on which were embroidered different shapes, such as crosses, little hearts pierced with pikes, and other signs of that kind'[3] — might well have occurred in rural Ireland (not only in 1798 but during any of the agrarian disturbances common between 1760 and 1845). But while in the west of France the Catholic participants in such gatherings exhibited a distinctly royalist political orientation, in Ireland their undoubted religious feelings, though not devoid of politically traditional elements, were often expressed in more noticeably radical terms.

Certainly some of those involved in the rising of 1798 seem to have been motivated by a contradictory mixture of sectarianism, rural protest, and a simple belief that 'my enemy's enemy is my friend'. But such 'primitivism' was largely confined to the western province of Connacht (the rising's least successful theatre) where General Humbert's 1,000-strong force of French revolutionary troops was greeted by local peasants anxious to 'take up arms

---

[1] K. T. Hoppen, *Elections, politics, and society in Ireland, 1832–1885* (Oxford, 1984), pp. 211–24; J. Sperber, *Popular Catholicism in nineteenth-century Germany* (Princeton, 1984), pp. 10–38; T. Nipperdey, *Germany from Napoleon to Bismarck, 1800–1866* (Dublin, 1996), pp. 363–6; Y.-M. Hilaire, *Une chrétienté au XIXe siècle? La vie religeuse des populations du diocese d'Arras (1840–1914)*, (2 vols, Lille, 1977), I, pp. 373–416 and passim.

[2] J. Devlin, *The superstitious mind: French peasants and the supernatural in the nineteenth century* (New Haven, 1987), especially pp. 1–42.

[3] C. Tilly, *The Vendée* (London, 1964), p. 317.

for France and the Blessed Virgin'.[4] However, the rebellion obtained an altogether greater purchase in the economically advanced south-eastern parts of Ireland where its progress proved far more than merely chaotic and spontaneous in character. Neither did it emerge primarily out of agrarian or sectarian issues, being instead based upon a widespread politicization brought about by the spread of the United Irish movement and the deliberate creation of a mass revolutionary policy.[5] Although, therefore, the rebellion was eventually crushed, its radicalizing impact upon the political culture of substantial parts of south Leinster and east Munster was very considerable indeed.

Such developments might suggest that the popular political life of Ireland in the decades immediately after the union with Britain in 1800 would follow an increasingly revolutionary path. That this did not happen can be attributed largely to the manner in which O'Connell effectively invented and successfully marketed entirely new types of reform-orientated political discourse and activity. This was no simple process, involving as it did the creation of mass political movements, the integration of the Catholic Church and clergy into the work of those movements, and — most difficult of all — success in mobilizing the more prosperous and 'modern' elements in both urban and rural Ireland (merchants, professionals, larger farmers, and the like) without irretrievably antagonizing (indeed, while drawing a good deal of additional support from) the poorer tenant farmers and landless labourers of the countryside.

O'Connell's first entry into public politics was as one of the few educated Catholics to take a firm line against the passage of the Act of Union shortly after the failure of the rebellion of 1798. But while opposition to the union and demands for its repeal were thereafter never far from his thoughts, the immovable opposition of successive British governments made it difficult (perhaps impossible) to base a continuing political career upon this one object alone. O'Connell was, in any case, perfectly willing to pursue a wider range of issues for more positive reasons, his earliest formation as a student of politics — in particular his reading of Godwin, Wollstonecraft, and Paine — having firmly set him upon the path of reform. For a time, indeed, he even adopted deism in response to such influences. But this proved a passing phase and by 1809, if not earlier, he had returned to orthodox Catholicism, becoming thereafter more devout by the year.[6] By

[4] T. Pakenham, *The year of liberty: the story of the great Irish rebellion of 1798* (London, 1969), p. 306. Pakenham's suggestion that such things were more generally true is no longer convincing.
[5] K. Whelan, 'Reinterpreting the 1798 rebellion in County Wexford' in D. Keogh and N. Furlong, eds, *The mighty wave: the 1798 rebellion in Wexford* (Dublin, 1996), pp. 9–36.
[6] O. MacDonagh, *The hereditary bondsman: Daniel O'Connell, 1775–1829* (London, 1988), pp. 41–2, 60–1, 101, 158.

contrast, his early lessons in politics as such remained fixed in O'Connell's mind, so much so that the chief argument he generally chose to deploy in favour of repeal was that only an Irish parliament could deliver full and adequate *reforms* and above all 'cheap government, and a just administration of the laws'.[7] Looking back over his political career as a whole, one might, indeed, conclude that, while repeal constituted the frame within which that career found its being, the painted canvas which it encompassed chiefly depicted a series of campaigns, negotiations, compromises, and achievements, pursued within the general world of early nineteenth-century Irish (and British) reform.

The fact that O'Connell entered the wider arena of reform politics through the issue of Catholic emancipation gave his subsequent activities that Janus-faced ambiguity which constituted at once their strength and their weakness. Emancipation was not, after all, a matter purely of reform (as, for example, many whigs liked to believe), but carried with it complex intimations of a religious and sectarian kind. The establishment of the Catholic Association in 1823 and its dramatic growth in 1824 when O'Connell introduced the penny-a-month contribution scheme at once hugely increased the campaign's popularity and (almost by accident) involved the bulk of the Catholic priesthood as collectors and organizers.[8] These developments not only inaugurated the clergy's definitive entry into public politics, but effectively established a set of reciprocal compromises between the church's religious and O'Connell's more secular priorities.

As a result, it became less and less possible for the clergy to maintain that their political activities could (or, indeed, should) be entirely confined to specifically 'religious' issues. The simple logic of events over the next quarter-century meant that they were to be inexorably drawn from involvement in the primarily religious issue of emancipation, through involvement in a range of partly religious and partly secular reforms in the 1830s, into what (for all its Catholic resonances) was the primarily secular matter of repeal in the 1840s. Not that the mass of the clergy needed much encouragement — as can be seen in the failure of the bishops' attempts to withdraw their troops to barracks after the granting of emancipation in 1829.[9] The overwhelmingly Catholic character of the emancipation campaign also, however, tended to encourage O'Connell to emphasize the denominational aspects of his political mentality and in effect muddy the waters of his oft-proclaimed (and, in

---

[7] *Hansard*, IV, 652 (4 July 1831). All references are to the 3rd series unless otherwise indicated.

[8] J. A. Reynolds, *The Catholic emancipation crisis in Ireland, 1823–1829* (New Haven, 1954), pp. 14–30.

[9] D. A. Kerr, *Peel, priests and politics: Sir Robert Peel's administration and the Roman Catholic Church in Ireland, 1841–1846* (Oxford, 1982), p. 68; *Ballyshannon Herald*, 31 Oct. 1834; Hoppen, *Elections, politics, and society in Ireland*, pp. 234–6; J. F. Broderick, *The Holy See and the Irish movement for the repeal of the union with England, 1829–1847* (Rome, 1951), passim.

many ways, perfectly genuine) liberalism. Not only did his repeated emphases upon the inclusiveness of the Irish 'nation' occasionally slide into more sectarian modes — as when in 1833 he denounced certain Protestants as 'foreigners to us, since they are of a different religion'[10] — but the heat of combat could lead him to declare (as he did in 1826) that it was the Catholics who were 'the people, emphatically the people', that, indeed, 'the Catholic people of Ireland are a nation'.[11] In private he was prepared to go further still, telling the future Cardinal Cullen in 1842 that Protestants 'would not survive the Repeal ten years' and that (despite his well-known support for the separation of church and state)[12] the Catholic majority in any Irish parliament would certainly move a long way towards endowing Catholicism out of official funds.[13] What, then, O'Connell seems in part to have been doing was to make use of what remained of the politicization achieved by the United Irishmen to push political life into less clearly inclusive channels and then to develop 'a highly effective form of trench warfare from within them'.[14] While, therefore, the clergy were certainly demonstrating that in Ireland Catholicism and reaction were far from synonymous,[15] the popular image of O'Connell was that of an Old Testament leader shepherding a Catholic nation into its promised and rightful inheritance.

> The bondage of those Israelites,
> Our Saviour he did see,
> He then commanded Moses,
> To go to set them free,
> And in the same we did remain
> Suffering for our own,
> Till God has sent O'Connell
> To free the Church of Rome.[16]

That this should have been the case had everything to do with O'Connell's relationship with the rural masses of the time. Although his campaigns undoubtedly attracted a good deal of (not always uncritical) support from urban dwellers, the very fact that, as late as 1841, less than

---

[10] *Hansard*, xv, 325 (7 Feb. 1833).

[11] F. O'Ferrall, *Catholic emancipation: Daniel O'Connell and the birth of Irish democracy, 1820–30* (Dublin, 1985), p. 144.

[12] O. MacDonagh, *The emancipist: Daniel O'Connell, 1830–47* (London, 1989), pp. 23–4.

[13] O'Connell to Cullen, 9 May 1842, in M. R. O'Connell, ed., *The correspondence of Daniel O'Connell* (8 vols, Dublin, 1972–80), vii, pp. 155–60.

[14] K. Whelan, *The tree of liberty: radicalism, Catholicism and the construction of an Irish identity, 1760–1830* (Cork, 1996), p. 153.

[15] A. de Tocqueville, *Journeys to England and Ireland*, ed. J. P. Mayer (London, 1958), pp. 130–5.

[16] Ballad of c.1830 cited in R. uí Ógáin, *Immortal Dan: Daniel O'Connell in Irish folk tradition* (Dublin, [1995]), p. 104.

14 per cent of the Irish population lived in towns of 2,000 or more inhabitants (and less than 18 per cent even in places with 500 or more)[17] meant that any political leader anxious to mobilize a popular following could hardly avoid a direct engagement with the countryside. And in the early decades of the nineteenth century that half of the countryside lying west of a vertical line drawn from Derry to Cork sustained a demotic culture in which the traditions, rhythms, and language of a Gaelic society had by no means evaporated. Indeed, the kinds of image presented in the ballad cited at the end of the last paragraph owed much to the cultural nexus which such a state of things implied. In this respect O'Connell's well-known statement that he was 'sufficiently utilitarian not to regret' the 'gradual abandonment' of the Irish language — still in his time spoken by perhaps 40 per cent of the population — did not significantly reduce his popularity in what survived of the Gaelic world.[18] Few Irish speakers felt otherwise about their language and even the handful who regretted his views took trouble to emphasize their admiration for his person and their support for his political demands.[19]

What mattered was that O'Connell's anchorage within Gaelic society was so firm and obvious that — quite apart from his own inclinations — there was simply no political need for him to take up issues of cultural nationalism in the way that, for example, his non-Gaelic-speaking critics in the Young Ireland movement would have liked him to do. Indeed, the proof of this particular pudding lay in the eating, it being noteworthy that O'Connell attracted a uniquely large amount of attention in ballads and oral tradition generally — far more, certainly, than other prominent Irish nationalists such as Wolfe Tone, Emmet, Davis, or Parnell.[20] Nor, unsurprisingly, was O'Connell unaware of this, telling his utilitarian mentor, Bentham, that the County Clare freeholders of 1828 were prepared to 'risk their all to vote for me as a fellow Catholic and a man long the theme of *ballads* and conversation'.[21] Given the governing values and traditions of Gaelic Ireland,

---

[17] 2,000 and more = 13.9 per cent; 500 and more = 17.8 per cent: W. E. Vaughan and A. J. Fitzpatrick, eds, *Irish historical statistics: population, 1821–1971* (Dublin, 1978), p. 27; H. Mason, 'The development of the urban pattern in Ireland, 1841–1881', unpublished PhD dissertation, University of Wales, 1969, p. 104.

[18] W. J. O'N. Daunt, *Personal recollections of the late Daniel O'Connell, M.P.* (2 vols, London, 1848), I, p. 14.

[19] G. Ó Tuathaigh, 'The folk hero and tradition' in D. McCartney, ed., *The world of Daniel O'Connell* (Dublin, 1980), p. 38; J. A. Murphy, 'O'Connell and the Gaelic world' in K. B. Nowlan and M. R. O'Connell, eds, *Daniel O'Connell: portrait of a radical* (Belfast, 1984), pp. 43–4.

[20] uí Ógáin, *Immortal Dan*, p. 1.

[21] O'Connell to Bentham, 26 Oct. 1828, in O'Connell, ed., *Correspondence of Daniel O'Connell*, VIII, p. 208 (O'Connell's emphasis). It is significant that the period 1829–48 marked the high point of official concern about the seditious nature of popular ballads as a political genre (M. Murphy, 'The ballad singer and the role of the seditious ballad in nineteenth-century Ireland: Dublin Castle's view', *Ulster Folklife*, 25 (1979), p. 80).

O'Connell's obviously 'Gaelic' character and origins helped to assign him a position of admired leadership by sheer force of a personality made manifest by confidence, courage, success, a golden tongue, by a host of intuitive gestures which persuaded very large numbers of people to see in him the incarnation of their aspirations and hopes.

When residing on his own County Kerry estate, O'Connell was inclined to behave much as an Irish chieftain might have been expected to do, and this reinforced such attitudes. Montalembert called on him at Derrynane in 1830, found '100 to 150 peasants waiting at his door for his advice', no less than thirty-four members of O'Connell's extended family in the house, and was then entertained at a large dinner party and by the playing of traditional Irish music.[22] 'He delighted', recorded William Fagan of O'Connell in the 1840s, 'in playing the Irish Tanist among his dependents. He was Judge, Jury, and Executive in all their disputes... Often, on the top of a mountain crag, while the hounds were at fault, would he sit on one of nature's rude imperishable benches, to hear and determine the disputes'.[23] Although O'Connell did not often use the Irish language in his speeches, he did not hesitate to deploy scattered phrases designed to emphasize his identification with those listening to him. At the enormous assemblages which gathered to hear him speak throughout the 1820s, 1830s, and 1840s, banners were carried emblazoned with Irish texts while addresses in Irish were delivered by his supporters at meetings concerning emancipation, reform, and repeal.[24] What, however, seemed to count for most in the construction of the relationship between O'Connell and Gaelic Ireland was not so much his attitude to it as its attitude to him. While he had little time for the nostalgia of traditional Aisling poetic fantasies in which Ireland was depicted as a virtuous and wronged maiden waiting to be rescued from Saxon clutches by a heroic deliverer (possibly with foreign help), those who still thought in such tropes preferred to remain unaware of the fact and simply ignored his denunciations of violence, his belief in liberal reform, and his support for a continuing (though devolved) connection with the British empire and crown. For them O'Connell, at bottom, was envisaged as the hero who was going to favour Catholics and destroy the privileges of the 'descendants of lying Luther and crooked avaricious Calvin' and to do so by banishing 'English-speaking boors, English-speaking

---

[22] J. Hennig, 'Continental opinion' in M. Tierney, ed., *Daniel O'Connell: nine centenary essays* (Dublin, 1948), p. 252.

[23] W. Fagan, *The life and times of Daniel O'Connell* (2 vols, Cork, 1847–8), II, p. 180.

[24] Murphy, 'O'Connell and the Gaelic world', pp. 37–8; S. P. Ó Mórdha, 'An anti-tithe speech in Irish', *Eigse*, 9 (1960–1), pp. 223–6; B. Ó Buachalla, 'A speech in Irish on repeal', *Studia Hibernica*, 10 (1970), pp. 84–94; G. J. Lyne, 'Daniel O'Connell, intimidation and the Kerry elections of 1835', *Journal of the Kerry Archaeological and Historical Society*, 4 (1971), p. 84; O'Ferrall, *Catholic Emancipation*, pp. 128 and 194; uí Ógáin, *Immortal Dan*, p. 42. O'Connell may — unusually — have been able to read as well as speak Irish (ibid., p. 21).

churls'.[25] And this, it was constantly affirmed, would be achieved by means of blood and the sword. Tomás Rua Ó Súilleabháin (a Kerry poet patronized by the O'Connell family) saw him in exactly these terms.

> Dónall, the strapping fellow, is in form and ready,
> The sword of blood in his fist ready for slaughter,
> And his mouth affirmed that before the end of autumn
> He would lift the sorrow from the Irish people.[26]

And the same was true — to an even more fanciful extent — of an anonymous balladeer whose productions were sent by an anxious County Cork magistrate to Dublin Castle in 1833.

> A large fleet is coming over from France,
> With young O'Connell with them as their leader,
> And then we will have bonfires over the country for joy,
> And beat them to hell.[27]

To a considerable extent O'Connell's Gaelically generated status as chieftain was acknowledged well beyond the west. In the east of Ireland, too, the folklore that came to surround him found its most characteristic expression, not in precise references to reform, emancipation, or repeal, but in a concern for cosmic deliverance, on the one hand, and for the hero's immediately personal attributes and successes — his ability to outwit oppressive landlords, magistrates, and treacherous Englishmen — on the other. And, indeed, the intense demonstrations which broke out in north-east Munster to celebrate emancipation's 1828 electoral triumph in County Clare were largely orchestrated by local factions determined to sink their own long-standing differences into a single, militant, and universal campaign.[28] Above all, O'Connell's unsurpassed skill and cunning as a lawyer were so widely celebrated that the title accorded him by the rural masses was more commonly that of 'Counsellor' than that of 'Liberator'.[29] And to a very large extent it was precisely this disjunction between the details of O'Connell's programme and the generalized manner in which that programme and

---

[25] Murphy, 'O'Connell and Gaelic Ireland', pp. 44–5 (translated from the Irish).

[26] úi Ógáin, *Immortal Dan*, p. 102 (translated from the Irish).

[27] National Archives Dublin (NAD), Outrage Papers 1833/2454/1.

[28] Ó Tuathaigh, 'The folk hero and tradition', pp. 33–4; idem, 'Gaelic Ireland, popular politics and Daniel O'Connell', *Journal of the Galway Archaeological and Historical Society*, 34 (1974–5), pp. 21–34; G. Owens, 'A "Moral Insurrection": faction fighters, public demonstrations and the O'Connellite campaign, 1828', *Irish Historical Studies*, 30 (1997), pp. 513–41.

[29] D. Ó Muirithe, 'O'Connell in Irish folk tradition' in Nowlan and O'Connell, eds, *Daniel O'Connell*, p. 55; also N. Ó Ciosáin's review of *Immortal Dan* in *Irish Historical Studies*, 30 (1996), pp. 282–4.

its author were perceived that made it possible for him to retain widespread popularity even when — as was not infrequently the case — the implications of his statements and views were anything but neutral as between the various social and economic groups which gave him their support.

The agrarian situation which O'Connell — as indeed all contemporary Irish politicians — faced was at once disturbed and unstable. Since the 1760s large parts of rural Ireland had experienced the violent activities of various secret societies bent upon redressing what they perceived to be injustices regarding the occupation, availability, and price of land.[30] These societies varied considerably as to membership and aims. The rents demanded from farmers; 'landlord attempts at reorganization; conacre rents; labourers' wages; the abandonment of tillage for pasture; the employment of "strangers" from outside the immediate locality; tithes, taxes, and tolls at fairs', any or all of these could 'become the cause of violence and intimidation in a society where the rural poor sought desperately to maintain a foothold in an increasingly overcrowded agrarian system'.[31] Three aspects of the make-up and activities of such societies bear especially upon their relationship with O'Connell's wider political priorities: first, the appearance of an overtly millennial frame of mind among many of those involved; second, the manner in which divisions between the various secret organizations reflected economic divisions within agricultural society in general; and third, a clear difference between their members' behaviour in distressed times (when discontent encompassed a very wide range of farmer and labourer interests) and in better times (when violence tended to be dominated almost entirely by the landless and the land-poor).[32]

[30] J. S. Donnelly Jr, 'The Rightboy movement 1785–8', *Studia Hibernica*, 17/18 (1977–8), pp. 120–202; idem, 'The Whiteboy movement 1761–5', *Irish Historical Studies*, 31 (1978), pp. 20–54; idem, 'Irish agrarian rebellion: the Whiteboys of 1769–76', *Proceedings of the Royal Irish Academy*, Section C, 83 (1983), pp. 293–331; M. J. Bric, 'Priests, parsons and politics: the Rightboy protest in County Cork, 1785–1788', *Past & Present*, 100 (1983), pp. 100–23. See also note 32 below.

[31] S. J. Connolly, 'Union government, 1812–23' in W. E. Vaughan, ed., *A new history of Ireland, V: Ireland under the Union, 1: 1801–70* (Oxford, 1989), p. 58. Conacre consisted of very small parcels of land let by tenant farmers to otherwise landless labourers for intensive potato cultivation, usually at very high rents.

[32] J. S. Donnelly, Jr, 'The social composition of agrarian rebellions in early nineteenth-century Ireland: the case of the Carders and Caravats, 1813–16' in P. J. Corish, ed., *Radicals, rebels and establishments*, Historical Studies, xv (Belfast, 1985), pp. 151–69; idem, 'Pastorini and Captain Rock: millenarianism and sectarianism in the Rockite movement of 1821–4' in S. Clark and J. S. Donnelly, Jr, eds, *Irish peasants: violence and political unrest, 1780–1914* (Manchester, 1983), pp. 102–39; P. E. W. Roberts, 'Caravats and Shanavests: Whiteboyism and faction fighting in east Munster, 1802–11' in ibid., pp. 64–101.

The growth of millennial feeling during the first quarter of the century was associated particularly with the so-called 'prophecies' of 'Pastorini', the latter a pseudonym adopted by the eighteenth-century English Catholic bishop, Charles Walmesley, to disguise his authorship of an apocalyptic *General History of the Christian Church* which went through numerous editions in Ireland in the years after 1790. Popularized versions caused considerable excitement among the rural masses and persuaded many that a dramatic and cataclysmic event would take place in the 1820s by means of which the oppressed Catholics of Ireland would be freed from English Protestant domination. Although O'Connell publicly belittled the impact of Pastorini, his own sudden manifestation as the major focus of Catholic aspirations in the mid-1820s drew upon himself many of the hopes of the millennialists.[33] For a time, indeed, he succeeded in transferring some of the energies previously devoted to the agrarian conspiracies of groups such as the Rockites (widely active in east Munster in the early 1820s) into the emancipation campaign, in part at least because millennial expectations came to infuse the latter no less urgently than they had the former.

However, at first sight, one major obstacle might still be seen as having stood in the way of O'Connell's achieving a *sustained* mobilization of rural Ireland: namely, the deep economic inequalities which divided its constituent parts: large, middling, and small farmers, cottiers, labourers with conacre land, labourers without access to land of any kind. In the years immediately before the Great Famine of 1845–9 the general relativities with regard to adult males (each of whom was usually required to support a large number of dependants) was roughly as shown in the table on p. 131.[34] O'Connell himself, who often (if somewhat inaccurately) called himself a utilitarian, had few personal doubts that economic progress and political stability could only be attained if the more substantial and successful agriculturalists were allowed to achieve a position of dominance in rural life. Although he ran his own property in Kerry along rather casually paternalistic lines,[35] on the wider stage he favoured what he called the agrarian 'middle classes' and as a result denounced the Sub-Letting Act of 1826 in terms that would have done credit to Samuel Smiles, insisting it should more properly be called an act 'to prevent a farmer from becoming a gentleman, [and] to prevent a gentleman

[33] *Minutes of evidence taken before the select committee ... appointed to inquire into the state of Ireland*, House of Commons paper 1825 (181), IX, 167; O'Ferrall, *Catholic emancipation*, p. 39. See also P. O'Farrell, 'Millennialism, messianism and utopianism in Irish History', *Anglo-Irish Studies*, 2 (1976), pp. 45–68.

[34] K. T. Hoppen, *Ireland since 1800: conflict and conformity* (2nd edn, London, 1999), p. 38 adapted from Donnelly, Jr, 'The social composition of agrarian rebellions', p. 152.

[35] MacDonagh, *The emancipist*, pp. 281–2; O'Connell to J. Primrose, 3 Mar. 1834, in O'Connell, ed., *Correspondence of Daniel O'Connell*, V, p. 109.

	No.	Percentage
Rich farmers (mean holdings 80 acres)	50 000	2.9
'Snug' farmers (mean holdings 50 acres)	100 000	5.9
Family farmers (mean holdings 20 acres and rarely employing outside labour)	250 000	14.7
Cottiers (mean holdings 5 acres)	300 000	17.7
Labourers (mean holdings 1 acre, though often without any land)	1 000 000	58.8

from acquiring Property'.[36] In areas where farmers of 'industrious habits' abounded, he told the House of Commons in 1830, there Whiteboyism found little purchase because such men 'have something to lose, and are therefore the friends of good order'.[37] O'Connellite activists were encouraged to inform labourers of the Liberator's hatred of combinations in general and of agricultural combinations in particular. In 1837 O'Connell's General Association even reproved a branch in Kildare for wanting to allow poor labourers to sit on its committee, while in the county constituencies generally the supporters of repeal tended to be depicted by headquarters as consisting largely of 'honest and respectable *farmers*'.[38]

A number of reasons can be put forward as to why such things did not prevent the rural masses from flocking to O'Connell's banner. Clearly O'Connell's status as Gaelic and millennial chieftain proved especially attractive to the poorest members of rural society, many of whom believed — however unrealistically — that their hero was about to lead them into an armed revolt, perhaps even that, as a ballad put it in 1831, 'Bony [sic] and O'Connell will set old Ireland free'.[39] Not only that, but millennialism, which attracted both farmers and labourers, provided a connection of expectation between groups otherwise separated by purely economic considerations. Again (as has already been pointed out) the onset of hard times had the effect of submerging the divergent interests of

[36] O'Connell to the Knight of Kerry, 27 Feb. 1828, in O'Connell, ed., *Correspondence of Daniel O'Connell*, III, p. 377.
[37] M. F. Cusack, ed., *The speeches and public letters of the Liberator* (2 vols, Dublin, 1875), I, p. 52.
[38] *Dublin Evening Post*, 24 Jan. and 18 May 1837; *Kilkenny Journal*, 4 Jan. 1837.
[39] Donnelly, Jr, 'Pastorini and Captain Rock', p. 136; Ó Muirithe, 'O'Connell in Irish folk tradition', p. 63.

labourers, cottiers, and farmers into a generalized discontent which then provided a kind of reservoir from which O'Connell could draw the waters of mass mobilization.[40] And hard times were frequent enough, with especially serious and widespread depressions occurring in 1800–1, 1813–16, 1821–4, and in the early 1830s. In particular, discontent about the payment of tithes for the support of the Protestant Church of Ireland proved especially effective in attracting larger farmers into common cause with lesser agriculturalists. Legislation in 1824 extended the requirement to pay tithes from arable land (where small farmers predominated) to pasture (generally the preserve of the more substantial operators), while the so-called Tithe War of the 1830s enjoyed overwhelming support from virtually all sections of the rural community.[41]

At the same time O'Connell, whether deliberately or not is far from clear, maintained so high a level of vagueness with regard to the 'land question' as such that he usually managed to avoid giving offence to any of the disparate groups enrolled under his command.[42] For a long time such thoughts as he addressed to economic matters in general tended more to the grandly banal than the usefully specific, as when in 1828 he laid it down that 'the greatest part of Ireland does not contain one-tenth of the population it could and ought to support in comfort'.[43] It was not until 1844–5 that he put any real flesh upon the bones of his agrarian rhetoric and even this amounted to no more than a series of modest proposals concerning matters such as compensation for improvements, an absentee tax (a particular — and politically safe — passion of his), the provision of agricultural schools, and the reclamation of unproductive land.[44]

None of this was designed to make any category among O'Connell's following feel either especially privileged or especially disadvantaged or to interfere with their amalgamation into what were primarily political (rather than economic or social) campaigns. Of course from time to time particular groups did come to the conclusion that emancipation, reform, or repeal had

[40] Donnelly, Jr, 'The social composition of agrarian rebellions', pp. 154–5.

[41] O'Ferrall, *Catholic emancipation*, pp. 48–9; G. Ó Tuathaigh, *Ireland before the famine, 1798–1848* (Dublin, 1972), p. 177.

[42] It is noteworthy that the United Irishmen in the 1790s had also been cautious about developing any kind of detailed — or indeed revolutionary — land policy for fear of upsetting particular interests (N. J. Curtin, *The United Irishmen: popular politics in Ulster and Dublin, 1791–1798* (Oxford, 1994), pp. 120–1 and 128–9).

[43] O'Connell to P. Mahony, 17 Sept. 1828, in O'Connell, ed., *Correspondence of Daniel O'Connell*, III, p. 406.

[44] J. Lee, 'The social and economic ideas of O'Connell' in Nowlan and O'Connell, eds, *Daniel O'Connell*, p. 71; also MacDonagh, *The emancipist*, pp. 26–7; O'Connell to C. Buller, 9 Jan. 1844, in O'Connell, ed., *Correspondence of Daniel O'Connell*, VII, pp. 234–7; O'Connell to P. Mahony, 25 Apr. 1845, ibid., VII, p. 313; R. B. McDowell, *Public opinion and government policy in Ireland, 1801–1846* (London, 1952), pp. 238–9.

yielded very little in terms of improved conditions or hard cash. As one cottier forcefully asked in 1832, 'What good did emancipation do us...Are we better clothed or fed, or our children better clothed and fed?'[45] But, in general, all sections of the rural population of Catholic Ireland were — sometimes to a greater, sometimes to a rather lesser extent — swept along by the O'Connellite tide. Thus labourers, for reasons that must have had more to do with communal emotion than economic self-interest, collaborated with farmers in agitating on O'Connell's behalf.[46] At the County Clare election of 1831 the Terry Alts (another agrarian secret society) even turned out shouting 'Hey for O'Connell and hey for Clare'.[47]

Furthermore, O'Connell repeatedly attracted enormous crowds at the vast meetings called to publicize his cause; and, although contemporary estimates ranged as high as a million for that held at Tara in August 1843, more sober calculations of 500,000 in the case of Tara and 300,000 or so in that of many others are impressive enough.[48] At what were, in effect, huge popular festivals, numerous altars were set up upon which priests said mass as the people arrived, platforms were provided for eminent clerics and politicians, songs were sung, and 'warm-up' speakers enthused the crowds before the Liberator himself arrived. O'Connell, though his own voice could presumably only be heard by a small number of those present, enlivened his more formal remarks with a kind of relaxed bantering that today would be condemned as mere stage-Irishry. At the famous Clare election of 1828 called because his opponent, Vesey Fitzgerald, had been appointed president of the board of trade, he was, for example, phonetically recorded as lapsing into what Oliver MacDonagh accurately enough calls 'proto-Kiltartanese': 'Arrah, bhoys, where's Vasy Vijarld at all, at all?...sind the bell about for him. Here's the cry for yez:–

> Stholen or sthrayed,
> Losht or mishlaid,
> The President of the Boord of Thrade!'[49]

And those who heard him responded with a matching enthusiasm. They shouted and groaned and sang and cheered, and when on one occasion a singer rendered a 'melody' by Thomas Moore about a slave freeing himself from chains, O'Connell leaped to his feet, raised his arms wide and exclaimed

[45] G. C. Lewis, *On local disturbances in Ireland, and on the Irish church question* (London, 1836), p. 109. See also Lady Gregory, ed., *Mr Gregory's letter-box, 1813–1835* (2nd edn, Gerrards Cross, 1981), p. 167.

[46] See, for example, Report of Chief Constable Hutton, 13 Feb. 1832, NAD Outrage Papers, 1832/2175/255; Report of Chief Constable Wright, 29 Dec. 1834, ibid., 1835/47/152.

[47] Hoppen, *Ireland since 1800*, p. 51.

[48] MacDonagh, *The emancipist*, pp. 227–30.

[49] MacDonagh, *The hereditary bondsman*, p. 253.

'I am not that slave!', upon which those present themselves again and again shouted 'We are not those slaves! We are not those slaves!'[50] Nor was such enthusiasm at all surprising at a time when priests too could sometimes adopt a similar kind of approach in front of their congregations which, in turn (recorded a visitor), expressed 'their sympathy with the preacher, as the Methodists in England do, by a deep and audible breathing'.[51] Although, therefore, O'Connell never found the process of mobilization an easy one — he had particular difficulties in identifying the precise location of his support in the still very restricted electorate of the time[52] — at the moments of his greatest impact he undoubtedly displayed a quite remarkable skill in holding together forces of a distinctly disparate kind. As the Irish-speaking draper and schoolmaster, Humphrey O'Sullivan, remarked, 'It is on O'Connell's advice this renewal of friendship and this peace is being made among the children of the Gael but the English do not like it; for they think it easier for them to beat people at variance than people in friendship'.[53]

And what — equally remarkably — these forces were being held together *for* was, at least in O'Connell's view, the furtherance of a programme of liberal and utilitarian reform. Thus, while religion, national feelings, and a shared sense of disadvantage provided the engines powering the O'Connellite machine, the destination towards which the driver was pointing was, above all, a reformist one. Religious matters and, indeed, questions of national identity tended to be confined to the realms of rhetoric and broad-brush generalization; but when it came to reform O'Connell was much more often prepared to enter into details and occasionally (though by no means invariably) to do so with a surprising degree of consistency. In this respect the early influence of Godwin provided him with an extensive — and at times even an extreme — programme of individual rights, both in the negative sense of 'freedoms from' and, more positively, in a firm adhesion to the pursuit of civil equality.[54] The influence of Bentham was less substantial, despite O'Connell's linguistically extravagant relationship with the great utilitarian during the last years of the emancipation campaign: 'BENEFAC-TOR OF THE HUMAN RACE' began one of O'Connell's letters, 'Dear, honest, supremely public-spirited, truly philanthropic, consistent, persevering, self-devoting Friend' began one of Bentham's.[55] Yet, however often he

---

[50] MacDonagh, *The emancipist*, p. 230.

[51] J. E. Bicheno, *Ireland and its economy* (London, 1830), p. 173.

[52] K. T. Hoppen, 'Politics, the law, and the nature of the Irish electorate, 1832–1850', *English Historical Review*, 92 (1977), pp. 773–6.

[53] O'Ferrall, *Catholic emancipation*, p. 228.

[54] MacDonagh, *The emancipist*, p. 19.

[55] O'Connell to Bentham, 30 July 1829, in O'Connell, ed., *Correspondence of Daniel O'Connell*, VIII, p. 216; Bentham to O'Connell, 15 Feb. 1829, in J. Bowring, ed., *The works of Jeremy Bentham* (11 vols, Edinburgh, 1843), XI, p. 12.

declared himself a utilitarian, O'Connell could never hide his distrust of 'big government', with the result that he opposed both the new English poor law of 1834 and the Irish poor law of 1838, not because he believed that a better *system* had existed before, but because both would lead to higher taxation and excessive state intervention and because he could not overcome an intuitive belief that they would also do 'away with personal feelings and connexions'.[56] In so far, therefore, as he was a Benthamite, O'Connell was so in an ethical rather than a doctrinal sense. Thus, while opposing the poor laws, he none the less favoured a wide-ranging reform of the legal system and was by no means as inimical to either factory reforms or the granting of certain strictly limited privileges to trade unions as he is sometimes supposed to have been.[57] And in the end, of course, the two men fell out, largely because Bentham had little sympathy with the kind of liberal Catholicism which O'Connell espoused or, indeed, with any policy that involved giving priority to Irish affairs.[58]

Whatever his deficiencies as a Benthamite, O'Connell's support for most of the central tenets — as well as some of the lesser aims — of contemporary British radicalism was extraordinarily tenacious, even sometimes to the extent of permanently antagonizing those who might otherwise have supported him. Although initially his trimming over the concessions demanded in the 1820s in return for emancipation (the disfranchisement of the forty-shilling freeholders for example) irritated radicals like Cobbett and Hunt, O'Connell took pains to mend his fences by addressing a meeting of Westminster electors in May 1829 in order to confirm his political credentials before an English audience. 'First, then, Englishmen', he began a rousing speech on the franchise question, 'I appear before you as a reformer, a radical reformer'.[59] The following year he spoke in the Commons in favour of extending the right to vote and again announced that he was doing so as 'a radical reformer' appealing 'to the great principle of democratic liberty which made England the great and productive country which she had been for centuries'.[60] And this was to prove a parliamentary song he was to sing

---

[56] *Hansard*, XXIV, 1060 (1 July 1834); O'Connell to Archbishop MacHale, [c. 18 Feb. 1838], in O'Connell, ed., *Correspondence of Daniel O'Connell*, VI, p. 136; A. Macintyre, *The Liberator: Daniel O'Connell and the Irish party, 1830–1847* (London, 1965), pp. 201–26; J. Lee, 'The social and economic ideas of O'Connell', pp. 75–6.

[57] J. Lee, 'The social and economic ideas of O'Connell', pp. 76–7, 80; F. D'Arcy, 'The artisans of Dublin and Daniel O'Connell, 1830–1847: an unquiet liaison', *Irish Historical Studies*, 17 (1970), pp. 242–3; R. B. McDowell, *Public opinion and government policy in Ireland*, p. 127.

[58] J. E. Crimmins, 'Jeremy Bentham and Daniel O'Connell: their correspondence and radical alliance, 1828–1831', *Historical Journal*, 40 (1997), pp. 359–87.

[59] F. D'Arcy, 'O'Connell and the English radicals' in D. McCartney, ed., *The world of Daniel O'Connell* (Dublin, 1980), p. 62.

[60] *Hansard*, 2nd Series, XXII, 720 (18 Feb. 1830).

without ceasing, no less at the end than at the beginning of his career as an MP.[61]

Gladstone's recollections of O'Connell published in 1889 are, in this respect, entirely to the point.

> He was an Irishman, but he was also a cosmopolite. I remember personally how, in the first session of my parliamentary life [1833], he poured out his wit, his pathos, and his earnestness, in the cause of negro emancipation. Having adopted the political creed of Liberalism, he was as thorough an English Liberal, as if he had had no Ireland to think of. He had energies to spare for Law Reform, for Postal Reform, ... for secret voting, for Corn Law Repeal, in short for whatever tended, within the political sphere, to advance human happiness and freedom.[62]

O'Connell's reformist interests were perhaps wider than those of any other leading politician of his day, encompassing, as they did, concerns of a British, Irish, and at times even a world nature. Unusually for a devout Catholic in good standing with early nineteenth-century ecclesiastical authority — and despite occasional equivocations in the 1840s — he generally supported both the separation of church and state and individual liberty of conscience.[63] If, on the issue of parliamentary and franchise reform he did not agree with the Chartists on every point, he agreed with them on most things. He urged English radicals to mobilize 'pressure from without' in favour of the ballot, short parliaments, and an increase in the number of voters. During a debate on the Charter in May 1842 he declared himself 'a decided advocate of universal suffrage' because he believed that no one could properly fix 'where the line should be drawn which determines that servitude should end and liberty commence'.[64] And he bitterly denounced the House of Lords for resisting reform, asking

> What prospect had the working classes, who had no votes for electing Members of Parliament, of finding redress? Who took care of their interests? They had no representatives ... You have deprived them of the franchise, and you suppose that they will be contented and satisfied under that system. They would not deserve to be Englishmen if they were satisfied. They are a slave class, and you a master class; and so long as this state of things existed, it was their right and duty to be dissatisfied.[65]

---

[61] See, for example, *Hansard*, LXXXI, 1097 (23 June 1845).

[62] W. E. Gladstone, 'Daniel O'Connell', *Nineteenth Century*, 25 (1889), pp. 156–7.

[63] Cusack, ed., *The speeches and public letters of the Liberator*, II, p. 285; MacDonagh, *The hereditary bondsman*, pp. 99–100; idem, *The emancipist*, pp. 19–23, 266–7; Macintyre, *The Liberator*, pp. 38–9.

[64] O'Connell to J. A. Roebuck, 23 Sept. 1837, in O'Connell, ed., *Correspondence of Daniel O'Connell*, VI, 86; *Hansard*, LXIII, 85 (3 May 1842).

[65] *Hansard*, XLIX, 961 (29 July 1839).

References to 'slavery' and its opposite, 'freedom', constituted key usages in O'Connell's rhetoric and argumentation, not least because they allowed him to universalize the Irish case into something of more than merely Irish significance. In no important manner, however, was he extending their relevance beyond Ireland on merely pragmatic grounds. He believed in 'freedom' for all men and (when he thought of it) for all women too.[66] He relentlessly opposed the existence of formal slavery throughout the world and never wavered even when it became clear that he was thereby doing his cause no good among important sections of opinion in the United States. In 1843 a black man stood up at a meeting of the Repeal Association in Dublin to thank O'Connell before a cheering crowd for saving 'the life of black people'. Having been — he went on to even greater cheers — 'brought up a Protestant, I am now a Catholic, and will die in that religion for the sake of Massa Dan O'Connell'.[67] Regardless, therefore, of the racist views of many Irish-Americans, O'Connell's abolitionism remained firm enough to earn him the title of 'the single most important supporter that American anti-slavery' had in the Europe of his day.[68]

The same notions of personal liberty drove O'Connell to embrace the cause of all those damaged by the spread of western colonialism. In denouncing the exploiters he burst into one of his (comparatively few) public attacks upon the British as such: 'There', he declared, 'are your Anglo-Saxon race! your British blood!... the vilest and most lawless of races. There is a gang for you!... the civilizers, forsooth, of the world'.[69] That he espoused a modified form of 'free trade' (he came to favour some protection for infant Irish industries) was perhaps both unsurprising and — in most radical circles — popular.[70] That he promoted, with even greater vigour, the cause of Jewish emancipation inevitably produced more brickbats than applause. 'I think', he told Isaac Goldsmid in 1829, 'every day a day of injustice until that civil equality is obtained by the Jews'.[71] And while it might be considered logical that a supplicant for Catholic emancipation should extend a similar demand on behalf of Jews, there were not a few contemporaries who saw no necessary connection between the liberties of Christians (however benighted) and those of the rest of humanity. O'Connell, however,

---

[66] O'Connell to L. Mott, 20 June 1840, in O'Connell, ed., *Correspondence of Daniel O'Connell*, IV, pp. 337–40.

[67] L. J. McCaffrey, *Daniel O'Connell and the repeal year* (Kentucky, 1966), pp. 74–5.

[68] D. C. Riach, 'Daniel O'Connell and American anti-slavery', *Irish Historical Studies*, 20 (1976), p. 24.

[69] Cited G. Osofsky, 'Abolitionists, Irish immigrants, and the dilemmas of romantic nationalism', *American Historical Review*, 80 (1975), p. 892.

[70] J. Lee, 'The social and economic ideas of O'Connell', p. 81.

[71] O'Connell to Goldsmid, 11 Sept. 1829, in O'Connell, ed., *Correspondence of Daniel O'Connell*, IV, p. 95.

followed a clearly different line of thought, one in which it was precisely the imperatives of his religious beliefs that underpinned the universal nature of the cause of liberty. 'Christianity', he told the Commons in May 1830, 'bade him do as he would be done by, and he only fulfilled that duty when he gave this [Jewish Relief] Bill his most hearty support'.[72]

Yet though O'Connell was so prominent among the advanced liberals of his time — he welcomed the collapse of the Bourbons in 1830, the success of the Belgian revolt in the same year, he grieved over the failures of the 'cause of liberty' in Poland and Spain and over the excessive use of capital punishment at home[73] — after 1829 he received little in the way of return from the leaders of radicalism in Britain. Only three English MPs (William Cobbett, Henry Hunt, and Thomas Wakley) ever gave any kind of public support to repeal, and only one of them ever voted in its favour.[74] Altogether more typical was G. F. Muntz, first vice-president of the Birmingham Political Union and MP for that city between 1840 and 1857, who in 1843 prefaced his contribution to a debate on an Irish Arms Bill with the observation that he 'had not the slightest intention to take part in the present debate merely respecting the Arms Bill, of which he knew nothing, such a measure never having been connected with the Government of England'.[75] Not long after O'Connell's death Richard Cobden was asked about his seven-year silence in the Commons on Irish affairs. 'I will tell you the reason', he replied,

> I found the populace of Ireland represented in the House by a body of men, with O'Connell at their head, with whom I could feel no more sympathy or identity than with people whose language I did not understand. In fact, *morally* I felt a complete antagonism and repulsion towards them. O'Connell always treated me with friendly attention, but I never shook hands with him or faced his smile without a feeling of insecurity; and as for trusting him on any public question where his vanity or passions might interpose, I should have as soon thought of an alliance with an Ashantee chief.[76]

And yet, even during his period of closest alliance with the whigs between 1835 and 1841, O'Connell was still prepared to go against Melbourne's ministry on radical-raised issues such as the ballot, flogging in the army, the sentences passed on the Tolpuddle Martyrs, and the abolition of newspaper stamp duty. That occasionally he failed to do so (on, for example, the Canadian question and on the details of tithe legislation) seems very small

---

[72] *Hansard*, 2nd Series, XXIV, 796 (17 May 1830).

[73] O'Connell to his wife, 5 July 1823, in O'Connell, ed., *Correspondence of Daniel O'Connell*, II, p. 498; to C. Fitz-Simon, 11 Sept. 1830, ibid., IV, pp. 203–4; to Lord Duncannon, 2 Oct. 1834, ibid., V, p. 187; MacDonagh, *The emancipist*, p. 62.

[74] D'Arcy, 'O'Connell and the English radicals', p. 65. Wakley voted for repeal on a motion introduced after O'Connell's death by Feargus O'Connor in 1848.

[75] *Hansard*, LXX, 139 (19 June 1843).

[76] J. Morley, *The life of Richard Cobden* (2 vols, London, 1881), II, p. 27.

beer indeed in comparison with the refusal of most British radicals to offer him even a tenth of what he gave to them.[77]

All the more remarkable, therefore, was O'Connell's persistence — and comparative success — in eliding the two causes most closely associated with his name — emancipation and repeal — into a general agenda of liberal reform. Already on the Clare hustings in 1828 he had connected emancipation with 'every measure favourable to radical Reform'.[78] The following year he was more specific still and produced an election address in which emancipation was presented as a kind of lever that would help to bring about parliamentary reform, the repeal of the Vestry and Sub-Letting Acts, the removal of restrictions on monastic orders, a charitable trusts act, a reform of grand jury assessments, codification of the law, improved internal communications, free trade, and much else besides.[79] But especially did he then rejoice — in words that some at least among his mass following would hardly have appreciated — that emancipation was 'a bloodless revolution more extensive in its operation than any other political change that could have taken place. I say *political* to contrast it with *social* changes which might break to pieces the framework of society'.[80] And in much the same manner was repeal of the union also put forward as a matter of *political* reform: 'in short, salutary restoration without revolution, an Irish parliament, British connection, one king, two legislatures'.[81] 'I do not', he declared in 1832, 'urge on the Repeal when it could interfere with Reform'.[82] Indeed, as the repeal movement developed in the early 1830s, O'Connell ensured that it became more and more closely linked with 'the full radical reform programme'.[83] Like emancipation, so repeal too was envisaged as making possible a vast array of practical improvements in everything from taxation to the rents paid by farmers and the wages received by agricultural labourers.[84]

However devoted O'Connell was to repeal as an issue, that reading which divides his career into two 'authentic' episodes — emancipation in the 1820s and repeal in the early 1830s and the 1840s — separated by a period of reluctant reformist pragmatism in the middle and late 1830s when O'Connell allied himself with the whigs and suppressed the repeal campaign in return for concessions on specific questions such as patronage, tithes, and local government, obscures more than it reveals. Although on the surface

[77] McDowell, *Public opinion and government policy in Ireland*, pp. 168–9.
[78] Reynolds, *The Catholic emancipation crisis in Ireland*, pp. 131–2.
[79] McDowell, *Public opinion and government policy in Ireland*, pp. 127–8.
[80] O'Connell to E. Dwyer, 14 Apr. 1829, in O'Connell, ed., *Correspondence of Daniel O'Connell*, IV, p. 45.
[81] O'Connell to P.V. Fitzpatrick, 21 Feb. 1833, ibid., V, p. 11.
[82] O'Connell to J. Dwyer, 17 May 1832, ibid., IV, p. 417.
[83] MacDonagh, *The emancipist*, p. 81.
[84] McDowell, *Public opinion and government policy in Ireland*, p. 126.

O'Connell's parliamentary course in the early 1830s might possibly be seen as an alternative to the whig alliance eventually formalized by the Lichfield House compact of 1835, in truth it constituted merely a 'variation in the method of consummating it'.[85] Long before 1835 O'Connell was putting out feelers to the whigs and there is no real evidence to suggest that he entered into an alliance with them reluctantly, hesitantly, or as a consciously perceived second-best. Indeed, in 1835 he let it be known that he was even ready to take office in Melbourne's new administration.[86] Nor, in the event, did he experience any great difficulties in carrying the mass of Irish public opinion with him.[87] More remarkable still, given the disappointments and difficulties of the next six years (though there were gains too as far as O'Connell was concerned), was his overall loyalty to the whigs as long as they remained in office.[88]

What changed everything was the return to power of Peel in 1841; but not simply because the tories refused to grant repeal — the whigs, after all, were no less antagonistic — but because they seemed also to oppose any and every Irish reform. If, however, in the short run O'Connell was now left with no alternative but to mount a mass campaign for repeal, he never abandoned hope that eventually the whigs might again help him to revert to more clearly reformist paths. In the last months of 1841 local O'Connellites were still organizing meetings of 'the clergy and other *reformers*' in the constituencies, and by September 1843 O'Connell was once again dropping hints to the effect that he might welcome a new alliance with the whigs. Indeed, in January 1844 (only three months after Peel's proclamation of the great repeal meeting planned for Clontarf) O'Connell was beginning to float the idea that a distinct programme of further reforms might yet enable a future whig administration to shunt repeal into the sidelines of political concern.[89] Nor should any of this be seen as surprising, for O'Connell's own understanding of repeal was highly elastic, not to say kaleidoscopic. While he undoubtedly imbued the concept (or, perhaps more properly, the term) with a certain mantra-like symbolism, he as frequently seemed willing to use repeal as little more than a device for the extraction of specific reforms. As he put it in 1840 — 'If we get the justice we require, then our Repeal Association is at an

---

[85] O. MacDonagh, 'O'Connell in the House of Commons' in McCartney, ed., *The world of Daniel O'Connell*, p. 50.

[86] McDowell, *Public opinion and government policy in Ireland*, pp. 153–4, 156–8, 160–1, 164–5.

[87] Macintyre, *The Liberator*, p. 145.

[88] McDowell, *Public opinion and government policy in Ireland*, p. 176; S. H. Palmer, 'Rebellion, emancipation, starvation: the dilemma of peaceful protest in Ireland, 1798–1848' in B. K. Lackner and K. R. Philp, eds, *Essays in modern European revolutionary history* (Austin, 1977), p. 20.

[89] O'Connell to Lord Campbell, 9 Sept. 1843, in O'Connell, ed., *Correspondence of Daniel O'Connell*, VII, p. 223; O'Connell to C. Buller, 9 Jan. 1844, ibid., VII, pp. 234–7.

end'; though, intent as always to keep his options open, he immediately added that the chances of this happening were slim.[90] One option that was, however, firmly closed was any kind of effective co-operation with the tories, not least because of the deep personal antagonism that existed between O'Connell and Peel. When, therefore, Peel began in 1844 to inaugurate a policy of 'killing repeal by kindness' O'Connell found it both personally and (in the event) politically impossible to respond.[91]

The failures of his last years, exacerbated as they were by the onset of the Great Famine and by increasing personal infirmity, should not, however, be allowed to place O'Connell's achievements in any but the most brilliant of lights. His combination of religious devotion and liberal principles gave both his personality and his politics a public European dimension that was, for its time, unusual, perhaps unique. For many (though not all) continental liberals he provided a much-discussed model. Above all, for Catholic liberals, in Germany no less than in France, he seemed to offer a third way between the extremes of revolution, on the one hand, and reaction, on the other.[92] Certainly Prussian officials had, by the late 1830s, become distinctly agitated about the frequency of the contacts between O'Connell and Catholic liberals in the Rhineland. Indeed, according to one authority, the mere mention of the name 'O'Connell' in the Rhineland or Westphalia was capable, at this time, of awakening '*in der Bevölkerung ebensosehr wie auf der Regierungsseite die Vorstellung der Gegenschaft zum bestehenden Staate*'.[93] Not only that, but liberals calling for a unified Germany had come to see Ireland's demands for religious and political freedom almost as a 'holy cause'.[94] Their admiration reached its peak in the early 1840s when, for example, the politician and journalist, Ludwig Wittig, produced his poem 'Der Harfner' published in *Vorwärts! Volkstaschenbuch auf das Jahr 1845*, whose editor was the well-known liberal, Robert Blum, later executed by order of a court martial during the 1848 revolution in Vienna:

[90] P. O'Farrell, *Ireland's English question: Anglo-Irish relations, 1534–1970* (London, 1971), p. 100.

[91] Kerr, *Peel, priests and politics*, passim.

[92] P. Joannon, 'O'Connell, Montalembert and the birth of Christian democracy in France' in M. R. O'Connell, ed., *Daniel O'Connell: political pioneer* (Dublin, 1991), pp. 98–109; P. Alter, 'O'Connell's impact on the organisation and development of German political Catholicism', ibid., pp. 110–18; G. F. Grogan, *The noblest agitator: Daniel O'Connell and the German Catholic movement, 1830–50* (Dublin, 1991).

[93] K. Holl, *Die irische Frage in der Ära Daniel O'Connells und ihre Beurteilung in der politischen Publizistik des deutschen Vormärz* (Johannes-Gutenberg-Universität Mainz, printed PhD thesis, 1958), p. 83.

[94] Alter, 'O'Connell's impact on the organisation and development of German political Catholicism', p. 114.

Der Harfner is ein alter Mann,
Doch blitzt sein Auge hell;
Kennt ihr ihn nicht als König Dan,
So nenn[e]t ihn O'Connell.
Grün Erin ist die Harfe sein,
Und meisterhaft sein Spiel,
Voll durch der Treuen dichte Reihn
Erschallt sein Lied: 'Repeal!'[95]

But in the end the continental political environment of the time made it impossible to translate O'Connell's particular marriage of Catholicism and liberalism into a dominant European force. In the first place, continental state power functioned very differently from the modes characteristic of the contemporary United Kingdom. In the second place, too many continental liberals despised Catholicism (and often, indeed, religion generally), while too many Catholics (and especially ecclesiastics) despised liberalism. And in this latter respect, it is, for example, notable that even so *theologically* advanced a figure as Ignaz von Döllinger deeply disapproved of O'Connell's repeal campaign because, just like Metternich, he feared the revolutionary potential of mass movements of any kind.[96]

In Ireland, however, O'Connell's pioneering agenda created resonances at once powerful, lasting, and unexpected. No observer of the Irish scene in 1800 could possibly have foreseen the manner in which O'Connell would succeed in galvanizing the Catholic people of Ireland into mass political action along constitutional and fundamentally reformist lines. And this in a country at the edge of Europe: poor, rural, in many ways backward, and occupying a distinctly inferior and ancillary position within a wider polity which many of its inhabitants regarded as at best alien, at worst oppressive.[97] By making use of the unique place which Catholicism occupied in Ireland, by playing so skilfully upon his own cultural affinities with those he sought to represent, by furnishing a politics of both spectacle and organization, O'Connell was able to introduce into Irish life a tradition of popular, non-violent, and constitutional action that was as novel as it was to prove significant. And he did all this by the deployment of what were, in conception at least, fundamentally pre-romantic ideas of individual rights and individual liberties. The critic Walter Benjamin once described the nineteenth-century *Bildungsroman* as 'integrating the social process with the development of a

[95] Ibid. p. 114: 'The harpist is an old man,/ But his eye still flashes brightly;/ If you don't recognize him as King Dan,/ Then call him O'Connell./ Green Erin is his harp,/ And masterly his playing,/ Right through the dense ranks of the true/ His song resounds "Repeal!"'
[96] Grogan, *The noblest agitator*, pp. 21–2.
[97] K. T. Hoppen, 'A double periphery: Ireland within the United Kingdom, 1800–1921' in H.-H. Nolte, ed., *Europäische innere Peripherien im 20. Jahrhundert*, Historische Mitteilungen im Auftrag der Ranke-Gesellschaft: Beiheft 23 (Stuttgart, 1997), pp. 95–111.

person'.[98] For his part, O'Connell was able to integrate the social and economic processes of early nineteenth-century Ireland into a new form of politics by, in effect, integrating them first into his own unique and extraordinary personality.

[98] W. Benjamin, *Illuminations*, ed. H. Arendt (London, 1970), p. 88 ('The Storyteller'). I was led to Benjamin by a reference in R. F. Foster, *The story of Ireland: an inaugural lecture delivered before the University of Oxford on 1 December 1994* (Oxford, 1995), p. 5.

1848:
Reform or Revolution in Germany and Great Britain

PETER WENDE

THE TITLE OF MY PAPER points to the two questions I want to address. The first is: are events in Britain and Germany in the year 1848 at all comparable? The second is: how does the revolution of 1848 relate to the concept of reform? The two questions are linked. As most textbooks will tell you, one cannot compare England and Germany in the year of the European revolution of 1848 because of the gulf that separates reform and revolution. Just as Russia on the eastern fringe of the continent was not affected by revolutionary upheaval because its backwardness did not yet provide the soil on which revolutionary forces can grow, so, on the western periphery, England had already taken the highroad of reform and was on a *Sonderweg* which rendered revolution superfluous, whereas the continent was once again lost in the chaos of revolution. Thus in his famous article 'Why was there no revolution in England in 1830 or 1848'[1] George Rudé concludes that this question is not actually worth asking. And in the latest book on *The European revolutions, 1848–1851* by Jonathan Sperber even the index does not mention Chartism.[2]

But, on the other hand, the whole argument can be turned round. Some modern scholars such as John Saville and David Goodway[3] argue that in England Chartism represented a revolutionary potential which has been underestimated and that Chartists intended a revolution which was pre-vented at the last minute by determined government action. According to this view the London events of 10 April 1848 form a link in the chain of that

---

[1] George Rudé, 'Why was there no revolution in England in 1830 or 1848', in Manfred Kossok, ed., *Studien über die Revolution* (Berlin, 1969), pp. 231–44.

[2] Jonathan Sperber, *The European revolutions, 1848–1851* (Cambridge, 1994).

[3] See John Saville, *1848: the British state and the Chartist movement* (Cambridge, 1987); David Goodway, *London Chartism 1838–1848* (Cambridge, 1982).

Proceedings of the British Academy, **100**, 145–157. © The British Academy 1999.

year's revolutionary uprisings, even though this was nipped in the bud. Unfortunately I have not the time to draw a detailed comparison between the events of 18 March in Berlin and of 10 April in London, when the military state of Prussia acknowledged defeat by the masses, whereas in Britain, where the slogan 'No Standing Armies' was still widely accepted, government was able to quell the threat of revolution by the mere threat to put superbly organized armed force into action.

In any case, there can be no doubt that when Chartists resumed their campaign in 1847–49 and again presented their six points in a new mass petition, they were in fact presenting revolutionary aims and demanding the introduction of mass democracy. Not only in the view of conservative contemporaries did Chartism stand for the threat of the red revolution,[4] but Friedrich Engels also observed, in his book on the *Condition of the working class in England*, that 'These six points, which are all limited to the reconstitution of the House of Commons, harmless as they seem, are sufficient to overthrow the whole English constitution, Queen and Lords included'.[5] And in 1848, Chartists as well as government and establishment felt that they were caught up in the maelstrom of the continental revolution.

'France has the Republic, England shall have the Charter' ran the Chartists' national slogan and the Halifax Chartists let their resolution culminate in the threat: 'Should this measure of justice be much longer withheld, nothing can prevent the people from aspiring after...a similar change in the constitution to that which the French people have so recently obtained'.[6] And though it will always be a matter of dispute to what extent those threats of revolution were actually based on a determination to take firm direct and even violent action, they provided ample reason to arouse the fears of the middle classes and cause them to close ranks with a government which made more than adequate preparations against any possible violence in the streets of London. Apart from the riots of 6 March in London and Glasgow, in which five people were killed, the Chartists' demonstrations of 1848 were the most striking repercussion in Britain of the revolutionary movement on the continent. When contemporaries such as Robert Peel were 'considering the events that are taking place in foreign countries, and considering the excited state of the public mind at home',[7] they argued that England was on the brink of revolution. And consequently, when the demonstration of 10 April did not come off and it became evident that the greatest mass movement of the nineteenth century had ended in failure,

---

[4] See Gareth Stedman Jones, 'The language of Chartism', in James Epstein and Dorothy Thompson, eds., *The Chartist experience* (London, 1982), p. 3.
[5] Saville, *1848*, p. 214.
[6] Dorothy Thompson, *The Chartists* (London, 1984), pp. 311f.
[7] Commons Debate, 7 June 1848, *Hansard*, 3rd. ser., XCVIII (1848) cols. 20f.

Prince Albert wrote next day to Baron Stockmar, 'We had our revolution yesterday, and it ended in smoke'.[8]

Of course, historians more or less unanimously agree — which in itself is quite a noteworthy fact — that there existed neither cause nor chance for a successful revolution in Britain in 1848. But there was a scenario of widespread fear, a heightened awareness of lurking danger so common on the eve of revolutions, that it remains legitimate to ask 'why was there no revolution in Britain in 1848?' — the more so, as the revolutions on the continent without exception also ended in failure.

On the other hand — and this is the second point I want to make — one might compare Britain and Germany because what actually happened in Germany was not a revolution but rather a widespread powerful movement for reform.

It is a commonplace that German liberals, the driving force behind the events of 1848, abhorred revolution; at most they were unwilling revolutionaries. They demanded change, even fundamental change, but it had to be achieved by peaceful means. Especially after having witnessed terror and bloodshed in the wake of the French Revolution, the only form of drastic change they would accept was by 'revolution from above' as proclaimed and partly put into practice by Hardenberg and the rest of the Prussian reformers. Revolution 'as fundamental change against the will of the ruling power',[9] even brought about by sedition and rebellion, by violence 'from below', was not on the political agenda of middle-class liberalism. So when in March 1848 violence did break out and blood was shed, especially in Vienna and on the barricades of Berlin, the immediate aim of the liberals who now took over in the states and who formed the majority in newly elected assemblies was the containment of revolution or rather, to 'overtake revolution by the way of reform'.[10] Thus the Prussian liberal Friedrich Harkort exclaimed, full of indignation and in spite of what had happened on the streets of Berlin: 'We — revolution; we in Prussia! This is absolutely impossible. We in Prussia want a peaceful, popular reform and a liberal constitution, but by no means a revolution'.[11] And later on, during the great debate of the Paulskirchen Assembly on the installation of a German provisional government in June 1848 which at the same time was a debate on the consequences of the German revolution, Friedrich Daniel Basserman declared: 'We have no tabula rasa in Germany, but we have given conditions [*gegebene Verhältnisse*] and the

---

[8] Saville, *1848*, p. 126.

[9] See below, p. 153.

[10] See Helga Grebing, *Der deutsche Sonderweg in Europa, 1806–1945* (Stuttgart, 1986), p. 90.

[11] Ibid.: 'Wir Revolution? Wir in Preußen? Das ist ganz unmöglich. Wir wollen in Preußen friedliche, volkstümliche Reform und liberale Verfassung, aber unter keinen Umständen Revolution.'

essential thing is to reform, not to revolutionize'.[12] After the two great national assemblies in Frankfurt and Berlin had finally gathered in May, revolution was at most discussed, but not made, and the majority always decided in favour of reform, as it had already done in the preparatory assembly (*Vorparlament*) on 31 March when the attempts of some radicals to perpetuate revolution by installing a revolutionary government had been stalled by an overwhelming liberal majority.

To the same extent to which liberalism dominated political thought and political action during 1847–8, the concept of reform was at the heart of politics and provided the dominant topic of contemporary political discourse. This holds true even if we turn to the left: that is, the minority of democrats and republicans who advocated radical change of political constitution and thorough social reforms, whose programme was the equivalent of the People's Charter in Britain.

Here, especially for the disciples of Hegel such as Karl Marx and Arnold Ruge, revolution in principle ranked high on their agenda. Their philosophy of history defined revolution as the key element of progress, as the often violent readjustment and bringing together of disparate historical developments at different levels. Thus, according to Arnold Ruge, revolution was, 'die äußerliche Darstellung der Rückkehr des Bewußtseins aus der Entfremdung des Geistes in sein präsentes Selbstbewußtsein'.[13] ('The outward representation of the return of awareness from the alienation of the spirit to its present self-awareness'.) And Julius Fröbel in his important book on the 'System of social politics' coined the gripping formula: 'Die Revolution hat recht, die Reaktion hat unrecht, die Revolution ist rechtmäßig, die Reaktion ist unrechtmäßig — denn die Revolution ist der Fortschritt.'[14] ('Revolution is right, reaction is wrong, revolution is legitimate, reaction is illegitimate — for revolution is progress'.)

But, on the other hand, Fröbel concedes that the legitimacy of revolution does not imply that it will not lead to disaster in the end because the lessons taught by history do not confirm the conclusions drawn by theoretical deduction. The experience of 'the cursed French Revolution'[15] in particular has dashed beyond repair all the hopes placed in revolution in general. Thus even the democrats on the left hold conflicting views concerning revolution,

[12] Franz Wigard, ed., *Stenographischer Bericht über die Verhandlungen der deutschen constituierenden Nationalversammlung* (9 vols, Frankfurt/Main, 1848–9), I, p. 381 (19 June 1848): 'Wir haben keine tabula rasa in Deutschland, wir haben gegebene Verhältnisse und es gilt zu reformieren und nicht zu revolutionieren.'

[13] Arnold Ruge, *Gesammelte Schriften*, (10 vols, Mannheim, 1846), III, p. 465.

[14] Julius Fröbel, *System der sozialen Politik* (2 vols. Mannheim, 1847), I, pp. 110f.

[15] Ludwig Bamberger in *Mainzer Zeitung* (30 March 1848), cited in Peter Wende, 'Der Revolutionsbegriff der radikalen Demokraten', in Wolfgang Klötzer, ed., *Ideen und Strukturen der deutschen Revolution 1848* (Frankfurt/Main, 1974), p. 65.

the more so as revolutions are to be made and accomplished from below, by the common people who, at present, are not to be trusted to meet the demands which the course of history makes on them. In 1848 only a minority of that minority, men such as Friedrich Hecker and Gustav Struve called for direct action and tried to accelerate the revolutionary progress by not only proclaiming, but taking up arms for, a German republic.

The majority of the left also took the way of reform, though they were not in step with the liberals. They often called for more drastic measures and though they refrained from revolutionary action, they were always prepared to invoke revolution, to 'talk swords and daggers'[16] as Ruge called it, in order to press successfully for more and decisive reforms. The closest the national assemblies in Berlin and Frankfurt came to revolution was when they debated whether they should, as a formal pledge to revolution, put that revolution on record — I will come back to this later. The fact that even these modest attempts at revolution were blocked by liberal majorities puts the whole story of the German revolution into a nutshell.

Anyone who talks of the failure of the German revolution should bear in mind that there were hardly any revolutionaries in 1848, and that revolution had not been put on the agenda by the overwhelming majority of the political opposition which was at most prepared to invoke revolution in order to press on with reform.

And at the same time, wherever and whenever revolution raised its head, it was sought to contain and canalize it by reforms. Friedrich Daniel Bassermann made this point when he told the Paulskirchen Assembly that in April, after the session of the preparatory assembly and the appointment of the Committee of the Fifty, the right to revolution had been lost and the duty to reform had begun.[17]

Obviously the political discourse of the German revolution is dominated by the concept of reform to such a degree that we need to define it more carefully by asking to what extent its close relationship with the concept of revolution may have changed its meaning or perhaps even tainted its essence.

I cannot possibly give a complete history of the concept of reform here and I need not do so, because this has already been done[18] — though one might add that further work needs to be done in this field. Instead I intend to concentrate on 1848 and the years leading up to it. But in order to do this, and to discover shifts and changes of meaning, let me first outline once again

[16] See Arnold Ruge, ed., *Anekdota zur neuesten deutschen Philosophie und Publizistik* (2 vols, Zürich, 1843), II, p. 15.

[17] Wigard, *Sten. Ber.*, I, p. 1417:'[hat] das Recht der Revolution aufgehört und die Pflicht der Reform begonnen'.

[18] See mainly, Eike Wolgast, 'Reform, Reformation', in Otto Brunner, Werner Conze and Reinhart Koselleck, eds, *Geschichtliche Grundbegriffe, Historisches Lexikon zur politisch– sozialen Sprache in Deutschland* (9 vols, Stuttgart, 1972–97), V, pp. 313–60.

the essence of the concept of reform in the late eighteenth and early nineteenth century.

As in the case of the term 'revolution', new and different meanings of the word 'reform' signal the fundamental change which affected political and social thought and discourse around the middle of the eighteenth century, thus providing further evidence for the epoch-making importance of what Reinhart Koselleck has labelled 'die Sattelzeit', that is the great turning point in modern European history. Originally both terms under discussion here implied a return to the past, revolution in the form of a circular movement, reform in the sense of a reformation, that is the restoration or renewal of past conditions. During the eighteenth century, in the wake of a new understanding of the course of history, the terms 'revolution' and 'reform' began to imply special modes of change in the realm of law, constitution, or society, in the context of history conceived as the unfolding of evolution and progress. But as with so many other notions and ideas, the concept of reform was redefined in the light of the experience of the French Revolution. Reform now came to stand more or less for the opposite of revolution. 'Reforms, but no revolutions' Ludwig Schlözer admonished his compatriots in 1793,[19] and especially in England, since Burke's criticism of the events taking place in France, reform had become the conservative alternative to revolutionary change and upheaval. This finally led to the standard textbook comparison between the revolutionary anarchy of France and Britain as the model for the success of reform.

Thus the list of meanings and connotations of the term 'reform' comprises: change, especially gradual change without violence from below, initiated from above in order to adapt laws and constitutions to changing conditions, in order to achieve necessary improvements, and all to prevent the abrupt and fundamental change, brought about by violence from below, which is the essence of revolution.

But as soon as one takes a closer look at the thick web of meanings of the concept of reform, especially during the period of the 'Vormärz' in Germany, such simple attributions of certain words to certain matters no longer hold, but dissolve into a complicated pattern of convergent and divergent lines.

Though as a rule reform is seen as the opposite of revolution, at the same time a strong affinity between reform and revolution can be registered, until both concepts seem to merge. To give just one example, let me quote from the speech which the student Karl Heinrich Brüggemann gave in his defence at his trial where he stood accused of preaching sedition at the Hambach Rally in 1832: 'Deutschland will und muß eine Revolution haben; zeigt das Volk

---

[19] August Ludwig Schlözer, *Allgemeines Staatsrecht und Staatsverfassungslehre* (Göttingen, 1793), p. 162, quoted in Wolgast, 'Reform', p. 343.

sich entschieden, so ist es befähigt, seine Revolution gesetzlich durchzuführen, wie es eben England tut'.[20] ('Germany wants a revolution and must have it. If the people is determined, then it is capable of carrying out its revolution lawfully, as England is doing'.) Again and again liberals of a more radical disposition, such as Karl von Rotteck for example, when demanding reform instead of revolution were actually advocating revolution in the guise of reform. Radical change, even radical change in the realm of the constitution, was to be brought about by lawful means. On the other hand, reforms, even those initiated by princes like Joseph II, have been judged revolutionary, by contemporaries as well as by historians. Legal reform was supposed to take on the task of illegal revolution whenever reform was announced as 'eine Revolution im guten Sinn'.[21]

The German revolution of 1848, as a movement for reform, must be seen and judged as the result of this close relationship between reform and revolution during the *Vormärz*. Since the French Revolution it had become a commonplace argument that reform and revolution actually served the same end: the adaptation of laws and constitutions to changed conditions. Therefore they differed only in *how* necessary change was brought about, and it was widely accepted that timely reforms would render revolutions unnecessary, whereas thwarted or even delayed reforms were sure to cause revolutionary upheaval. Karl Heinrich Ludwig Pölitz put it into a nutshell when he argued in 1823 'daß den meisten, wo nicht allen, Revolutionen durch zeitgemäße Reformen hätte vorgebeugt werden können' ('that most, if not all, revolutions could have been prevented by timely reforms') and more than fifty years later the economist Gustav Schmoller maintained: 'Der ganze Fortschritt der Geschichte besteht darin, an die Stelle der Revolution die Reform zu setzen'.[22] ('Progress in history consists entirely in putting reform in the place of revolution'.)

As soon as this argument was taken up by those who actually favoured revolution, certain essentials of the classic concept of reform were not only left out but even changed. Whereas the reforms at the beginning of the century, which Wehler for example has labelled acts of defensive modernization, were measures inaugurated by governments in order to prevent further change which might endanger the sovereignty of the rulers, during the *Vormärz* the call for reform could stand for aggressive modernization, for the attempt to force rulers into conceding far-reaching, even fundamental reforms under the threat of impending revolution.

[20] Cited in Reinhart Koselleck, 'Revolution', in Brunner, Conze and Koselleck, eds, *Geschichtliche Grundbegriffe*, v, p. 746.
[21] Hardenberg's 'Rigaer Denkschrift' (12 September 1807), in Georg Winter, ed, *Die Reorganisation des Preußischen Staates unter Stein und Hardenberg* (2 vols, Leipzig, 1931), i, p. 306.
[22] Cited in Koselleck, 'Revolution', pp. 752f.

Now reforms were no longer to be initiated from above, but brought under way by pressure being exerted from below. At the same time a new element was introduced into the discussion of reform politics: the principle of agreement ('das Prinzip der Vereinbarung'), in other words reforms were no longer to be one-sided acts by the government, executed without public debate, but negotiated between the ruler and his subjects, or rather the representatives of his people. Characteristically the official title of the Prussian National Assembly was 'Versammlung zur Vereinbarung der Preußischen Staatsverfassung' ('Assembly for the Agreement of the Prussian Constitution'). Here constitutional change on a grand scale was to be achieved by 'transaction between the crown and the people', as the Prussian minister Hansemann called it.[23]

But political negotiations always take place in the context of power politics, especially when a shift of sovereignty is put on the agenda, as in 1848 when German states were expected to become part of a new nation-state and rulers were expected to share power with their subjects. This was the dilemma of the liberal majorities in the assemblies. The power they could draw upon was the power they had renounced, because it was the power of revolution. On the other hand, the democratic minorities, which gained strength in the course of the events, at least tried to invoke the threat of revolution. They tried to conjure up that alternative to reform in order to press on for fundamental change by agreement. This was the difference, and the contest which lay behind the often passionate debates on the range of the revolution which had taken place in the days of March.

The great example for this was set by the Berlin Assembly, when it discussed the motion proposed by the left: 'Die hohe Versammlung wolle in Anerkennung der Revolution zu Protokoll erklären, daß die Kämpfer des 18. und 19. März sich wohl um das Vaterland verdient gemacht haben.'[24] ('In recognition of the revolution, the assembly wishes to have it put on record that the fighters of 18 and 19 March rendered the fatherland great service.') The proposers of this motion also wanted to stress that the assembly was the child of revolution and that its existence implied the recognition of the revolution[25] and of the sovereignty of the people, whereas their liberal opponents maintained that the rights of the people and the existence of the National Assembly were the result of an act of grace by the king. In the heat of this debate Riedel, a liberal member of the assembly, stated the true point at issue: 'We all know: revolution is constitutional change taking place

---

[23] *Verhandlungen der Versammlung zur Vereinbarung der Preußischen Staats–Verfassung* (2 vols, Berlin, 1848), I, p. 160.

[24] Ibid., p. 156.

[25] Ibid. 'Die Versammlung selbst ist aus dieser Revolution hervorgegangen, ihr Dasein ist also faktisch die Anerkennung der Revolution.'

against the will of the ruling power whereas reform means change taking place with the assent of that power'.[26] The left resorted to revolution at least in order to enforce a one-sided bargain in their favour, trying to assume the position of the victor who dictates the terms of the treaty. The liberals also wanted a 'fundamental change in the constitution to take place; but for the reformation to take effect only through conviction acted upon conviction, within the law and without the use of violence' ('daß eine prinzipielle Änderung der Verfassung stattfindet, aber die Art und Weise, wie die Reformation wirkt, ist keine andere, als die, durch die lebendige Überzeugung auf die lebendige Überzeugung, innerhalb der Formen des Gesetzes und ohne Anwendung materieller Gewalt').[27]

To achieve fundamental constitutional change by negotiating an agreement with their sovereigns: this was the essential aim of liberals during what has been called the German revolution.

I should now like to put three final questions: Though revolution foundered, did reform also end up in failure? If so, what were the reasons for the failure of reform? And can the failure of German reformers and of British Chartists be compared, and can any conclusions be drawn from this which could help us define some limits for reform in general?

In Germany Manfred Hettling has recently argued that though revolution in 1848 was to prove an illusion, reforms were actually achieved. In most of the German states, especially those which already had constitutions and popular assemblies, non-violent demonstrations achieved 'reform without revolution' (this is the title of Hettling's important book on Württemberg during the *Vormärz* and the revolution).

Popular liberal governments, the so-called 'March ministries' were installed, liberty of the press was granted, the emancipation of the rural population (*Bauernbefreiung*), begun during the Napoleonic era and then often interrupted, was finally completed. And one could go further than Hettling and argue that even where revolution failed and reaction triumphed, as was the case in Berlin, reform on a grand scale was achieved by the the installation of the Prussian constitution in December 1848, whose original version did hardly differ from what liberals had put on their constitutional agenda.

But this was not the result of deliberations and transactions, not reform by way of mutual agreement (*Vereinbarung*), but by way of octroi simply imposed from above. It was not the outcome of a bargain between two parties, not a compromise, as finally became obvious during the constitutional crisis of 1862.

---

[26] Ibid. p. 166. 'Revolution ist eine Staats–Veränderung, welche gegen den Willen der herrschenden Gewalt geschieht, und Reform ist eine Staats–Veränderung, welche mit dem Willen der herrschenden Gewalt geschieht, das wissen wir Alle.'
[27] Ibid.

Revolution foundered in Germany in 1848. Events were dominated by the concept of reform — but revolution was not the only illusion. There was also the illusion of reform. As soon as the heart of the matter was touched, as soon as the question of sovereignty was raised, reform by agreement had to turn out to be an illusion. Fundamental constitutional change was to be the touchstone of the strength and depth of the reform movement and whenever this question was raised, sovereigns remained adamant in their rejection of any compromise.[28] And this was also to contribute heavily not only to the failure of constitutional reform in the member states of the German Federation, but also to the failure of the national revolution; in other words: the foundation of a German nation-state which would have more or less abolished the sovereignty of the thirty-something German princely rulers.

The hope of being able to compromise on sovereignty, and to divide supreme political power evenly between the ruler and his popular assembly would prove to be the illusion of reformers which led to the failure of reform in 1848.

But — and this is my second point — this kind of failure was not accidental. It was the outcome of an attempt to achieve certain aims by inadequate means. Or, rather, it was a failure that resulted from attempts to ignore the limits of reform. And this, at the same time, was the consequence of that peculiar concept of reform which equated reform with revolution minus violence, and which argued that revolution might be replaced by reform.

The illusion of achieving revolution by reform sprang from an inadmissible mixture of aims and means, from the belief that as long as one adhered to the principle of non-violent change, even radical measures could be put through.

It was the radicals who clearly saw that revolution was doomed to failure as soon as it switched to reform, and it was this idea which underlay their efforts at least to ensure the recognition of the principle of revolution by formal declarations, to establish a reign, not of revolutionary terror, but of revolutionary rhetoric. And it was Karl August Varnhagen von Ense, the liberal essayist of the *Vormärz*, who, now at the age of 63, made this point in a running commentary in his diaries. On 19 May he noted: 'Deutschland scheint nicht zu retten als durch den Sturmschritt auf dem Wege der Revolution. Wer weiß, ob wir nicht bald bedauern müssen, daß Struve und Hecker gescheitert sind'. ('It seems that Germany cannot be saved except by

---

[28] See Wolfram Siemann, *Die Revolution von 1848 in Deutschland* (Frankfurt/Main, 1985), p. 226: 'Kein Herrscher der führenden deutschen Staaten war willig zu einem konstitutionellen Kompromiß auf der demokratischen Basis von 1848.' And Hettling has to concede the same even for Württemberg (Manfred Hettling, *Reform ohne Revolution: Bürgertum, Bürokratie und kommunale Selbstverwaltung in Württemberg, 1800–1850* (Göttingen, 1990), p. 191).

revolution on the double. Who knows — we might soon regret that Struve and Hecker failed'.) One month later (17 June): 'Jeden Tag wird es klarer, daß der König nur dem Zwange nachgeben hat, daß er beschämt und ergrimmt darüber ist, daß er die Richtung, die er zu halten versprochen hat verwünscht und haßt'. ('Every day it emerges more clearly that the king has merely given way to pressure, that he is humilated and infuriated, that he curses and hates the direction which he has promised to take'.) Again, four weeks later (10 July): 'Die Sachen gehen einen schlimmen Weg. Die Einheit der Deutschen wird nicht mit und bei den Fürsten zustandekommmen. Nur das Volk allein kann sie bewirken und genießen. Ob das aber ohne die Fürsten zu handeln versteht, reif dazu ist?' ('Things are taking a bad turn. German unification will not be achieved with and by the princes. The people alone can effect it. But can the people act without the princes, is it mature enough?') And finally, on 12 August: 'Bei uns zeigt sich diesmal recht, daß unsere Revolution keine ganze war.'[29] ('This time it has become crystal clear that our revolution was not a proper one.')

And as my final witness I again call on Manfred Hettling, the advocate of 1848-reform, when he concedes: 'Da eine Revolutionierung der Verhältnisse abgelehnt wurde, war auch die Reform ohne Revolution zum Scheitern verurteilt.'[30] ('As a revolutionizing of conditions was rejected, reform without revolution was also condemned to failure.')

Whereas the replacement of revolution by reform could easily prove to be an illusion, on the other hand revolution and reform might get on very well together. Quick, radical, and fundamental change cannot be brought about by peaceful reforms; but the achievements of revolutions, if they are to last, must be cast into the mould of legal reforms, because, as Hegel observed, 'Revolution cannot last without reform'.[31]

Though I have mainly concentrated on some aspects of reform and revolution in 1848 Germany, I would, nevertheless, like to make some attempt to compare the failure of reform movements in Britain and Germany, even though, on closer inspection, striking differences seem to render every comparison futile. At a very general level one might argue that in both cases attempts were made to enforce rapid and radical political and constitutional change by way of reform. Both movements foundered because the policy of reform aimed at targets beyond what might be called the limits or boundaries of reform. In both cases the reigning sovereign was expected to assent to a transfer of power which would affect the constitutional framework and *de facto* revolutionize the political system.

[29] Karl August Varnhagen von Ense, *Journal einer Revolution. Tagesblätter 1848/49* (Nördlingen, 1986), pp. 149, 165, 173, 185.

[30] Hettling, *Reform*, p. 211.

[31] See Heinz Monhaupt, ed., *Revolution, Reform, Restauration*, (Frankfurt/Main, 1988), p. 6.

In England the movement miscarried in the teeth of resolute and unanimous resistance of the political nation in Parliament and outside Parliament where more than 100,000 special constables put on an intimidating display of force on behalf of the establishment. In Germany the movement miscarried because it lost its initial unanimity and resolution when facing the threat of revolution and thus opened up chances for the sovereign powers of the *ancien régime* to initiate their policies of defensive reforms and political reaction. In Britain, moreover, those resisting the claims of the Chartists could point to a whole catalogue of successful reforms, thereby demonstrating that Parliament was always 'ready to act according to the enlightened opinion of the people', as Lord Russell argued, when he spoke against a further extension of the franchise in June 1848.[32] It was not to be no further reform, but only no further reform *now*, because, it was argued, the Chartists did not represent the majority of the people. Not only the great Reform Act of 1832, but also the Factory Acts as well as the repeal of the Corn Laws, testified to the fact that within the framework of the British constitution there were ample means 'to introduce those changes which the "great innovator Time" has rendered expedient'.[33] Thus the failure of the Chartists and the failure of German revolutionaries and reformers was of a different quality. In Germany the actual transfer of political power to the nation had still to take place and would finally be brought about only by 'blood and iron', by the wars of unification and the First World War and revolution. In England, by contrast, since the end of the seventeenth century, political modernization had meant adapting parliamentary representation to the changing scope of the political nation. In this respect the debate on extending the franchise in the House of Commons on 6 July 1848 was most revealing. Nearly everyone consented that this had to take place as soon as the majority of the people were to press for it because Parliament, it was stressed, is nothing but the agent of the people. As the advocate for further reform, Osborne, put it: 'In fact . . . all are for progress now-a-days; the only question appears to be, what is to be the pace, and who the drivers of the new vehicle?'[34]

The many labels which can be attached to the nineteenth century certainly include that of reform. Because of continuous and often rapid change in many areas 'the great moving power of reform' becomes the essence of politics in order to adapt laws and institutions — as was pointed out in an article on reform in the *Edinburgh Review* of 1859. To remove abuses, to reorganize, to improve, to amend, to expand, to recast was to become the daily bread of politics to such an extent that nowadays reform is

[32] *Hansard*, 3rd ser., XCIX (20 June 1848), col. 930.
[33] 'Reform', *Edinburgh Review*, 109 (1859), col. 284.
[34] *Hansard*, 3rd. ser., C (6 July 1848), cols. 157f.

almost synonymous for politics. Nineteenth-century Britain already possessed the necessary framework for this process of adaptation which allowed the six points of the People's Charter to be put on the agenda of some future Parliament,[35] and which puts the failure of the Chartists into perspective: England's 'monarchy, limited as it is, is a republic under another name; and need not change its appelation in order to obtain universal suffrage, or after it has got it' as a 'Superior Spirit' put it in his *Reflections on the European revolution of 1848*, published in May of that year.[36] In Germany this framework had yet to be introduced. In Britain the failure of radical reform in 1848 meant the postponement of reform, in Germany the failure of reform meant waiting for a future revolution.

---

[35] See John Russell, *Hansard*, 3rd. ser., XCIX (20 June 1848), col. 930: 'I think that a time may come — perhaps it is not distant — when reform may be usefully introduced . . . for the improvement of the representation.'

[36] *Reflections on the European revolution of 1848, by a superior spirit* (London, 1848), pp. 180f.

The Idea of Reform in British Politics, 1829–1850*

DEREK BEALES

I

ALMOST ALL RECENT HISTORIANS of the period 1829 to 1850 habitually, and as a matter of course, describe many of its laws and its private initiatives as 'reforms'. The Reform Bill of 1832 always has a special place in their accounts, and the word 'Reform', standing alone and with a capital letter, is understood as meaning parliamentary reform; but the term is applied also without hesitation to measures such as Catholic emancipation, the Metropolitan Police Act, the abolition of slavery, the Irish Church Temporalities Act, the New Poor Law, the reduction of capital punishment, the Bank Charter Act, the repeal of the Corn Laws, the Ten Hours Act and the Public Health Act; and with these laws are commonly bracketed certain changes that were not imposed by parliament, especially in education, for example the churches' campaign to build schools and Cambridge University's partial modernization of its curriculum in 1850. Some of these laws and social developments are regularly referred to as 'social reforms'. Further, 'reform' in the singular, standing on its own and probably without a capital letter, is nowadays frequently used to embrace all these laws and developments, as in E. L. Woodward's volume in the old *Oxford history of England* entitled *The age of reform*.[1] In this formulation a sub-set of generalized reform is called 'social reform'.

When I agreed to give this paper, my intention was to discuss the idea of

* Most of the text of this paper and the main thrust of its argument remain unchanged since I delivered it to the Reform conference on 27 September 1997. But in the discussion after the paper it was pointed out that I had revealed almost complete ignorance of an important strand of the discourse on reform in my period, namely that of the Owenites. I am most grateful to Professor G. Claeys and Dr E. Royle, who not only made this point but proceeded, with great generosity, to pass on to me a number of references which have enabled me to take some account of this usage. See pp. 170–2 below. I also owe thanks to Dr J. P. Parry and Professor G. Stedman Jones, who kindly read and commented on earlier versions.
[1] 2nd edn, Oxford, 1962.

reform that inspired, influenced and was embodied in these various developments, and then to consider the relationship between the idea and the
reality of reform. But, as I read the sources of the period, I began to notice
that, in many contexts where modern historians naturally use the word
'reform', contemporaries did not. (Whenever I use 'contemporary' and
'contemporaries' in this paper, I shall always be referring to the period
between 1829 and 1850 and to persons who were alive at that time, and when
I use 'modern' I shall mean 'twentieth century'.) It became apparent that the
meaning of the word 'reform' had changed between the early Victorian
period and the present day, not totally, but significantly, and more than I had
realized. To my further surprise, I have not been able to find in the scholarly
literature any extended discussion of the *idea* or meaning of reform in its
application to Britain between 1829 and 1850, or indeed at other dates. I am
speaking of the idea of reform in general. There exists of course a large and
impressive corpus on the idea of parliamentary reform with special reference
to the Reform Bill of 1832,[2] and another one on the ideas that inspired and
influenced social reform.[3] What appears to be lacking is a survey of the
history of the concept of reform as employed in the English language
comparable with the discussion of German usage which is to be found in
the article 'Reform' in *Geschichtliche Grundbegriffe*.[4] You might expect to
find something in the *Encyclopaedia of the social sciences*. But the recent
version of that work offers no articles on any topics falling alphabetically
between 'Reference groups' and 'Refugees'. The version published in the
1930s is slightly more helpful: it contains an article 'Reformation' entirely
devoted to religion, followed by a brief article 'Reformism' by H. M. Kellen.
This latter piece begins reasonably enough, declaring for example that 'the
reformer operates on parts where the revolutionist operates on wholes'. But
it contains also this slashing passage:

> Sheer reformism [whatever that might be] ... goes, as a rule, with psychopathic
> traits of the personality, of the kind commonly to be observed in official and
> volunteer censors, in spelling reformers, in professional patriots, and in similar
> riders of hobbies which give the impression of being compulsive.[5]

[2] N. Gash, *Politics in the age of Peel* (London, 1953); M. G. Brock, *The Great Reform Act*
(London, 1973) and J. Cannon, *Parliamentary reform, 1640–1832* (Cambridge, 1973) remain
fundamental. Valuable recent discussions are I. Newbould, *Whiggery and reform, 1830–41*
(London, 1990) and J. Parry, *The rise and fall of Liberal government in Victorian Britain*
(London, 1993).
[3] Perhaps the most compendious general account is in J. P. C. Roach, *Social reform in England,
1780–1880* (London, 1978), though, like virtually every other discussion, it shows little interest in
contemporary usage of 'social reform'.
[4] O. Brunner, W. Conze and R. Koselleck, eds, *Geschichtliche Grundbegriffe* (8 vols, 1972–97), v
(1984), esp. pp. 340–60.
[5] R. A. Seligman, ed., *Encyclopaedia of the social sciences* (15 vols, London, 1930-5), XIII, pp.
194–5.

The best discussion that I know in English is the entry in Raymond Williams's *Keywords*, but it is only brief.[6] What I am going to try to do is to survey and characterize the idea of reform in contemporary usage and then to suggest some possible wider implications of my findings.

In the writings and speeches of the period 1829 to 1850 'reform', as now, was both noun and verb. Among its derivatives 'reformer' was common and 'reformist', with virtually the same meaning, fairly common; but 'reformism', according to the *Oxford English dictionary*, was unknown before the twentieth century, when it appeared in the context of debates within socialism.[7] 'Reform' was of course mentioned and discussed *ad nauseam* during the period, at least in certain contexts, and I have been able only to scratch the surface of the huge materials available. But I hope, on the basis of a limited selection of sources, and with the help of other scholars, to have arrived at a fair impression of contemporary usage, or at least to have reached the point where I can justifiably challenge some assumptions of modern writing.

My first and unsurprising conclusion is that, then as now, if the word was unqualified by an adjective or its context, and especially if it had a capital R, it almost invariably meant *parliamentary* reform, or at any rate constitutional reform; and people wishing to speak of other types of reform had to put an adjective in front of the word. From the time when the first Reform Bill was presented to the Commons in May 1831 the word 'Reform' often referred simply to that or to its aims and/or to its effects. I should make the obvious point that the phrase 'the Reform Bill', which has established itself permanently in the language, is an odd one. 'The Reform Bill' was never an official or accurate title. In the first place, there were separate bills for England and Wales, for Scotland and for Ireland, all of which became acts in 1832. The formula 'the Reform Bill' sometimes seems to refer to the whole package of the three acts and sometimes just to the act for England and Wales. This last, the most important and best known of the three acts, was headed 'An act to amend the representation of the people in England and Wales' — that is, 'the People' got in on the act, but 'Reform' did not — and the text talks of 'correcting divers abuses' and 'extending the Elective Franchise', but never of reform. The Scottish act of the same year has the title, 'Representation of the people (Scotland) act', and talks of amending

---

[6] R. Williams, *Keywords* (Glasgow, 1976), pp. 221–2. The growing literature on the use of political language in the period 1750–1850, though a stimulus to this sort of research, has not yet, so far as I know, seriously attacked 'reform'. See e.g. O. Smith, *The politics of language, 1791–1819* (Oxford, 1984); M. Weinzierl, *Freiheit, Eigentum und keine Gleichheit* (Munich, 1993); D. Wahrman, *Imagining the middle class: the political representation of class in Britain, c. 1780–1840* (Cambridge, 1995).

[7] It must surely have arrived a little sooner, as Williams suggests (ibid. p. 222), but in any case it is irrelevant to my paper.

that representation, but it too fails to mention reform. I have not, incidentally, found the word 'reform' in the title or text of any well-known
contemporary act of parliament.

Furthermore, the struggle for the bill loomed so large in people's minds
that the members of the parliamentary coalition formed by Earl Grey in 1830
between whigs of various kinds, former tories of various kinds and some Irish
and radical MPs were usually designated not by the old party names but as
Reformers. 'Reformer' clearly signified parliamentary reformer, supporter of
the Reform Bill, rather than an advocate of reform in a general sense —
though of course it is the case that persons in favour of the Reform Bill were
more likely to be proponents of further changes than were its enemies, that
many supporters of the bill confidently expected it to lead to other changes,
and that some supported it only for that reason. It was not until after the
break-up of the reforming ministry and coalition in 1834–5 that the term
'Liberal' gradually displaced 'Reformer' as the designation for the party as a
whole.[8]

The understanding that 'Reform' with a capital R continued to mean
parliamentary reform, especially the settlement of 1832, is also to be found in
modern usage. But the proportional weight of parliamentary reform in the
meaning of the word was much greater then than it is now, because, first,
there were many types of what we call reform that were seldom so styled by
contemporaries, and secondly, 'reform' in the singular was seldom or never
used on its own to embrace the full range of reforms. On the other hand,
'reform' was used, even in talking about parliamentary reform, relatively less
frequently and in a less broad sense than we would use it. The Six Points of
the Chartists are all parliamentary reforms to us, but they were rarely so
described by the Chartists, and then probably as 'Radical Reform'. The word
'reform' figures nowhere in their petition of 1842.[9] This is one of many
contexts where contemporaries seem to be deliberately avoiding the word.
They could easily do so, since they had at their disposal a vast battery of
alternative words which could mean something very like reform, many of
which we no longer employ in this sense. The commonest of all, I think, is
'improvement'; and Lord Briggs's title *The age of improvement*[10] is closer to
the language of the period than Woodward's *The age of reform*. But here is a
list of other words that I have found doing duty for what we call reform:
'amelioration', 'melioration', 'amendment', 'modification', 'correction',
'innovation', 'promotion', 'reformation', 'renovation', 'restoration',
'remedy', 'regulation', 'relaxation', 'relief', 'redress', 're-edification', 'regeneration', 'reconstruction', 'reorganization', 'restructuring'. Moving a little

[8] Parry, *Rise and fall of Liberal government*, pp. 130–1 and n. 11 on p. 353.
[9] Cf. D. Thompson, ed., *The early Chartists* (London, 1971), p. 55.
[10] London, 1959.

further away from the normal meaning of reform, there are 'repeal', 'removal', 'abridgment', 'concession', 'interference', 'intervention', and 'interposition'. Many of these words were applied to parliamentary reform, while some were appropriate only to other types of what we call reform. Here are just two examples: the Chartist petition of 1842, shunning 'reform', talks of 'amendment', 'remedy', and 'removal'; Disraeli in *Coningsby* normally treats 'reform' as something to deplore or scoff at, whereas changes that he applauds he calls 'reconstruction'.

To continue for a moment destructively, there are many other contexts in which I had expected 'reform' to be used and rarely or never found it. Sir George Cornewall Lewis's *Remarks on the use and abuse of some political terms*, a compilation with a high reputation in its day, has no discussion whatever of reform. Perhaps this is not so surprising in view of its other omissions, such as political parties, but the book was first published in the very year 1832.[11] I have looked again through many standard modern studies of what are now universally known as reforms — other than parliamentary. Their authors repeatedly call them so, but their quotations from contemporary sources seldom or never contain that word. This is true for example of S. E. Finer's *Life and times of Sir Edwin Chadwick*,[12] in which the author describes as reforms the changes which his subject promoted, factory regulation, the New Poor Law, public health legislation and so forth, but the sources he quotes hardly use the word. Chadwick himself rarely employed it, and the first use I have found of the phrase 'sanitary reform' is in *The Times* of 1847. The same applies to Royston Lambert on *Sir John Simon and English social administration*,[13] to David Roberts's *Victorian origins of the welfare state*[14] and to W. C. Lubenow's *The politics of government growth*.[15] In Lubenow's chapter on the New Poor Law, which he describes as a reform, he quotes no contemporary who gives it that appellation, while citing two who call it a revolution, Nassau Senior because

---

[11] Lewis's book has been reprinted with an introduction by C. F. Mullett (Columbia, 1970). I am grateful to one of those who came up to me after I had given my paper — I am sorry that in the *mêlée* I did not take a note of who it was — for a reference to D. Urquhart, *Familiar words as affecting the character of Englishmen and the fate of England* (London, 1855) and what amounts to its second, much expanded edition of 1856 entitled *The effect of the misuse of familiar words on the character of men and the fate of nations*. There is no entry for 'reform' in the first edition, but 'Reform and Remedy' occupies pp. 326–30 of the second. It is not so much an attempt to define reform as a violent attack on the movement for parliamentary reform: 'Reform and Remedy are terms antithetical... Reform was a delusion, and Reformers sycophants.' This no doubt represents in strident form the views of some radicals, but it seems not to merit discussion here, especially since it was published after the end of my period.

[12] London, 1952.

[13] London, 1963.

[14] New Haven, 1960.

[15] Newton Abbot, 1971. See for the next sentence pp. 39, 51.

he approves of it and Disraeli because he loathes it. The most remarkable instance I have found is J. T. Ward's *The factory movement*,[16] in which he classes the acts of 1833 and 1847, and other lesser or attempted measures, all as reforms, successful or failed as the case may be. But his numerous quotations virtually never do so. It is a frustrating characteristic of the literature that 'reform' is practically never indexed, but Ward's book is an exception: he supplies an index entry under each of the major participants, Fielden, Oastler and Shaftesbury, for their connection with 'industrial reform'. Scores of pages are cited in these entries, but on only one of them is a contemporary quoted as actually calling for 'reform'. This was the apocalyptic J. R. Stephens, who said in 1839: 'If they will not reform this, aye uproot it all, they shall have the revolution they so much dread' (p. 183). Even this reference is dubious, because it seems from the context that he might in fact have been thinking of the New Poor Law, or the situation of the poor in general, rather than of factories, as in need of 'reform'. Another activist did say in 1833: '[Factory regulation] will be [carried] by the People adopting the same means as ensured the passing of the Reform Bill, by an extensive combination of the physical and moral power of the PEOPLE' (p. 99). But that is neither to applaud the Reform Bill itself nor to identify factory legislation with reform. The most telling quotation of all is introduced by Ward with this sentence: 'Oastler urged that factory reform should dominate everything.' Yet this is what Oastler actually said: 'Don't be deceived! You will hear the cries of "No Slavery", "Reform", "Liberal principles", "No Monopoly", &c. But let your cries be — 'No Yorkshire Slavery", "No Slavery in any part of the Empire", "No factory mongers", "No factory monopolists". Thus, what Ward calls 'factory reform' is explicitly set by Oastler over against what he calls 'reform', which is seen as a deceiving, whig cry. The two organizations set up to fight for factory regulation were called the Factory Reformation Society and the National Regeneration Society. Neither *The Times* nor any of the great quarterlies published articles entitled 'factory reform', though they often addressed the problem under other headings. It cannot be accidental that 'reform' was so little used in this connection.

My final negative point concerns the phrase 'social reform'. Despite the freedom with which historians have applied it to the period, I have found no example of its use in what might be called upper-class discourse during these years. The first pamphlet in the British Library catalogue whose title contains the phrase was published in 1859 and called *Social versus political reform*. It urged that social reform should be treated as more important than the parliamentary reform bill that was before parliament at the time. Its idea of

[16] London, 1962.

social reform is clarified by its subtitle: *The sin of great cities; or, the great social evil, a national sin.* The only social problem it mentions as needing reform is prostitution. Not a word in the pamphlet suggests that the phrase 'social reform' has any other signification. According to the *Oxford English dictionary*, 'social evil' meant — and indeed still means — prostitution and nothing else. This was not entirely true even in my period,[17] but it was evidently natural to think in those terms in 1859.

II

Now I turn to the constructive side of my story. I shall begin by discussing an article published in *Blackwood's Magazine* early in 1831, evidently before the contents of the first Reform Bill were known; its title is 'Correction, Melioration, Reformation, Revolution'; and it was written by John Herman Merivale.[18] It is unique, so far as I have discovered, in that it discusses the concept of reform in general and compares it with related concepts. Despite the title, 'reform' is more frequently mentioned in it than 'reformation' and they are not really distinguished. The author claims that the four concepts of his title correspond to political options available at the moment. To 'correct' is merely to remedy some defects. To 'meliorate' or improve is to render some existing materials more useful. To reform implies belief in the existence of 'defects too deep-seated, too radically inherent, to be removed, without the previous destruction of that something to which they are attached', or that things 'are so essentially bad as to be incapable of any improvement'. It is wrong, he further claims, to use 'reform' except in the senses of 're-edification', 're-construction'. 'To reform . . . implies that there is something which has been, or must be, previously subverted.' 'Revolution', finally, involves violence and means 'total change in the fundamental laws and institutions of a nation.' What happened in 1688, therefore, was not a revolution, but presumably a reform.[19] This article appears to me exceptionally cool and objective both for its date and for the periodical it appeared in. While it would be absurd to suggest that all users of the word 'reform' had Merivale's fine distinctions in mind, I think it did have for many, especially in the early 1830s, the sense of the greatest change possible short of violent revolution. Further, the article brings out that the word still conveyed, as it

[17] I have found a work called *Social evils and their remedy* (2 vols, London, 1833), by C. B. Tayler, which recommends Christian faith as the remedy for many personal weaknesses, such as hobnobbing with trade unions.

[18] The article is in vol. 29, pp. 593–602. My authority for its authorship is the *Wellesley index of Victorian periodicals*, vol. III.

[19] See J. Burrow, *A liberal descent* (Cambridge, 1981), esp. ch. 2. This work, stimulating though it is, suffers from what seems to me the serious defect of never asking what contemporaries meant by the terms 'liberal' and 'whig'.

scarcely does now, the notion of a return to a pristine or better past. Just as successive church reforms or reformations claimed to revive the practices of the primitive church, so parliamentary reformers claimed that they wished to revert to an old system that had been less corrupt, perhaps in the late middle ages, perhaps in the reign of William III. In making these points Merivale seems to me to contribute to explaining the reluctance of contemporaries to bandy the word 'reform' about too freely, especially in contexts where the problem to be resolved was new, as with factories and the health of towns. The normal modern meaning of reform, a mere 'change for the better', without the implication that a former situation was being restored, had not yet become dominant.

Merivale seems to be thinking only of parliamentary or constitutional change. But the application of 'reform' to other fields had already begun. The titles of works in the British Library catalogue and of articles in the great quarterlies give a crude indication of this development. 'Economical reform' seems to have been forgotten by 1829. Radical reform, on the other hand, was a common expression. It is of course different in character from nearly all the other phrases I am going to cite, in that the adjective does not specify an area of reform but refers to the degree of extremism in advocating reform, meaning usually parliamentary reform. A number of articles appeared early in my period on aspects of law reform. Debate about church reform under that name dates back well before 1829, and in the early years of the period this was clearly the most frequently mentioned brand of reform other than parliamentary. 'Financial reform' is the title of a *Westminster Review* article of 1830 and an article in *Blackwood's* of the following year. But this appears to be the limit of the expansion of the term 'reform' before 1832.

It would be possible to spend a long time on the ideas behind the Reform Bill. I can hardly ignore them but, since historians have already discussed them so much,[20] I shall deal with them summarily. Almost all parliamentarians and persons of social standing regarded the measure proposed in May 1831 as, to say the least, far-reaching — radical with a small r. Its relationship to revolution was the subject of anguished discussion. Grey declared that 'the principle of my Reform is to prevent the necessity for revolution,'[21] and a large number of the bill's supporters echoed him. Brougham tried to sway the House of Lords to support the Reform Bill by urging them that this was the way to perpetuate the constitution.[22] Macaulay famously elaborated

---

[20] See the works cited in n. 3 above and the useful symposium on 'Political reform in Victorian England' in *Albion*, 12 (1980), esp. E. A. Wasson, 'The spirit of reform, 1832 and 1867', pp. 164–74.

[21] Quoted in Brock, *Great Reform Act*, p. 336.

[22] Quoted in E. P. Thompson, *The making of the English working class* (revised edn, Harmondsworth, 1968), p. 901.

the theme. The bill avoided giving 'any violent shock to the institutions of the country'. The constitution must be shown to have within it 'the means of self-reparation'.

> Then will England add to her manifold titles of glory this, the noblest and the purest of all — that every blessing which other nations have been forced to seek, and have too often sought in vain, by means of violent and bloody revolutions, she will have attained by a peaceful and a lawful reform.[23]

Much was said by ministers and their advocates about preserving the just role of the aristocracy, and much also about enfranchising the people, meaning the well-off and intelligent, the middle classes. The measure was certainly less radical than Radical Reformers with a capital R demanded: it did not bring household or manhood suffrage, the secret ballot, shorter parliaments, payment of members, equal electoral districts or the abolition of the House of Lords. On the other hand, any idea that the government was unwilling to make fundamental changes should be dispelled by the declaration of Jeffrey, minister in charge of the bill for Scotland, that 'no shred or rag, no jot or tittle [of the old system] was to be left' standing.[24] The bill's tory opponents said that it overstepped the bounds of reform and amounted itself to revolution, and some others who had supported it came to think it had been too extreme. Lord Fitzwilliam wrote in 1840: 'We have been through one revolution, for now that we can speak of these events historically, it is idle to call by any other name the events of 1830, 31 and 32'.[25] King Leopold of the Belgians declared to Queen Victoria in 1847 that, whereas in the 1830 Revolution in France 'they changed nothing but the dynasty, in 1832 England had abolished the very spirit of the old monarchy'.[26] For almost all the 'parliamentary classes' the Reform Bill was reform at its most extreme, teetering on the verge of revolution, perhaps actually going over the edge.

The drawing of the distinction between reform and revolution led naturally to a consideration of foreign relations and to comparisons such as Macaulay and Leopold drew between the experiences of Britain and of other countries. It was the excesses of the French Revolution that had evoked the coalition of Pitt and Portland in 1792–4 and persuaded many erstwhile reformers not to risk tampering with the British constitution, no doubt delaying reform for decades. The most conspicuous facet of the liberal toryism of the 1820s had been Britain's withdrawal from the congress system and her consequent readiness to support some rebellions against

[23] T. B. Macaulay, *Speeches parliamentary and miscellaneous* (2 vols, London, 1853), pp. 12, 75.

[24] Gash, *Politics in the age of Peel*, p. 38.

[25] J. T. Ward, ed., *Popular movements, c. 1830–1850* (London, 1970), p. 47.

[26] *Letters of Queen Victoria* (3 vols, London, 1908), II, p. 118: Leopold to Victoria, 15 January 1847, from the Tuileries. D. Southgate, *'The most English minister'... Palmerston* (London, 1966), p. 188.

established monarchs. The French revolution of 1830 had had some effect on
the parliamentary reform movement in England, making moderate change
look more necessary, but more containable and so less alarming. Another
article in *Blackwood's*, from the second half of 1833, is of particular interest
because it puts an extreme view contrary to that of the reformers, the sort of
view for which the magazine was notorious, about the relation between
reform and revolution in other countries. It is entitled 'Prussia, or the
progress of rational reform' and was written by George Moir, an acolyte
of Thomas Carlyle.[27] It takes up the theme of the reformers that only
constitutional change could stave off revolution and bring improvement,
an argument that they were now applying to the German situation. The
author, by contrast, maintains that the revolutions that have recently
occurred in German states have taken place precisely in those states where
constitutions have been established and concessions made. In Prussia, on the
other hand, where a wonderful series of rational reforms has been imposed
from above, neither constitution nor revolution has been found necessary.
The author thinks that the great error made by regimes is to allow parliaments the right to refuse taxation, 'the instrument of which popular
demagogues infallibly avail themselves in order to produce a crisis'. The
people are unwise to seek 'the boon of political power — fatal in general to
the wearer as the robe of Nessus.' In fortunate Prussia 'the mental and moral
character of her subjects' has been 'elevated' by benevolent rulers. Therefore
the entire whig theory of reform was false.

  This can have been the view of only a small minority in England, but
something like it was prevalent among ultra-tories. Such an article helps to
put into perspective the Tamworth manifesto — another topic of such
importance that it cannot be ignored, and yet hardly needs further elaboration from me.[28] As is well known, at the very end of 1834, after the king had
dismissed the government of reformers and put the tories, now renamed
Conservatives, in power, Peel announced in this address to his constituents
that he accepted the Reform Bill as a final settlement, that he was against
reform if it meant 'a perpetual vortex of agitation', but in favour of 'a careful
review of institutions, civil and ecclesiastical, undertaken in a friendly
temper', of 'the corrrection of proved abuses and the redress of real
grievances'. He spoke at length of his readiness to promote church reform
in England and Ireland in so far as it tended to enhance the efficiency of the
church establishment And he appealed to his own record of supporting
'judicious reforms', especially in the criminal law. Thus in his manifesto Peel
espoused almost every type of reform that had so far been christened. He not

[27] Vol. 34, pp. 55–71.
[28] See esp. N. Gash, *Reaction and reconstruction in English politics, 1832–55* (Oxford, 1965) and
R. W. Davis, 'Toryism to Tamworth: the triumph of reform', *Albion*, 12 (1980), pp. 132–46.

only tried to steal the whigs' clothes; he also repudiated the toryism of *Blackwood's*. If he was to be believed, reform was now bipartisan; and he did much to persuade people of his sincerity by collaborating with Melbourne's ministry in carrying municipal reform in 1835 after having secured important amendments to the government's plan.

However, the whigs, liberals, radicals and Irish MPs who made up Melbourne's following, which Russell wished to rename 'the Liberal Party', were not prepared to surrender their proprietary right to reform. The foundation of the Reform Club early in 1836 illustrates their attitude. The club was intended as a meeting-place for all supporters of Melbourne's government, and it became so; but it had been a liberal and radical rather than a whig initiative. It was called 'the Reform Club' after a previous attempt to found a 'Liberal Club' with virtually the same agenda had failed. The sole qualification for membership was to be 'proposed as a "Reformer" ' (capital R and inverted commas in the original). To count as a 'Reformer' it was only necessary to give general support to Melbourne's government, to be a 'Liberal'. There was no requirement to espouse any particular measure, and of course the party leadership had laid down that the act of 1832 was the final reform of Parliament. This minimal definition of 'Reformer' remained prominent for some years, and was enshrined in the rules and decisions of the club for at least half a century. So the word 'reformer', which in 1831 had been identified with advocacy of a bold measure of constitutional reform, seemed in this usage to have been shorn of ideological content and reduced to a mere party label.[29]

It appeared that, between them, the two great parties had rendered the concept of reform so narrow or anodyne that other words were called for to describe any proposals for significant change. But there was one group that persisted in propagating the notion of continuing reform, the utilitarians and radicals who ran the *Westminster Review*. In 1833 it published a piece on 'corporate reform', in 1834 one on 'Post Office reform', then in 1835 'municipal reform', and in 1837 'military reform'. Even for this group[30] there ensued a gap of eleven years before another new brand of reform was the subject of an article in 1848 — 'road reform'! Then in 1849, vindicating the *Encyclopaedia of the social sciences*, arrived 'spelling reform'. Other periodicals yield little in the way of novelties, from the *Quarterly* only 'Liturgical reform' of 1834, and from the *Edinburgh* 'Poor Law Reform' in 1841 (which was in fact a plea not to reform the New Poor Law), and two

---

[29] G. Woodbridge, *The Reform Club, 1836–1978* (New York, 1978), chs I–III and Appendix III. I am most grateful to the Librarian of the Reform Club, Mr Simon Blundell, for checking the text of the 1836 rules for me.

[30] But see e.g. W. Molesworth in *London and Westminster Review* 26 (1836–7), pp. 280–318, and J. S. Mill in *Westminster Review*, 32 (1839), pp. 476–7, demanding further reform.

articles on university reform in 1849. We have to go beyond the confines of the period to find in these periodicals essays on 'administrative reform', 'sanitary reform', and 'social reform'.

The unwillingness of the two main parties to support further fundamental reform after 1832, and the limitations of even the radicals' ideas of continuing reform, go far to explain the reluctance of the Chartists to adopt the term. Their entire programme was a rejection of the notion that the Reform Bill was a final settlement. Moreover, the harshness of the New Poor Law, which had done so much to rouse their indignation against the political system, had been deliberately willed at Westminster by a combination of Conservatives, liberals and radicals, among whom some radicals were particularly prominent and dogmatic. Advocates of factory regulation, too, had compelling reasons for avoiding the word 'reform', since self-consciously reforming radicals were their most fervent enemies, and tories who disliked the Conservative reformism of Peel were their most determined friends.

There was a further, less obvious reason why Chartists and agitators for factory regulation shied away from the concept. They had to contend with another quite different discourse of reform that flourished below the level of parliament, the quarterlies and *The Times*: that of Robert Owen and his followers.[31] As early as 1823 was published *A new theory of moral and social reform; founded on the principal and most general facts of human nature; or, essays to establish a universal criterion of moral truth . . . and to found thereon a plan of voluntary association and order . . . by a friend of the utmost reform.* Many later uses of the phrase 'social reform' in much the same sense can be found. Owen and his followers insisted that they intended to proceed by peaceful reform rather than by violent revolution, but they nonetheless sought a total change in society, the establishment of property-sharing communities, 'co-operation', and universal education to create a new morality. This was the core of what they meant by 'social reform', which was seen by them and others as virtually synonymous with 'socialism'. The movement was further identified, especially by its enemies, with hostility to the family, marriage, and religion. These views were considered totally impractical and deeply objectionable by many working-class activists as well as by the 'Establishment'. An editorial in Owen's *New Moral World* of 1837, anticipating the pamphlet of 1859 already discussed, explicitly contrasted '*Political versus social reform*', but used the phrase 'social reform' in a totally different sense:

> The Social Reformer proposes to take no wealth or privileges from any individual or bodies now in existence, but to purchase, borrow, and shortly

---

[31] This paragraph depends on material generously supplied to me by Professor G. Claeys and Dr E. Royle. See n. 1 above.

repay, the materials for creating new wealth for themselves and society at large. The Political Refomer proposes to abolish the privileges and distinctions now possessed by the most powerful portion of our fellow countrymen — to take and keep all the wealth they can under the system of individual accumulation, their aim being not to create new wealth, but to insure, according to their notions, the more equal distribution of that already in existence[32]

Whether radicals and Chartists would have accepted this categorization may be doubted, but most of them certainly wished to keep their distance from the Owenites. In particular, the pre-emption by the latter of the designation 'social reform' for their own programme would seem for a long time to have ruled out its use by other groups whose aims were different. A usage similar to that of the Owenites is to be found in French socialist writing,[33] at least by the 1840s, and it was in a work about French socialism by Lorenz Stein that the term *Sozialreform* was first used in German in 1850, again in a Utopian socialist spirit.[34] 'Social' had to shed this socialist identification — to be 'neutralized'[35] — before it could be employed, in conjunction with 'reform', to refer either in general or in particular to piecemeal measures concerning such matters as public health, housing, and the provision of amenities.

III

Three works that appeared in 1850 are of special significance in illustrating both the degree to which the application of reform had expanded and the limits of that expansion. The first was the second volume of Harriet Martineau's *History of England during the thirty years' peace, 1816–1846*, the volume relevant to my period. In it she wrote of 'the noble series of reforms' carried by the 'whig' governments of the 1830s (p. 79). She counted the New Poor Law as a reform since its aim 'was to restore the principle and revert to the operation of the Law of Elizabeth' (p. 89). She called Edwin Chadwick's work for public health an 'enterprise of reform' (p. 711), and spoke of the repeal of the Corn Laws as a 'great reform of policy' if 'an inferior order of reform' to the act of 1832 (p. 685). Factory legislation, of which she disapproved, was not honoured with the name of reform. Some of

---

[32] *New Moral World*, III, 24 June 1837, p. 285.

[33] L. Reybaud, *Études sur les réformateurs ou socialistes modernes: Saint-Simon, — Charles Fourier, — Robert Owen* (2 vols, Paris, 1844–5) both uses the phrase 'réforme sociale' himself and finds it in Fourier (vol. I, p. 413). I am grateful to Professor G. Stedman Jones for telling me of this book.

[34] L. Stein, *Geschichte der socialen Bewegung in Frankreich von 1789 bis auf unsere Tage* (3 vols, Leipzig, 1850), esp. I, pp. cxxiv–cxxxi. Cf. *Geschichtliche Grundbegriffe*, v, p. 355.

[35] See G. Claeys, '"Individualism," "socialism," and "social science": further notes on a process of conceptual formation', *Journal of the History of Ideas*, 47 (1986), pp. 81–93. Professor Claeys kindly sent me a copy of this article.

these usages seem to be new, though in the spirit of the *Westminster Review*. She seems never to have used 'reform' in the singular for the whole range of such measures, or to have spoken of 'social reform'.

The second work of 1850 that I wish to cite is Carlyle's *Latter-day pamphlets*. The book amounts to a denunciation of reform as normally understood:

> Poor old Genius of Reform; bedrid this good while; with little but broken ballot-boxes, and tattered strips of Benthamite Constitutions lying around him; and on the walls mere shadows of clothing-colonels, rates-in-aid, poor-law unions, defunct potato and the Irish difficulty — he does not seem long for this world.

What is needed is 'not a better Talking-Apparatus but a better Acting-Apparatus', 'an infinitely reformed Governing-Apparatus', 'expurgating Downing Street'.[36] Carlyle evidently regards the Reform Bill as the core of the word's meaning, but various other measures as related to it, though not, apparently, the Factory Acts, the repeal of the Corn Laws or the Public Health Act. He plainly thinks he has invented the notion of large-scale administrative reform.

The third work is far less well known. It is a brief article in the radical Joseph Barker's periodical *The People* entitled 'The comparative usefulness of different classes of reformers', which salutes all those who work for reform of any kind, whether to build schools, lecture-rooms or reading-rooms, to promote temperance, or to agitate for financial or parliamentary reform.[37] J. F. C. Harrison used it to exemplify the enlargement by this date of the meaning of 'reform', and Barker is certainly remarkable in grouping such a wide range of good works under that name, including many that did not involve legislative changes. Even so, it is striking how limited the range is by later standards — there is no reference, for example, to housing, medical provision or pensions — and, though Harrison quotes the article under the heading 'Social reform in Leeds', Barker himself does not use the phrase.

A fourth utterance of 1850 is more typical of normal usage:

> It has always been the fate of advocates of temperate reform and of constitutional improvement to be run at as the fomenters of revolution. It is the easiest mode of putting them down; it is the received formula... Now there are revolutionists of two kinds in the world. In the first place there are those violent, hot-headed and unthinking men who fly to arms, who overthrow established Government, and who recklessly, without regard to consequences, and without measuring difficulties or comparing strength, deluge their country with blood

---

[36] T. Carlyle, *Latter-day pamphlets* (London, 1888), pp. 59, 78–9, 198.
[37] *The People* (Wortley nr. Leeds, 1849–51; reprinted Westport, Conn., USA, 1970), 2 (100), pp. 378–9. Cf. J. F. C. Harrison, 'Social reform in Victorian Leeds: the work of James Hole, 1820–1895', *Publications of the Thoresby Society, Monographs III* (Leeds, 1954), p. 42 and his *The early Victorians, 1832–1851* (London, 1971), p. 152.

and draw down the greatest calamities on their fellow-countrymen . . . But there are revolutionists of another kind; blind-minded men, who, animated by antiquated prejudices, and daunted by ignorant apprehensions, dam up the current of human improvement until the irresistible pressure of accumulated discontent breaks down the opposing barriers, and overthrows and levels to the earth those very institutions which a timely application of renovating means would have rendered strong and lasting. Such revolutionists as these are the men who call us revolutionaries.[38]

This was Palmerston in the *Civis romanus* speech, defending himself against a powerful parliamentary attack on his interfering and hectoring foreign policy. The quotation reminds us again that the notion of reform was not in British minds applicable only to Britain. It is also a fine expression of the whig or liberal attitude to domestic reform, concerned essentially with constitutional questions. This kind of rhetoric continued to serve Palmerston well until he died in office in 1865. Many more years had to pass before the predominance of this approach was seriously challenged by the notion that social reform — in a sense still, it seems, unknown to the language in 1850 — was what mattered most in British politics.

IV

Does it matter that the word 'reform' was used in this period in ways rather different from what historians have suggested? I do not believe that the word is the action. I do not think it unreasonable for historians to explain the past with concepts not available to contemporaries. I speak as one who has done exactly that for this period. But I do think that they — and I — should have been more aware of contemporary usage. If it be true that contemporaries did not think of what we call factory regulation as reform and did not have the modern concept of social reform, then these are significant points that historians need to keep in mind. They can, for example, be related to, and they reinforce, the computations of W. O. Aydelotte which showed that, in the Commons during the 1840s, voting on constitutional and ecclesiastical issues followed one pattern, and voting on what we call social questions quite another.[39] If the semantic rift shows that there was a wide intellectual rift to be crossed between constitutional measures and social legislation, if the upper classes by and large just could not see the regulation of factories or even the repeal of the Corn Laws in the guise of reforms, and if there was no acceptance as yet of a generalized notion of reform such as we have, covering

---

[38] Quoted in Southgate, *'The most English minister'*, p. 57.

[39] E.g. 'The disintegration of the Conservative Party in the 1840s: a study of political attitudes' in A. Aydelotte, G. Bogue and R. W. Fogel, *The dimensions of quantitative research in history* (Princeton, 1972), pp. 319–46.

social as well as constitutional change, then these are additional reasons for the mutual incomprehension of liberals and Chartists, not to mention Owenites. Much later Disraeli was still bridling at Parliament so much as discussing social questions: 'We are a Senate', he declared, 'not a vestry.'[40] Might it be the case that only the word 'reform' — perhaps also 'concession' — triggered the full rhetoric of 'reform to stave off revolution', 'reform that you may preserve'? Did Liberal grandees, members of the Reform Club, perhaps need the concept 'social reform' to be invented in order to justify social legislation to themselves? It seems to me that it would be well worth while pursuing the meaning of 'reform' beyond 1850.

Things were, however, changing in our period. The notion of reform was being widened in certain directions. Professor Stedman Jones has brought back into currency the notion, widespread and important at the time, that it was the repeal of the Corn Laws which persuaded many of those disillusioned by the Reform Bill that Parliament was capable of acting in the interests of the poor and unenfranchised.[41] Fittingly, Macaulay himself ratified the deal when he told the electors of Edinburgh at the election of 1852 that Britain had been saved from the ruin other countries had experienced in 1848–9 by 'two great reforms': Russell's of 1832 and Peel's of 1846.[42] It was one of Lorenz Stein's main contentions that there must be absolute clarity about what 'social reform' meant, if there was not to be disappointment and discontent among the proletariat.[43] But the British case suggests that consensus can be assisted by broadening, conflating — even, to use Dr Mitchell's verb, muzzying — the meanings of words.

---

[40] Quoted in P. Smith, *Disraelian Conservatism and social reform* (London, 1967), p. 267. I am grateful to Professor Smith for help on this point.
[41] G. Stedman Jones, *Languages of class* (Cambridge, 1983), esp. pp. 167–8, 177–8.
[42] Macaulay, *Speeches*, II, pp. 388–93.
[43] See n. 35 above.

Index

absolutism, 8–9, 11, 16, 43–4, 49, 51, 53, 56–7, 66, 97, 116
agriculture, 14, 18, 73, 90
Albemarle, Lord, 30
Albert, Prince, 109, 147
Allen, John, 29
Allgemeines Landrecht, 44–5, 49, 53–5, 68
Altenstein, Karl von, 66, 72, 83, 86
America, 35, 68, 70, 101, 137
American War of Independence, 21, 92, 115
Amiens, Peace of, 97
Ancillon, Johann Peter, 85
Angiolini, Luigi, 107
armies, 13, 76, 87, 90–2, 94, 99, 105, 146
Arndt, Ernst Moritz, 61
Arnim, Achim von, 73
Ashton, Rosemary, 115
Association Movement, 21
Auerstedt, 82, 85
Austerlitz, 98
Austin, William, 105
Austria, 10–12, 14, 44, 48–9, 52, 74, 89, 98
Aydelotte, W. O., 173

Baden, 49, 56
Bagehot, Walter, 26, 41
Baring, Francis, 29
Bartlett, Thomas, 92
Bassermann, Friedrich Daniel, 147, 149
Bathurst, Earl, 86
Bavaria, 48, 56, 58
Beccaria, Cesare, 58
Beckmann, Gustav Bernhard, 46–7
Beckmann, Ott David Heinrich, 46–7
Belgium, 102, 138
Beltrami, Giacomo, 107
Benjamin, Walter, 142
Bentham, Jeremy, 126, 134–5
Berg, 65
Berlin, 69, 146–9, 152–3
Berlin, University of, 69

Berliner Abendblätter, 64
Bessborough, Lord, 32
Bismarck, Otto von, 62, 74–6
Blackwood's Magazine, 28, 35, 165–6, 168–9
Blanqui, Adolphe, 114
Blum, Robert, 141
Bonaparte, Napoleon (Napoleon I), 34, 65, 70, 82, 90, 95, 98–9
Boyen, Hermann von, 66, 68
Breihan, John, 21, 22
Brentano, Clemens von, 67, 73
Brewer, John, 8, 20, 80
Brissot de Warville, Jacques Pierre, 115, 116
Broglie, Duc de, 25–6
Brougham, Henry, Lord, 29, 38, 166
Brüggemann, Karl Heinrich, 150
Brüning, Heinrich, 76
Brunswick, 16
Bucher, Lothar, 110
Bulwer Lytton, 111
Burdett, Sir Francis, 30–1, 33, 37, 98
bureaucracy, 9–10, 14–17, 53, 66, 69, 71–2, 75
Buret, Eugène, 112
Burke, Edmund, 116–17, 150

Calvin, John, 127
Cambridge, 28, 107, 159
cameralism, 11, 18
Canning, George, 36
Captain Swing, 35
Carlyle, Thomas, 168, 172
Cartwright, John, 5, 98
Carus, C. G., 118
Castlereagh, Viscount, 86, 94
Catholic emancipation, 19, 92–4, 99–100, 108, 110, 121, 133, 159
Cavour, Count Camillo, 103
censorship, 13
Chadwick, Sir Edwin, 163, 171
Charles I, 104

Charles X, king of France, 109, 112
Chartism, 136, 145–6, 148, 156–7, 162–3,
    170–1, 174
civil liberties, 54
Clare election of 1828, 128, 133, 139
Clark, J. C. D., 5
Claudius, Matthias, 50
Cobbett, William, 20, 107, 135, 138
Cobden, Richard, 138
Confederation of the Rhine, 23, 65, 72
Cookson, J. E., 91
Cooper, James Fenimore, 103
Corn Laws, 172, 174
Cornewall Lewis, Sir George, 163
Cottu, Charles, 118
Cromwell, Oliver, 34
Cullen, Cardinal, 125

Dalberg, Karl Theodor von, 49
Devonshire, Duchess of, 32
Devonshire, Duke of, 34
Dickson, Peter, 15
Dipper, Christof, 9
Disraeli, Benjamin, 35, 163–4, 174
Dissenters, 19
Dohna, Count, 66
Dundas, Henry, 83, 86, 92
Dupin, Charles, 104
Durham, Earl of, 39

economical reform, 5, 21–2
economy, 13, 52–3, 75
Edinburgh Review, 29, 156
education, 13, 17, 23, 52, 65, 74, 107
Ehrman, John, 83
Eisenhower, Dwight D., 80
Eldon, Lord, 37
Engels, Friedrich, 62, 112, 146
Enlightenment, 52, 67–8
Erskine, Thomas, 31, 34, 41
Ertman, Thomas, 10
Establishment Act (1782), 21
Estates, 47, 51, 55

Faucher, Léon, 107
finance, 11, 50

Finer, S. E., 163
Fitzwilliam, Earl, 167
Fontane, Theodor, 103, 109
Fox, Charles James, 26–7, 31, 34–5, 116–17
France, 25–6, 44, 54, 66–7, 69–70, 74, 84,
    86, 98, 102, 112, 117, 121–2, 146,
    167
Frankfurt am Main, 148–9
Frederick the Great, 5, 16, 68, 81
Frederick William III, 61, 73, 84, 95, 109
Frederick William (the Great Elector), 87
freedom of trades, 71, 74
Freiburg, 49
French Revolution, 26, 28, 35, 65, 67, 70, 74,
    80–1, 88, 92, 104, 119, 147–8, 150, 168
Friedland, 98
Fröbel, Julius, 148

Geijer, Erik Gustaf, 110
General Directory, 84, 86
Gentz, Friedrich, 119
George I, 104
George II, 104
George III, 98, 116
George IV, 104
Gerstäcker, Carl Friedrich Wilhelm, 57
Giessen, 50
Gladstone, William Ewart, 136
Glasgow, 146
Glorious Revolution, 30
Gneisenau, August Wilhelm Anton, Count
    Neithardt von, 66, 69, 89, 97
Godwin, William, 123, 134
Goldsmid, Isaac, 137
Goodway, David, 145
Gourbillon, Joseph Antoine de, 101
Great Irish Famine, 130, 141
Great Reform Bill, 35, 37, 40, 110–11, 159–
    62, 164, 167, 170, 172
Grenville, William, Lord, 86, 93–4
Grey, Charles, Earl, 29, 38, 40, 162, 166
Guizot, François Pierre Guillaume, 111

Habermas, Jürgen, 18
Halifax, 112
Halle, 46–7
Hambach, 150
Hampden Clubs, 29

Hanover, 49, 56
Hardenberg, Karl August von, 61–2, 64–5, 66, 68, 70–1, 73, 75–7, 82–3, 85–7, 91, 95, 147
Hardy, Thomas, 31
Harling, Philip, 22
Harrison, J. F. C., 172
Harvey, Christopher, 111
Haussez, baron d', 102, 106, 112
Hazlitt, William, 31, 38
health, 14, 16, 18, 19, 52, 172
Hecker, Friedrich, 149, 155
Heine, Heinrich, 107, 110
Hertzberg, Ewald, Count von, 67
Hessen-Darmstadt, 49–50
Hessen-Kassel, 49, 56
Hettling, Manfred, 153, 155
Hintze, Otto, 80
Hitler, Adolf, 62
Holland House, 29, 31–2, 41, 98
Holy Roman Empire, 11, 17, 47, 50, 56
Holyoake, George, 115
Howard, John, 114
Huber, V. A., 107–8
Humbert, General, 122
Humboldt, Wilhelm von, 69, 71
Hunt, Henry, 29–30, 37, 135, 138

industrialization, 14, 18
Ingrao, Charles, 14, 16
Innes, Joanna, 19
Ireland, 35, 80, 92–3, 121–43, 168

Jackson, Sir Francis, 97
James II, 104
Jekyll, Joseph, 41
Jena, 69, 74, 82, 85, 88, 93, 98
Jesuits, 13
Jews, 90, 137–8
Johnson, Hubert C., 16
Joseph II, 5, 12–13, 15, 61, 151
judicial reform, see law

Kant, Immanuel, 57, 67
Kellen, H. M., 160
Kleist, Heinrich von, 64

Kohl, J. G., 103
Koselleck, Reinhard, 6, 63, 150
Kulturkampf, 75

Lafayette, Marquis de, 25, 36
Lamb, Lady Caroline, 32
Lambert, Royston, 163
law, 17, 43–4, 46–59, 64–5, 84, 136, 151, 166
Ledru-Rollin, Alexandre Auguste, 115
Leeds, 112
Leopold I of the Belgians, 167
Levinger, Matthew, 95
Lewin, Rahel, 68
liberalism, 148–9, 169, 174
Lieven, Prince, 102
Lindemann, Mary, 16–17
Liverpool, 112
Liverpool, Earl of, 86
Louis Philippe, king of France, 25
Louis XV, 117
Lubenow, W. C., 163
Luther, Martin, 127

Macaulay, Thomas Babington, 166–7, 174
Mackintosh, Sir James, 40
Maistre, Joseph de, 116
Mandler, Peter 22
Marat, Jean Paul, 114
Marengo, 98
Maria Theresa, 11–13, 15, 48
Martineau, Harriet, 171
Marwitz, Alexander von der, 68
Marwitz, Ludwig von der, 70
Marx, Karl, 148
Mayhew, Henry, 115
Mecklenburg, 49
Melbourne, Viscount, 33, 38–40, 138, 169
Merivale, John Herman, 165
Michelet, Jules, 112
military reform, see armies
Mill, J. S., 38
Mill, James, 38
Ministry of All the Talents, 93
Moir, George, 168
Moira, Earl of, 93
Molesworth, Sir William, 38, 40
monasteries, 13

Montesquieu, Charles de Secondat, baron de, 116
Montulé, Édouard de, 104
Moore, Barrington, 64
Moore, Thomas, 133
Moser, Friedrich Karl von, 50
Muir, Thomas, 31
Muntz, G. F., 138

Napoleon I, 34, 65, 70, 82, 90, 95, 98–9
Nassau memorandum, 85
National Socialism, 64
natural law, 11, 44–5, 51, 57, 59
Nettelbladt, Daniel, 47
Newman, Cardinal, 108
Newton, Sir Isaac, 105
Niebuhr, Barthold Georg, 88, 109
North, Lord, 21

O'Connell, Daniel, 121–43
O'Connor, Arthur, 31
O'Sullivan, Humphrey, 134
Owen, Robert, 170–1, 174
Oxford, 107

Paine, Tom, 5, 123
Palmerston, Viscount, 173
Parkes, Joseph, 39
Parliament, 19–21, 41, 96, 109–10, 116, 136, 146, 156, 161, 167
peasantry, 64, 70, 74, 87, 90, 153
Peel, Sir Robert, 36–7, 119, 140–1, 146, 168, 174
Peterloo, 29
Phillips, Sir Richard, 102
physiocracy, 11
Pietism, 11
Pillet, René-Martin, 116
Pitt, William, 'the Younger', 21–2, 31, 83, 86, 92, 98, 105, 167
Place, Francis, 33
Poland, 138
Pölitz, Karl Heinrich Ludwig, 151
Portland, Duke of, 167
Prussia, 10, 14, 16, 20, 44–5, 48–9, 53–4, 56, 61–100, 103, 121

Prussian Reform Movement, 23, 61, 63–4, 66–7, 70, 72, 74, 76–7, 79, 82, 147

radicalism, 37–40, 167, 169, 171
Reform Club, 169
religious toleration, 13–14, 19
Rémusat, Charles de, 116
Riesbeck, J. K., baron von, 109
Riga memorandum, 82, 87, 95
Roberts, David, 163
Robinson, David, 35
Rockingham, Marquess of, 21, 30
Rockingham whigs, 21
Rogers, Samuel, 40
Romilly, Samuel, 118
Roscoe, W. C., 37
Rotteck, Karl von, 151
Rousseau, Jean-Jacques, 69–70
Rubichon, Maurice, 109
Rudé, George, 145
Ruge, Arnold, 148–9
Rugge, Fabio, 80
Russell, Lord John, 26–8, 30, 33–4, 37, 41, 156, 174
Russia, 98, 145

Sachsenspiegel, 46
Sarrans, Bernard, 110
Savigny, Friedrich Carl von, 45
Saville, John, 145
Saxony, 49, 56
Scharnhorst, Gerhard Johann David von, 66, 76, 90
Schissler, Hanna, 80
Schleiermacher, Friedrich, 69
Schlözer, Ludwig, 150
Schön, Theodor von, 66, 87, 90
Scotland, 167
Scott, Sir Walter, 119
Seeley, J. R., 100
Selkirk, Earl of, 83
Senior, Nassau, 163
Seven Years War, 5, 11–12
Sheridan, Richard Brinsley, 31, 116
Silesia, 71, 84, 89
Smith, Adam, 70
Smith, Sydney, 32
social welfare, 14, 19, 23, 52, 75, 112

socialism, 75–6, 170
Sonderweg, 100, 145
Soult, Marshal, 114
Southey, Robert, 101
Spain, 138
Spence, Peter, 97
Sperber, Jonathan, 145
Spiker, Samuel Heinrich, 114
Spooner, Dick, 39
Staël, Madame de, 25
Staël-Holstein, baron de, 105, 108
Stedman Jones, Gareth, 174
Stein, Heinrich Friedrich Carl, baron vom,
	61–2, 64–5, 66, 69, 71, 73, 75–7, 85
Stein, Lorenz, 171, 174
Stephens, J. R., 164
Stockmar, Baron, 109, 147
Struve, Gustav, 149, 155
Sturm und Drang, 68
Sunday School Movement, 19
Süvern, Johann Wilhelm, 71

Talleyrand, Charles Maurice de, 36
Tamworth manifesto, 168
Tara, 133
taxation, 14, 16, 22–3, 50, 64, 71, 80, 95
Test and Corporation Acts, 19
Thatcher, Margaret, 7
Thibaut, Anton Friedrich Justus, 45
Tilsit, 65, 74
Tocqueville, Alexis de, 37, 39, 111
Tone, Theobald Wolfe, 126
Tooke, John Horne, 31, 38
tories, 30, 34, 36–7, 39–40, 140, 167, 169
torture, 53
Treitschke, Heinrich von, 62, 73
Tristan, Flora, 114
Trollope, Anthony, 36

Union, Act of, 123
United Irishmen, 83, 123, 125
United States of America, *see* America
universities, 13, 54

Varnhagen von Ense, Karl August, 154
Vendée, 122
Victoria, Queen, 167
Vienna, 147
Vierhaus, Rudolf, 9
Vincke, Friedrich Ludwig, 88, 117
Voltaire, 105, 116
Vossische Zeitung, 61

Wakley, Thomas, 138

Wales, 80
Walmesley, Charles, 130
Walsh, Joseph-Alexis, Vicomte, 110
Ward, J. T., 164
Watson, Richard, 28, 30
Weber, Max, 8, 62, 73
Wehler, Hans-Ulrich, 79
Weis, Eberhard, 50
Westminster Review, 38, 166, 169, 172
Westphalia, 65, 72, 141
whigs, 25–7, 29–31, 34, 35–41, 140, 169
Whiteboyism, 131
Wilberforce, William, 105
Wilkes, John, 5, 21, 31, 104
William III, 104, 166
William IV, 26, 34
Williams, Raymond, 161
Windham, William, 93–4
Wittig, Ludwig, 141
Wolff, Christian, 18
Wollstonecraft, Mary, 123
Woodward, E. L., 159, 162

York, Duke of, 93

Zachariä, Karl Salomo, 57